VFR Flight Review
A guide to better flying

To help you get the most out of your solo practice

To prepare you for the private pilot check ride

To sharpen your skills for the biennial flight review

To improve and maintain your proficiency as a single
engine or multi-engine pilot

With Self-Practice Exercises

With Self-Evaluation Score Sheets

Avram Goldstein, CFI, CFII

SECOND EDITION

Published by AvvA, Inc.
735 Dolores Street, Stanford, CA 94305

Other books by Avram Goldstein...

The Right Seat:
An Introduction to Flying for Pilots' Companions and Would-Be Pilots

Flying Out of Danger:
A Pilot's Guide to Safety

IFR Principles and Practice:
A Guide to Safe Instrument Flying

See the final pages of this book for more detailed information and how to order.

CONTENTS

0
INTRODUCTION

A. WHAT THIS BOOK IS ABOUT, AND HOW TO USE IT

You may be thinking that the last thing you need is another instructional manual for flying. That's not what this book is. I assume that you have had plenty of instruction already, from flight instructors and from textbooks and ground school.

This book is intended to meet the special needs of three kinds of pilot: the student pilot who has already soloed and is beginning to prepare for the check ride, the private pilot who is due soon for a biennial flight review, and the experienced pilot who is looking for new practical pointers on flying in order to improve their skills and be a safer pilot.*

Since there are no specific prescsribed guidelines for a biennial flight review, you may be uncertain what to expect. The purpose of the review is clear, however. You should be able to fly with at least the same level of competence as when you first got your ticket. Thus, the best way to prepare for a BFR is to imagine that you are going to take a check ride all over again. Likewise, if your BFR is past, and you just want to upgrade your piloting skill, the most comprehensive outline to follow is the same one that was used for your check ride.

Therefore, this book is arranged in exactly the same order as the FAA's PRIVATE PILOT PRACTICAL TEST STANDARD (FAA-S-8081-1). It contains all the procedures and maneuvers with which you should be familiar. In

---

*You may be surprised at my use of "they," "their," and "them" as singular pronouns. All aspects of aviation are of interest to men and women alike, and all the opportunities for professional as well as amateur flying are equally available to both sexes. Most authors who write "he," "his," and "him" have a mental image of a man, and the reader gets the same impression. To say that "he" really means "he or she" doesn't solve the problem of the subtle sexist influence of all-male personal pronouns. But I find "he or she" clumsy, especially when repeated again and again. The solution, which I have adopted throughout this book, is in every dictionary—even the venerable Oxford English Dictionary: "They" and "their and "them" can be used for the singular, meaning "he or she," "his or her," "him or her," when the sex is unspecified. And although it sounds odd at first, one soon gets used to it. After all, the same thing happened long ago with "thou," "thy," and "thee"; "you," which had been permissible only as a plural form, came into use in the singular, and now we think nothing of it.

fact, the entire text of this official guide is included here, broken down according to the different phases of flying. My practical commentary and explanations make up the main text of the book. Each of the next thirteen chapters is divided into a series of **tasks** (lettered A, B, C, etc.). Under each task, the verbatim extract from the FAA publication is reproduced, giving the **Objective**, and explaining the examiner's **Action** in evaluating the applicant's performance.

There are several key reference or training manuals that FAA considers essential for any pilot; these are the official guides to flight. Sometimes, in this book, I shall take issue with them on one or another small point, but on the whole these books are thorough and authoritative, and I recommend them strongly:

1. Flight Training Handbook (FAA AC-61-21A).

2. Pilot's Handbook of Aeronautical Knowledge (FAA AC-61-23).

3. Aviation Weather (FAA/NWS AC-00-6A).

4. Aviation Weather Services (FAA/NWS AC-0045B)—A supplement to the above.

5. Airman's Information Manual (FAA)—Basic Flight Information and ATC Procedures. This is a vast storehouse of information about procedures. It is issued semi-annually on a subscription basis. Most of the essential portions are also printed privately and sold at a reasonable price by the Aviation Book Co.

6. Airport/Facility Directory (National Ocean Survey)—Regional editions sold separately or by subscription.

7. AOPA's Handbook for Pilots. Published annually, this handy pocket-sized 450-page booklet contains a vast amount of information extracted from official publications, including the full text of relevant parts of the Federal Aviation Regulations (FARs)—Part 61 (Certification), Part 67 (Medical Standards and Certification), and Part 91 (General Operating Rules). It also contains a helpful **Glossary** in which one can find the correct official meanings of numerous terms. Every pilot should carry this handbook in their flight bag.

Some chapters begin with a discussion of general principles that apply to all the tasks covered in the chapter. All chapters include an explanation of the principles underlying the performance of the specific tasks, and sometimes problem sets are included. Finally, Chapter 14 contains explanations and discussions of selected advanced or controversial topics that should be of interest to most pilots.

A unique feature of the book is the inclusion of **Self-Evaluation Score Sheets**. These allow you to rate yourself every time you go out for a practice flight, to note your weaknesses, and to watch your improvement from one flight to the next. The scoring system is on a 10-point basis, with 1 for a really poor unsatisfactory performance, and 10 for a perfect one. With experience and self-critical honesty, you will be able to judge yourself on a consistent basis. Regard an average score of 7 as satisfactory, 8 as better than satisfactory, 9 as very good, and 10 as perfect. You should work toward attaining an average score of at least 8 before you put the particular exercise behind you. The important thing about self-scoring is that you will have a record of your strengths and weaknesses, which you can study and analyze from flight to flight as you progress.

A word of warning. **Don't** try to make entries on the score sheet while you are flying. All your attention should be outside, scanning for traffic, and any time left over from that task should be devoted to scanning the engine and flight instruments. If someone is in the right seat who knows a good deal about flying, they could discuss the scoring of each maneuver with you, and make entries on the score sheet. Otherwise, make mental notes as you go along. Then, when you are safely back on the ground, go over the various aspects of your flying performance, and score yourself accordingly.

In this book, all the prinicpal procedures and maneuvers for VFR flying at the private pilot level of proficiency are described. Before you fly, decide which few maneuvers you will practice, then work on those few exclusively. Resist the tendency to do these maneuvers "once over lightly," without being sufficiently self-critical, without demanding enough of yourself. The principle of successful practice, remember, is **repetition**, coupled with **analysis**, leading to **understanding**, and thus to **self-correction**. The satisfaction of doing a maneuver nearly perfectly is the reward that makes the session worthwhile. And your instructor will reinforce your feeling of satisfaction the next time you fly dual.

This book offers you an organized, planned, systematic way of practicing everything that you know how to do already but not yet perfectly, or that you once could do perfectly but now are rusty on. Read here, in advance, what errors to look for, and how to correct them. After your flight, as you fill out the self-evaluation score sheet, live the flight over again in your mind, and note what the problems were and what you could have done better. Read the explanatory material again. Then, if there are still difficulties you can't resolve, blocks to progress that you can't get past (that happens to everyone from time to time), get help from your instructor. Most instructors prefer an active, eager student to a passive one. Don't be afraid of instructors; their job is to help you become a better pilot.

It is assumed that you have good textbooks and manuals, so needless repetition is avoided here. This book is not a substitute for any other. It is a supplement—to your own books, to your ground school, to your instructor's teaching, and to your own experience as a pilot. The overriding consideration in flying is **safety**. The purpose of this book—and my aim in writing it, based on thousands of hours of pilot-in-command and instructing time—is to help you become a safer pilot. Good luck!

B. THE BASICS OF FLYING: STRAIGHT AND LEVEL, TURNS, CLIMBS, DESCENTS

Principles. Curiously, these basics of flying are not even listed in the FAA PRACTICAL TEST STANDARD. This is because they are implicit in all the procedures and maneuvers covered there. They are the foundation, without which you can accomplish nothing else. It is worthwhile, therefore, to begin with a review of these basics, and take a self-critical look at how well you perform them, just as the examiner or instructor would do at a check ride or BFR. I see pilots with hundreds of hours, who have been taught poorly or have forgotten what they've learned, and really don't have good command of the basics. But even if you are not one of them, and you fly very well already, new insights and new angles may be helpful to you.

Straight and Level Flight. An aircraft in straight and level flight should always be flying a definite **heading**—whether by the heading indicator or by outside reference is immaterial. You never just wander about the sky. At every moment in flight you should **know** what your heading is supposed to be. If your instructor suddenly asks "What's your heading supposed to be?," you should have an instant answer—and without looking at the heading indicator. You also have a definite altitude, which you are trying to maintain. This is done by having a definite power setting, and a definite airspeed for which you are properly trimmed.

Look at your left hand on the yoke. If you are gripping the yoke tightly, something is wrong. With correct trim, you should be able to control the yoke with a thumb and two fingers, at the most. A proficient pilot will barely touch the yoke at all, except for tiny corrections to keep the wings level, and slight pressure (a thumb or a finger is enough) or slight pull (a couple of fingers) to oppose updrafts and downdrafts. If there is a long-term trend of increasing or decreasing altitude, you can be sure the trim is not right, and you should correct it. An airplane is a very stable machine, aerodynamically, and if you let it fly without clumsy interference, its flight will be smooth and unvarying.

Even though it is not required for any flight test, you should be able to demonstrate for yourself the **longitudinal stability** of the airplane. Go up to a convenient altitude, say 3,000' AGL. Trim for level flight and wait long enough to satisfy yourself that the altitude remains constant. Now pull back gently on the yoke. The vertical speed indicator (VSI) will register a climb immediately, the airspeed indicator (ASI) will show a decrease, and the altimeter reading will begin to increase. Having disturbed the equilibrium, you should now release the yoke—just let it go, and sit back to observe what happens.

As soon as you release the back pressure, the nose will drop, the VSI will show a descent, the airspeed will begin to increase, and the altimeter will start to unwind. Don't be alarmed! Don't touch anything, except that you may very gently (with one finger on the yoke) keep the wings level; but be very careful not to pull or push the yoke even slightly.

What happens? As the airspeed picks up, the faster flow of air over the wings increases the lift, the airplane slows its descent, the nose comes up, and a climb begins again, but to a lesser extent than before. Each time the nose comes up, increasing the angle of attack, the airspeed falls off, reducing the lift, and this causes the nose to fall again. Each time the nose falls, reducing the angle of attack, the airspeed increases, lift is increased, and the airplane begins to climb again as the nose comes up. These are the famous "phugoid oscillations" that reflect the airplane's tendency to resist changes in the longitudinal axis, i.e., they reflect the airplane's longitudinal stability. This characteristic makes the airplane a safe flying machine; think how you'd have to fight for control if it were longitudinally unstable. The point to note here is that as the oscsillations become smaller and smaller, the airplane eventually flies level again—at 3,000' AGL and at the original airspeed for which it was trimmed.

Repeat the same exercise starting with forward pressure on the yoke. Initiate a gentle dive, then suddenly release the pressure. You will see the same sequence as before, and in the end you will be back to the initial altitude and airspeed. Since both versions of this exercise involve some sudden movement of the yoke, it had best be carried out at maneuvering speed.

I think this demonstration gives one a real feel for the fact that the airplane, when trimmed for level flight, will maintain that condition at a constant power setting and airspeed, unless it is disturbed by a ham-handed pilot. That is why thumb and forefinger of the left hand are more than enough to guide the airplane gently, to make it do whatever you want it to.

What about turbulence, updrafts and downdrafts? Don't you need to fight them constantly, pushing and pulling on the yoke to maintain your altitude? No, you don't. In most cases, if you respond promptly to indications on the VSI with slight thumb pressure or slight finger pull, you can counteract the disturbances before they result in any significant change of altitude. You may have read, even in some quite authoritative places, that the VSI has a significant lag, whereas the altimeter does not. This is certainly wrong, as you can easily prove to yourself. The VSI shows the **initiation** of a climb or descent well before the altimeter registers a detectable change of altitude. This is why the VSI, telling you what is **going to happen** before it does, can be such a useful tool in maintaining level flight. Monitor it, and respond promptly to its indications, but don't overcorrect.

For stronger turbulence, the correct technique is to hold a constant pitch **attitude**, and let the altitude vary as much as 50' or so above and below the desired level. Constant attitude is the safe way to fly; you don't want the nose pitching up and down, changing the airspeed from near-stall at one extreme to the yellow arc at the other. Remember that by and large, an area of downdrafts will be followed by an area of updrafts, and vice versa; all the air can't flow up or down continuously. So, in the long run, your average altitude will usually be maintained.

The limitation of this method is that you must not be wandering into altitudes where you don't belong. VFR and IFR traffic have assigned altitudes 500' apart, so a deviation of more than 100' is really not acceptable. I recommend that when the deviation approaches 50', you should use moderate yoke pressures to return toward your reference altitude, but take care not to let the pitch attitude change excessively. Here the VSI is an invaluable aid to prevent overcorrecting. Suppose you are 60' too low. The only thing you need to do is to establish a slight climb on the VSI **and maintain it**; the lost altitude will surely be recovered in time, and there's no great rush to get there. Watch the VSI continuously during such an altitude correction. The common error is to establish a climb (or descent), but then to relax the pressure. The reason for this error is that the longitudinal stability comes into play to oppose whatever you are trying to do. Thus, you must maintain the back pressure (or forward pressure) that is necessary to keep the VSI needle where you want it for a constant rate of climb (or descent), for long enough to return to the original altitude.

For deviations of 100' or more, my rule is to correct **immediately** with throttle—increasing power to climb, decreasing power to descend. The deviation is unacceptable, and it needs to be reversed as soon as possible, while keeping the pitch attitude and airspeed within acceptable limits. If there is more than light turbulence, remember to reduce to maneuvering speed to avoid overstressing the aircraft.

Turns to Headings. Turns to headings are among the easiest of maneuvers. The angle of bank will never exceed 15° to 20°, the bank angle for a standard-rate turn (360° in 2 minutes) at typical airspeeds of small aircraft. For turns of less than 30°, the bank angle will be even less, following the rule of using a bank angle about one-half the number of degrees to be turned. Thus, adverse aileron yaw in rolling into and out of the turn will be very slight, necessitating little or no rudder pressure to keep the ball centered. One problem in executing a smooth turn is leading the rollout by an appropriate amount, so as to have wings level exactly as you reach the new heading. For these moderate bank angles, starting the rollout 10° in advance of the new heading will suffice. The only other requirement is to apply slight back pressure to the yoke to maintain altitude during the turn, and to relax it smoothly with the rollout. But here, too, the modest bank angle makes it easy. Steep turns are another matter; they are discussed in Chapter 14.

Climbs. In small trainer aircraft, climbs are usually carried out at full power, provided the RPM does not exceed red-line. There are three kinds of climb, each with its own precise airspeed, which you must know for your aircraft. The steepest climb is the obstacle (best angle) climb, at V_x, to achieve the greatest gain in altitude with the smallest distance covered. Next is the normal (best rate) climb, at V_y. Finally, there is the cruise climb, at a faster airspeed and lower pitch attitude, for better visibility over the nose and better engine cooling. The special techniques for using V_x and V_y in maximum performance takeoffs will be discussed in Chapter 4. Here let us consider the technique of transition from cruising flight to climb, in order to move to a higher altitude.

Let us assume you wish to make the transition as rapidly as possible, and therefore that you will climb at V_y. Suppose your cruising airspeed is 95 k and your V_y is 70 k. The smooth way, as in all flying maneuvers, is to **do one thing at a time**. First, apply back pressure to raise the nose to the pitch attitude you know will correspond to about 70 k—a certain definite amount above the outside horizon or the artifical horizon. Immediately, the airspeed will begin to fall, and the climb will begin. Let the airspeed bleed off until it has very nearly reached 70 k. Then smoothly advance the throttle to full climb power, and trim out the back pressure. That's all there is to it.

Leveling off is also done in two distinct steps. When you have just reached the desired altitude (some pilots like to overshoot by 50′), push on the yoke to lower the nose to the normal cruising attitude (a certain amount below the horizon). Hold it there as the airspeed picks up, watching the altimeter. As the airspeed creeps up, it will take more and more pressure on the yoke to prevent a further climb. Finally, when the airspeed reaches 95 k, reduce the power to the normal cruise setting, and trim out the forward pressure. In the course of these manipulations, you will probably lose the extra 50' of altitude and wind up exactly where you want to be. As you become proficient in the level-off maneuver, you will find it unnecessary to climb above the desired altitude. Instead, you can **stop the altimeter** exactly where you want it, and hold it there with whatever forward pressure on the yoke is necessary, until the airspeed reaches cruise, and you throttle back to cruise power and trim out the forward yoke pressure.

Descents. One of the simplest maneuvers in flying is a cruise descent. You are in normal cruising flight, say at 95 k, and trimmed so you can fly hands off. To descend, you have only to reduce the power—nothing else. With less power, the nose will drop and descent will begin. The airspeed will remain very nearly unchanged. The rate of descent will be determined by the degree of power reduction, and you will soon discover exactly what power setting is needed to establish, let's say, a 500 fpm descent. Find it out in your airplane, write it down, and memorize it, so all your cruise descents can be established briskly and without hesitation.

This virtually automatic behavior of the airplane illustrates nicely how the trim setting determines the airspeed—at least approximately—regardless of what you do with the throttle. An airplane trimmed for 95 k will fly at that airspeed in level flight, will climb (at higher power settings) at only slightly lower airspeeds, and will descend (at reduced power settings) at airspeeds that are only modestly higher, right down to idle power. This point is explained very fully by Langewiesche in his classic text **Stick and Rudder**, which all pilots should read.

An **ideal** airplane, according to Langewiesche, would maintain exactly the same airspeed at a given trim setting, regardless of power changes. It would climb, fly level, or descend at this identical airspeed, depending on the power. As I show with actual flight data in Chapter 14, Section E, this is not quite true in real airplanes, but the deviation from ideal behavior is not great enough to spoil the usefulness of the concept. Most light trainers will respond to complete power reductions by dropping the nose a bit too much, so the airspeed in the glide will inrease by 10–20 k. But ordinary cruise descents can be handled very easily with a small power reduction and no re-trimming. Don't make the common mistake of trying to hold the nose up. That just defeats your purpose. Let the airplane have its way. Keep your hands off the yoke, except for a light touch with thumb and a few fingers to maintain the wings level.

If the aim is to descend at a reduced airspeed, as in a normal approach to landing, make the transition by steps, again changing one thing at a time. First, reduce power to less than you will need eventually in the descent. Learn this degree of power reduction by trial and error. Then, before the descent begins, gradually increase the back pressure to maintain altitude (watching the altimeter) until the airspeed falls off to the desired value. Then trim for this airspeed, and bring in whatever power is necessary for the rate of descent you want (watching the VSI). Remember the basic principle that trim (yoke position) controls the airspeed, while throttle controls the rate of descent (or rate of climb, or level flight).

To level off from a descent, you only need to advance the throttle. If your descent was at cruise airspeed, bring in power to the value you know is correct for level cruising flight. If your descent was at reduced airspeed, bring in just enough power for level flight at that airspeed. In either case, no re-trimming should be needed. It is a good idea to lead the desired level-off altitude by about 50′, because the airplane's momentum makes it impossible for it to stop its descent instantaneously.

A special case of descent at reduced airspeed, with which you need to be thoroughly familiar, is the power-off glide at best-glide airspeed, as in a simulated or actual forced landing. This will be discussed in Chapter 11.

Now look up and fill in the appropriate numbers for your airplane.

Descent at cruise airspeed.

Desired airspeed: ⎯⎯⎯⎯⎯⎯

Power settings for 500 fpm descent.

MP (variable pitch prop): ⎯⎯⎯⎯⎯⎯⎯

RPM: ⎯⎯⎯⎯⎯⎯

Descent at reduced airspeed.

Desired airspeed: ⎯⎯⎯⎯⎯⎯

Power settings for 500 fpm descent.

MP (variable pitch prop): ⎯⎯⎯⎯⎯⎯⎯

RPM: ⎯⎯⎯⎯⎯⎯

Power-off glide.

Best-glide airspeed: ⎯⎯⎯⎯⎯⎯

Score Sheet: 0B. Straight and Level Flight

Date										
Maintaining heading ± 10 degrees										
Choosing and maintaining correct manifold pressure and/or RPM										
Maintaining altitude ± 100 ft.										
Proper trim and gentle touch on yoke										
Timely corrections for up and down drafts										
Knowledge of maneuvering speed (V_A) for flight in turbulence										
Vigilant look-out for traffic at all times										
TOTAL SCORE										
Divide by 7 = AVERAGE SCORE										

Score Sheet: 0B. Turns to Headings

Date										
Smooth coordinated roll to standard rate turn										
Smooth roll-out to within 10 degrees of desired heading										
Small bank angles for turns of less than 30 degrees										
Maintaining altitude ± 50 ft. in turn										
Coordinated release of back pressure and no altitude gain in roll-out										
Searching for traffic **before** starting turns, lifting inside wing if necessary before banking										
TOTAL SCORE										
Divide by 6 = AVERAGE SCORE										

Score Sheet: 0B. Climbs

Date											
Knowing V_y before starting climb											
Raising nose **first** to the correct pitch attitude for V_y											
Smoothly advancing power when V_y has been reached											
Level-off by forward yoke to stop altimeter											
Smooth reduction to cruise power when cruise airspeed is reached in level-off											
New altitude established ± 50 feet											
TOTAL SCORE											
Divide by 6 = AVERAGE SCORE											

Score Sheet: 0B. Descents

Date									
Establishing cruise descent by smooth power reduction to appropriate new value for 500 fpm descent									
Level-off by power application, leading by 50 ft, returning to cruise airspeed									
Establishing descent at predetermined reduced airspeed by smooth power reduction to appropriate new value for 500 fpm descent, with re-trimming for new reduced airspeed									
Level-off by power application, leading by 50 ft, returning to level flight at reduced airspeed									
Power-off glide, throttle fully idle, carb heat if appropriate, trimmed for best-glide airspeed									
TOTAL SCORE									
Divide by 5 = AVERAGE SCORE									

1

PREFLIGHT PREPARATION

A. CERTIFICATES AND DOCUMENTS

---

1. **Objective.** To determine that the applicant:
   a. Exhibits adequate knowledge by explaining the appropriate -
      (1) pilot certificate privileges and limitations.
      (2) medical certificate and expiration.
      (3) personal pilot logbook or flight record.
      (4) FCC station license and operator's permit.
   b. Exhibits adequate knowledge by locating and explaining the significance and importance of the airplane's -
      (1) airworthiness and registration certificates.
      (2) operating limitations, handbooks, or manuals.
      (3) equipment list.
      (4) weight and balance data.
      (5) maintenance requirements and appropriate records.

2. **Action.** The examiner will:
   a. Ask the applicant to present and explain the appropriate pilot and medical certificates and personal flight records and determine that the applicant's performance meets the objective.
   b. Ask the applicant to locate and explain the airplane documents, lists, records, and other required data, and determine that the applicant's performance meets the objective.
   c. Place emphasis on the applicant's awareness of the importance of certificates, records, and documents as related to safety.

In order to fly an airplane legally, **you** must have in your personal possession both your pilot certificate and your current medical certificate (for a student pilot, both combined in one). You should know the expiration date of your medical certificate—the last day of the 24th month after its issuance for Class 3, of the 12th month for Class 2. Whenever you had your medical examination in a given month, you are due for another before the last day of the same month a year or two later. In order to operate a radio transmitter, you require from the Federal Communications Commission a Restricted Radiotelephone Operator Permit, and this must also be with you when you operate the radio.

For the airplane to fly legally, **it** must have aboard an airworthiness certificate bearing the assigned registration number, and this certificate must be displayed at all times. There must also be aboard a registration certificate, which is issued to the owner of the airplane. If the airplane has a radio transmitter, it must have aboard a radio transmitter station license issued by the FCC.

The FAA requires that certain information be made available to the operator concerning the operation of the airplane. The manufacturer of a heavy aircraft has to furnish an FAA-approved Flight Manual, which contains all the information. For light aircraft, however, the same information can be provided in various ways—by placards, an equipment list, an Owner's Manual, and even by separate sheets of paper such as typically contain Weight and Balance data. Wherever it is to be found, you should dig out the following information, become familiar with it, and know where to find it again if you should need it:

1. Data concerning the power plant and propeller, including operating ranges as shown on the various panel instruments, and any special limitations.

2. Airspeed limits for various flight conditions, as marked on the airspeed indicator, and also maneuvering speed, which is not marked there.

3. Information needed for weight and balance computations, described later in the chapter.

4. Recommended procedures for various operations, such as starting the engine, takeoffs and landings, climbs and descents, and emergencies.

5. Performance data, such as takeoff and landing distances, and stall speeds.

6. Limitations, usually shown by placards on the instrument panel or elsewhere.

The aircraft and engine logbooks are not required to be carried in the aircraft, but they should be available for inspection at a check ride, and you should understand and be able to explain the entries. The logbook entries provide the only means of knowing if the aircraft is really airworthy and legal for flight. Have all airworthiness directives (AD's) been complied with? Was a periodic inspection carried out, as required, within the preceding 12 calendar months?

Let me tell you a true story. A short while ago I signed off a student for his IFR check ride. Tom was an outstanding pilot, skillful and careful, and there was no doubt he would perform splendidly. The scheduled time arrived, and so did the examiner. "Let's start by your showing me how you would load the airplane. Get out your Weight and Balance sheets." End of check ride! Tom had failed to confirm that all his paperwork was in order. After the recent installation of a new radio, the repair shop had not returned the Weight and Balance material. "Sorry," said the examiner, "I can't fly with you until you take care of that." Weeks later, Tom got his IFR rating, but the lesson here is clear: Take the trouble to have all your papers in order before every flight, and especially before a check ride or BFR.

B. OBTAINING WEATHER INFORMATION

1. **Objective.** To determine that the applicant:
   a. Exhibits adequate knowledge of aviation weather information by obtaining, reading, and analyzing
      (1) weather reports and forecasts.
      (2) weather charts.
      (3) pilot weather reports.
      (4) SIGMETS and AIRMETS.
      (5) Notices to Airmen.
   b. Makes a sound go/no-go decision based on the available weather information.

2. **Action.** The examiner will:
   a. Determine that the applicant has obtained all pertinent weather information. (If curent weather materials are not available, the examiner will furnish samples for use.)
   b. Ask the applicant to analyze and explain the weather data, and determine that the applicant's performance meets the objective.
   c. Place emphasis on the applicant's ability to interpret the weather data and make a sound go/no-go decision.

The FARs stipulate that the pilot in command must be familiar with all information affecting the flight before starting. Weather is critically important because it affects course, fuel adequacy, terrain clearance, destination airports, alternates, enroute airports, and so on. Many pilots—even experienced ones—do not really know how to obtain a proper weather briefing. No doubt all flight service personnel do their best, but they have different styles and different approaches, so you may have to play an active role in seeking out the information you need. And what you need is a thorough understanding of the whole weather picture. After identifying your aircraft on the phone, and explaining that you want to go VFR, and what time you propose to leave, ask for the big picture first, get into details later. The briefer may want to jump right into the middle and tell you about the weather at your destination or the thunderstorm half way there, but unless you first get a more global synopsis, there's no way you can fit the pieces together. Satellite pictures offer the most vivid way to see what is going on over the whole country, so find out what the latest satellite picture shows, and when it was taken? Is there a frontal system, and if so, where is the front right now, and how fast is it moving? Are there squall lines and lines of thunderstorms, and where are they?

Weather charts present a visual impression of your whole route of flight, and they contain a wealth of information about what is likely to happen next. If you are visiting the FSS for your briefing, study the charts and ask the briefer to explain them. Ask for outdated copies of several kinds of charts, and take them home to study—they throw them away otherwise. If you have on-line access, through a modem and PC with graphics capability, you will have to read the charts yourself, and the same is true if you tune "AM Weather" on your local early-morning TV. The general ("synoptic") presentation comes from three charts—the surface analysis chart, the weather depiction chart and the radar summary chart, all of which are from one to four hours old. These charts are illustrated in the FAA's excellent manual, AVIATION WEATHER (AC 00-6). I am going to discuss charts at length—at too greath length, you may think. I have found that a great many pilots—I would even say most pilots—know too little about weather. And weather happens to be the direct cause of more than half of all general aviation accidents. Could there be a connection? My aim is to encourage you to take a greater interest in the weather, to visit the FSS or Weather Service office, to get them to go over the charts and sequence reports with you and explain them. I guarantee you the meteorologists will welcome your interest, and I promise you that you will become a safer pilot through knowing more about the weather.

The **Surface Analysis Chart** (Fig. 1-1) shows highs and lows and the positions of fronts and troughs. In my opinion, the main value of this chart for a pilot is that it shows these major features at a glance and clearly. In Fig. 1-1, for example, you can see that a cold front is moving toward the Atlantic coast, while a stationary front runs northeast from the Great Lakes region. There is a major low-pressure area where these two fronts converge, and there are two high-pressure areas, to the north and south. This chart promises you good flying west of the Mississippi and along the Gulf coast, but very dubious weather over the whole eastern part of the country. Wind direction and velocity are shown at each of the hundreds of reporting stations, as well as temperatures and dewpoints. The little wind indicator symbols tell surface wind strengths by the number of barbs on their shafts. They tell wind direction by the fact that the shafts point into

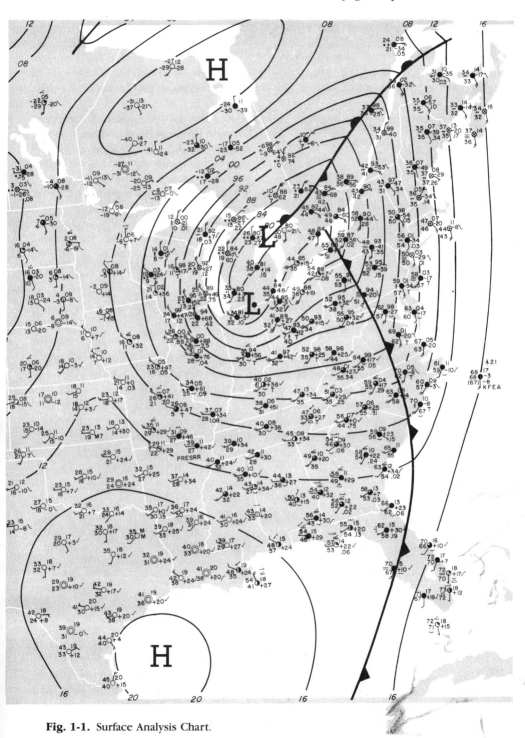

Fig. 1-1. Surface Analysis Chart.

the wind; but you know already that the pattern of circulation is counter-clockwise around a low, clockwise around a high, so no useful new information is conveyed. The truth is, the clutter of symbols and numbers on this chart makes it difficult to read, and besides, all the information from the same reporting stations is found in the teletype sequence reports.

The **Weather Depiction Chart** (Fig. 1-2) shows the actual surface weather by cloud cover, rain, snow, etc. It also outlines the areas that have marginal VFR conditions or worse. This chart presents the most direct way of finding out if you can make your trip in VFR conditions or not. The Weather Depiction Chart shown here was prepared at the same time as the Surface Analysis in Fig. 1-1. Here the cloud cover at each reporting station is shown as a little circle—solid black for overcast, black and white for broken, white for clear. You can see that the extensive low-pressure area at the Great Lakes is associated with overcast skies, rain showers ("RW"), and snow showers ("SW"), and that similar conditions prevail along the east coast. Solid outlines represent areas below VFR (ceiling less than 1,000' and/or visibility less than 3 miles). The larger areas, outlined by scalloped edges, depict ceilings of 1,000' to 3,000' and/or visibility 3 to 5 miles (marginal VFR).

You might think the Weather Depiction Chart by itself tells you everything you need to know. It might encourage you, for example, to fly in the north-south corridor that has VFR conditions behind the cold front. Remember, however, that the chart is a static picture of conditions several hours ago, and that you plan to be in the air several hours from now. Weather is dynamic; it can change radically in a few hours. The Surface Analysis Chart helps in predicting what will happen next. For example, it is likely that the low-pressure center will move eastward, possibly carrying all its miserable below-VFR weather right into the path of your proposed flight. This is exactly the sort of situation in which an expert briefer can help. If the FSS briefer sounds uncertain about predictions, ask them to connect you with a National Weather Service meteorologist. If you do plan to fly through an area shown as marginal VFR, you should be ready to make a 180 at the earliest sign that conditions are worse than were depicted, or that they are deteriorating as you continue the flight.

The **Radar Summary Chart** (Fig. 1-3) shows "echoes," i.e., areas of precipitation and of thunderstorm cells containing heavy precipitation. Increasing intensity of the radar echoes would be shown by concentric contours, but there are none in this chart because all the echoes here were weak to moderate. Echo intensity relates to how heavy the precipitation is. Radar also gives the tops of the echoes, but the actual tops of the clouds are probably a few thousand feet higher, because radar can not detect clouds that contain relatively little moisture. Radar charts are very impor-

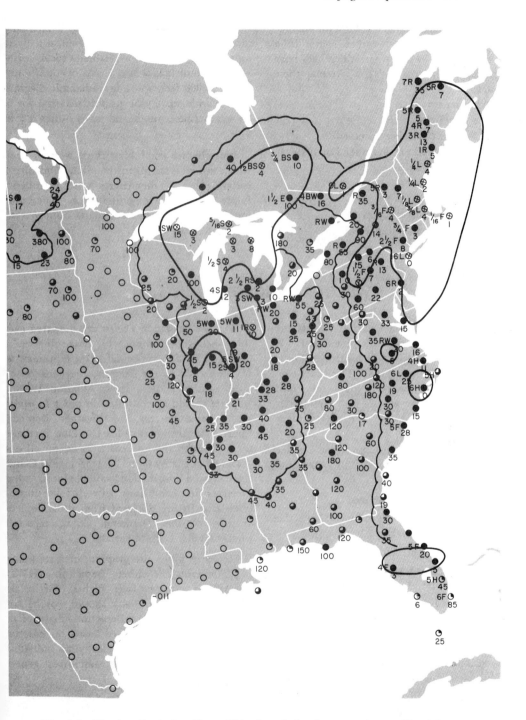

Fig. 1-2. Weather Depiction Chart. This chart is for the same time as Fig. 1-1.

tant to the VFR pilot, because they show everything; thunderstorms can no longer hide between weather reporting points, as used to be the case in the past. Areas where echoes were observed at the time the chart was prepared tell you where there was significant precipitation. The individual cells shown on the chart will long since have vanished—a thunderstorm usually builds, matures, and subsides in less than an hour—but new cells will usually be taking their place in the same general areas. The direction and speed with which the cells are moving is also indicated, by arrows and numbers (knots) next to the arrow shafts. This particular chart was compiled at the same time as Figs. 1.1 and 1.2. The areas of echoes are outlined by scalloped edges. Under each echo is given its top in hundreds of feet—a very important number if you are thinking of flying

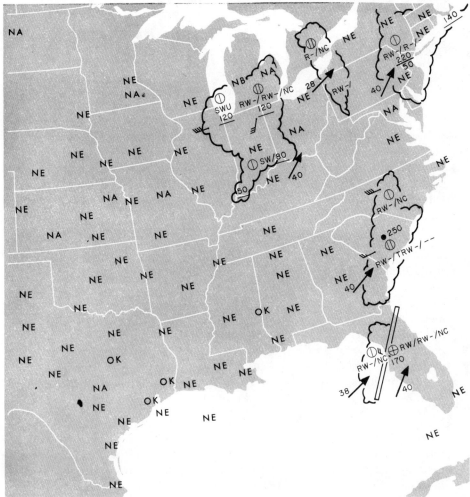

Fig. 1-3. Radar Summary Chart. This chart is for the same time as Fig. 1-1.

VFR on top. For example, the strong cell (solid black circle) in eastern South Carolina evidently represents a giant cumulonimbus with heavy precipitation extending upward to 25,000'. On the positive side, there is real assurance in a radar chart that shows nothing but "no echoes" (NE) over your entire route. That is the situation here for the whole central part of the country. "NA" means "observation not available."

The next things in a briefing are the current weather enroute reports and the terminal forecasts, both of which the briefer reads out from the teletype **sequence reports**. The briefer will tell you, in plain English, what you want to know, so you don't need to be able to decode the sequence reports. These curious sets of abbreviated symbols seem rather out of place in our modern era of communications, although they did serve a purpose in the early days of the teletype, when slow transmission of information was the rule. Today, the same information could just as well be conveyed in straightforward intelligible words and numbers. Besides, the FAA is installing an increasing number of automatic weather observing stations (AWOS), from which one can obtain—in the air or on the phone—a synthesized voice report, in plain English, of current conditions, obtained by automated instruments. On the other hand, some of the on-line weather services to which you can have access through a modem and a telephone line use essentially the same set of symbols as in the sequence reports. Whether or not it makes sense, the FAA requires that you be able to interpret the sequence reports, and they test your ability on written examinations and at check rides, so you'll have to learn how; but I certainly don't think that the ability to read these has much to do with one's skill as a pilot.

Sequence reports give actual conditions at the various observation points (usually airports) at a specified recent time. The format is always the same, and it corresponds to the order in which information is presented in an ATIS broadcast or by a control tower. This standard order is: location identifier, sky cover, visibility and weather conditions (rain, snow, fog, haze, etc.), sea-level pressure in millibars, surface temperature and dewpoint, surface wind direction and velocity, and altimeter setting. Runway visual range, primarily of interest to IFR pilots, may be given next. Finally, significant PIREPS may be added at the end, such as reports on the tops of an overcast, or of cloud layers not visible from the ground.

Next in the briefing, after the sequence reports, comes the **winds aloft forecast**. Winds aloft can make a big difference to your estimated flight time, but more often than not, unfortunately, they don't turn out as forecast. You should, of course, know how to apply a winds-aloft report or forecast to your planned course, in order to compute an appropriate heading, and also to estimate your probable groundspeed, because you will surely be required to do this on a check ride. However, I have found that what works well in actual practice is to start out with a heading that corresponds exactly to your course line on the sectional chart, and then monitor your progress very frequently, so you can build in heading corrections as you go, on a trial-and-error basis. It is also important to get an estimate of your ground speed after you level off at cruising altitutude, and to watch it closely while there is still plenty of fuel in your tanks, so you can plan timely changes of destination if necessary.

If the briefer says nothing about SIGMETS (warnings of severe weather that is significant for all aircraft) or AIRMETS (for small aircraft), or NOTAMS (notices to airmen, which are relevant to your proposed flight), ask and verify that there really are none. Missing a NOTAM and then discovering that your destination airport is closed for runway repairs, for example, would be impermissible and potentially dangerous.

A good plan, after you have listened to the briefing and copied down the information, is to draw a rough sketch map of your route, showing all the weather conditions along the way. This will give you a clear visual image of what lies ahead, and then you will be better sensitized to anything turning out different from what was expected. When the forecast turns out to be wrong in any respect, it often means that some major unexpected change in the weather has taken place, and you need to be prepared for a diversion if the route ahead goes sour. The sooner you recognize what is happening, the better; and you can't know anything has gone wrong unless you have a clear idea of what conditions are supposed to be.

Mountain passes present a special problem for the VFR pilot. Try to establish if the weather will allow good safe VFR flight through them, at a high enough altitude so there will surely be room for a 180° turn if required. Remember that passes are roughly V-shaped, with the narrowest part at the bottom, where a road or railroad or river may run, and the widest part up near the ridge line. If the mountain tops are obscured by a solid overcast, going through could be very dangerous, even though you can see to the other side, because you need plenty of room for reversing course if the clouds or fog settle in. An airplane making a 180° turn at 90 k with a 30° bank angle requires a full half mile of room, and since the turn diameter increases as the square of the airspeed, faster airplanes need substantially more room—two miles, for example, at 180 k. Thus, the width of the pass **at your altitude** is a very important consideration before you ever start the flight, unless conditions are absolutely CAVU.

If there are areas of broken clouds with poor visibilities enroute, you may want to consider flying on top, and to do that you will need estimates, during the briefing, of just where the tops are. The best sources for that informtion are PIREPS. Single-engine VFR flight on top of a solid overcast is a risky business for a pilot who is not IFR-rated; how will you get down if the broken clouds forecast at your destination turn to solid overcast before you get there?

If you have a taste for a more sophisticated understanding of the weather aloft, where you are actually going to be flying, read about the **Constant Pressure Charts** (Fig. 1-4), and get a few copies to study from your nearest FSS. These are constructed twice daily from measurements made with radiosondes—automatic measuring devices that are carried aloft by balloon or dropped from aircraft, and transmit data on pressure, temperature, humidity, and wind at every altitude. A separate chart is constructed for each "standard pressure surface"; the ones of chief interest to general aviation are the 850-, 700-, and 500-millibar charts, which correspond approximately to the 5,000', 10,000', and 18,000' levels, respectively. The 500-millibar chart in Fig. 1-4, for example, shows connected solid lines of altitude ("contours") corresponding to exactly 500 millibars of pressure. These contour lines are labeled in tens of meters of altitude, from 516 (5,160 meters, about 17,000') at the upper left to 588 (5,880 meters, about 19,000') at the lower right. Any "low-pressure area" extends through a large vertical segment of the atmosphere, so the 500-millibar contour line is found at a lower altitude in such an area than in a high-pressure area. The constant-pressure level could be imagined to be a sheet of rubber extending over the entire country, with dips and troughs and sinks and ridges representing the pressure variations.

Fig. 1-4 was compiled at about the same time as the previous charts. Picture this as a contour map, and imagine yourself somewhere southeast of Florida. As you look in a northwesterly direction, you can see how the pressure level slopes down quite steeply (lines close together) into a trough that is positioned over the Great Lakes, where the 5,220-meter line dips sharply down from Canada. This "trough aloft" overlies and influences the bad weather underneath, which you saw in the previous charts.

The winds flow parallel to the lines of equal altitude, and actual wind directions and velocities charted here are the source data for the briefer's winds-aloft information. Moreover, by noting abrupt changes of direction and velocity on a single constant-pressure chart or between two charts at different altitudes, turbulence (horizontal and vertical wind-shear) can be inferred.

At each reporting point there is a cluster of four numbers, representing the actual radiosonde measurements at the 500-millibar pressure level. The number at upper right of the cluster is the exact observed altitude (in tens of meters) at which the pressure is 500 millibars; it is from these numbers that the solid contour lines are drawn. The number at upper left is the temperature. Locations of equal temperature are connected by broken lines (isotherms) at intervals of 5°C. Just below the temperature number at each

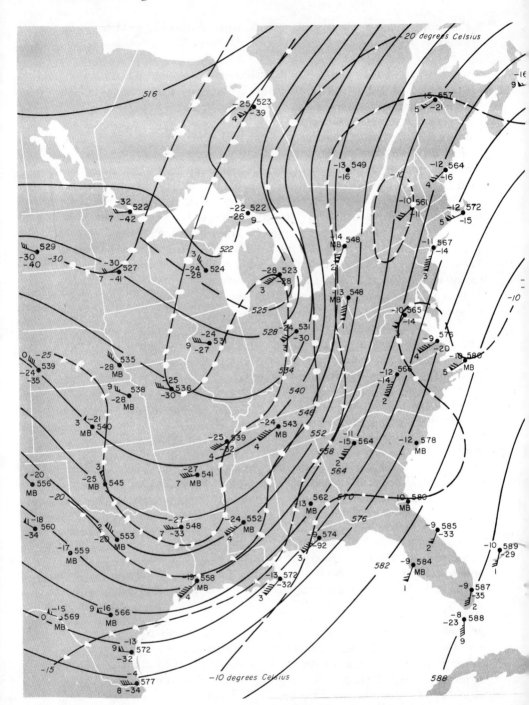

Fig. 1-4. Constant Pressure Chart (500 millibar). This chart is for the same time as Fig. 1-1.

reporting point is the very important temperature-dewpoint spread. When this number is only a few degrees, as in the low pressure area, precipitation can be expected—snow or rain, depending on the temperature at the altitude where you are flying. Freezing levels aloft are of more concern to IFR than to VFR pilots, but even though you are in VFR conditions under the clouds, freezing rain, hail, or snow from above could endanger your flight. Finally, the number at the lower right of the cluster gives the height change (in tens of meters) at that station since the previous reading 12 hours earlier. "M" means "missing observation."

Thunderstorms destroy airplanes in two ways—aloft and near the ground. An airplane that ventures into one is subjected to turbulence beyond belief, imposing forces that exceed the structural design limits. Moreover, in severe turbulence the airplane becomes uncontrollable, so that pilot-exerted forces can add to the damage. The second danger of thunderstorms is wind shear on takeoff or landing—downbursts and microbursts that have brought more than one large jet aircraft to grief. Pilots everywhere may have to deal with thunderstorms at some time or another, but the frequency of thunderstorms varies greatly across the country (Fig. 1-5). In the far west they are rare except over the high mountains and the deserts in the summer. In Florida and along the Gulf coast they are more frequent and more severe than anywhere else. July and August are the big months for thunderstorms, while there are relatively few in December and January. However frequent or infrequent, there is never an excuse for a VFR pilot to fly into one. Isolated thunderstorms—as over the western deserts—are easily circumnavigated at a safe distance, while solid lines of thunderstorms mean "stay on the ground."

The basic requirements for the development of thunderstorms are **unstable air**, **lifting action**, and a **high moisture content**. These features are displayed on a **Stability Chart** (Fig. 1-6), which is therefore extremely valuable in predicting where thunderstorms are likely to develop. Together with the Radar Summary Chart (which shows where thunderstorms actually were and which way they were moving), this chart offers good guidance for the go/no-go decision. Two indexes are shown, which are calculated somewhat differently, but which both reflect the degree of instability of the air. One is called the **lifted index**; it is shown above a short horizontal line on the chart. A large positive value indicates stable air, a small positive value or a negative one indicates unstable air. The other is called the **K index**; it is shown below the lifted index. High positive K values (10, 20, or greater) mean unstable and moisture-laden air. These indexes, which are worked out from the radiosonde temperature and moisture measurements, should be taken very seriously. If your proposed flight will pass through regions with negative lifted indexes and K values greater than about 20, you may expect thunderstorms, possibly severe ones. For

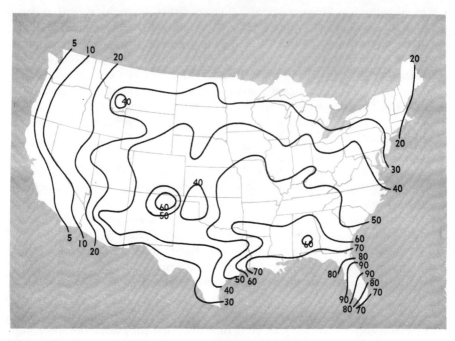

Fig. 1-5. The average number of thunderstorms per year.

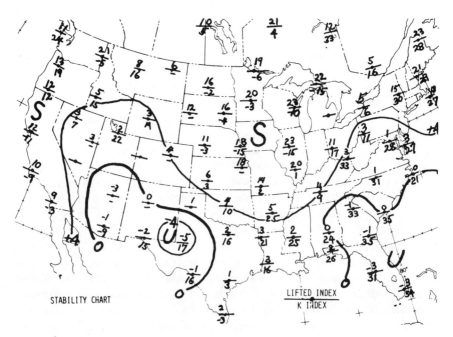

Fig. 1-6. Stability Chart. This chart is for a different date than Fig. 1-1.

example, in Fig. 1-6 (which does not correspond to any of the previous charts), the entry 22/-15 over the Great Lakes means very stable dry air and a smooth ride. The entries -5/17 on the Texas-New Mexico border, and -3/31 over Florida mean very unstable moist air, convective turbulence, and probable thunderstorms. The Stability Chart is a major element that enters into the **Convective Overlook** on the teletype circuit—a narrative prediction of thunderstorm development, written by expert meteorologists.

Forecasts on the teletype circuit or as given to you by the briefer over the telephone are derived from **prognostic charts**, affectionately called "progs." In general, these are the same kinds of charts we have discussed above, except that they are predictions for 12 and 24 hours hence, rather than actual observations. The surface progs look like a combination surface analysis (showing fronts) and weather depiction (showing conditions that are marginal VFR or worse.) Forecast winds and temperatures aloft are given on eight prog charts corresponding to various flight levels. Constant pressure progs show forecast contours, temperatures, and winds in the familiar constant-pressure format. Finally, there is a special prognostic chart called the **Severe Weather Outlook Chart** that shows areas forecast to have really dangerous weather (severe thunderstorms or tornadoes) in the next 12 to 24 hours. As these forecasts materialize, **severe weather watches** are issued for the affected areas.

C. DETERMINING PERFORMANCE AND LIMITATIONS

1. **Objective.** To determine that the applicant:

   a. Exhibits adequate knowledge by explaining the airplane's weight and balance, performance, and limitations including adverse aerodynamic effects of exceeding the limits.

   b. Uses the available and appropriate performance charts, tables, and data.

   c. Computes the weight and balance and determines that the weight and center of gravity will be within limits during all phases of the flight.

   d. Calculates the airplane's performance considering density altitude, wind, terrain, and other pertinent conditions.

   e. Describes the effects of seasonal and atmospheric conditions on the airplane's performance.

   f. Makes a sound decision on whether the required performance is within the airplane's capability and operating limitations.

2. **Action.** The examiner will:

   a. Ask the applicant to explain the airplane's performance and limitations including adverse effects of exceeding the limits and determine that the applicant's performance meets the objective.

b. Ask the applicant to determine the airplane's performance and limita-tions, and describe the effects of seasonal and atmospheric conditions on the airplane's operation, and determine that the applicant's perform-ance meets the objective.

c. Place emphasis on the soundness of the applicant's judgment based on complete and accurate performance calculations.

The "V numbers." In the oral portion of the checkride or biennial flight review you will be questioned about the critical airspeeds for your aircraft. These are to be found in the Owner's Manual. You must know them, and you must use them correctly in every appropriate flight condition. Look them up and fill them in here.

V_{so} is the power-off, full-flaps, gear-down stall speed, which is shown as the bottom of the white arc on the airspeed indicator (ASI). This speed relates to the flight characteristics of the aircraft in a fundamental way, because most of the other critical airspeeds are simply definite multiples of this speed. Remember the curious fact that V_{so} as shown on the ASI is **calibrated**, not **indicated** airspeed. Since ASI instrument error is greatest at low airspeeds, the airplane will actually show a significantly lower air-speed at the stall. If you don't know this from experience, go up and try it.

$$V_{so} = \underline{\hspace{2cm}}$$

V_x is the speed for best angle of climb, i.e., for the greatest increase of altitude **per ground distance covered**. It is generally about 1.3 times V_{so}. This is the only correct airspeed for climbing to clear an obstacle, as described later under Maximum Performance Takeoffs in Chapter 4.

$$V_x = \underline{\hspace{2cm}}$$

V_y is the speed for best rate of climb, i.e., for the greatest increase of altitude **per minute**, as would be shown on the vertical speed indicator (VSI). It is generally about 1.6 times V_{so}. This is the speed at which normal climbs are made after takeoff, and also in cruising flight when the aim is to reach a new altitude as quickly as possible.

$$V_y = \underline{\hspace{2cm}}$$

V_r is rotation speed, the speed at which gentle back pressure on the yoke will let the aircraft fly off the runway. This takeoff speed is close to the stall speed in the takeoff configuration, usually not very different from V_{so}.

Obviously, the speed at which an airplane starts to fly must be very nearly the same as the speed at which it stops flying. This fact suggests what an experienced pilot could do in a totally unfamiliar airplane. If no manual were available, so that none of the V numbers were known, they could set neutral trim and let the airplane accelerate and fly itself off the runway. By glancing at the ASI at the moment they become airborne, they could call that airspeed—at a rough approximation—V_{so}. Then they could work out approximate values for all the other V numbers, by using the right multipliers. V_y for initial climbout would be 1.6 times, V_x would be 1.3 times, and approach to landing would be 1.3 times the experimentally determined V_r, which was assumed to be the same as V_{so}. The purpose of this fanciful account is to show you how all the V numbers interrelate; it is not a recommended procedure for flying unfamiliar airplanes.

V_r = _____

Cruise climb airspeed is the speed recommended in the Owner's Manual for climb when maximum performance is not required. A convenient speed is about half way between V_y and normal cruise. It is better for the engine than V_y because higher airspeed means greater airflow for cooling. It is also safer because the higher airspeed is achieved by lowering the nose, thereby allowing better forward visibility.

Cruise climb airspeed = _____

Cruise airspeed is the speed you choose to use in level flight, within the limits recommended by the manufacturer. An economical choice often made is to fly at 65% power with manifold pressure (MP) and/or RPM as given in the performance charts of your Owner's Manual. The indicated airspeed (IAS) will decrease, the higher you fly; but the true airspeed (TAS) at 65% power will actually increase. Every model has an optimal flight altitude at which maximum TAS is achieved for a given percent of maximum power. In the Cessna 172, for example, at standard temperature (colder the higher you go, by 3.5° F per 1,000 ft), TAS at 65% power is 109 k at 2,000', 117 k at 10,000'.

If your airplane has a constant-speed (variable-pitch) propeller, there will be several combinations of MP and RPM that produce 65% power, but the TAS and fuel consumption are about the same for them all. In a Cessna 182, for example, at 6,000' and standard temperature you could use MP 19 inches at 2,400 RPM, 20 inches at 2,300 RPM, 21 inches at 2,200 RPM, or 22 inches at 2,100 RPM, and all of these combinations give 65% power, 133 k, and 11.1 gallons per hr.

Typical cruise TAS at 65% power = _____
MP (variable pitch prop) = _____
RPM = _____

V_a is the design maneuvering speed. It is the maximum airspeed at which abrupt maneuvers of the controls, producing sudden steep banks or sharp pull-ups, will result in a stall before the aircraft structure is overstressed. You can recover from a stall, but there is no recovering from a seriously broken airplane! It is important to understand the significance of this speed, which is determined by the design of each particular aircraft model. You know that the stalling speed increases sharply with increased g force, as in a bank or a pull-up. For example, in a Cessna 172, which stalls without flaps at a calibrated airspeed (CAS) of 53 k, the stall speed increases to 75 k in a 60-degree bank. There is a force of 2 g, equivalent to doubling the weight of the aircraft, in such a bank. Every aircraft is built to withstand a certain g force without breaking; in the Cessna 172 this "flight load factor" is +3.8 g. Obviously, the stall speed at 3.8 g will be considerably higher than the 75-k stall speed at 2 g. This stall speed at 3.8 g is V_a; in the Cessna 172 it is 96 k CAS. At this or any lower speed the airplane can not break, no matter what g force is applied, because it will stall first.

V_a is the correct airspeed to use in significant turbulence, since a gust, no matter how strong, will not break the airplane but will stall it instead. It is also the correct airspeed for maneuvers such as stalls, steep turns, chandelles, and lazy eights, in which unusual control movements will be required. From the standpoint of structural safety alone, a speed lower than V_a could be employed, but this is inadvisable in turbulence because it offers you less margin over the stall, and because aircraft control responsiveness will be sacrificed, as when the controls go "mushy" in slow flight. You may worry that by flying exactly at V_a you risk structural failure, but the design flight load factor actually allows a safety margin of about 50% over the stated value upon which V_a is based; this ensures that you will always and surely stall first.

Many pilots are surprised to discover that V_a is lower when the aircraft weight is less than maximum gross. Somehow, it seems, you ought to be safe flying faster if the airplane is light than when it is heavy. Not true! Remember that all stall speeds decrease with lighter loading, just as they increase with heavier loading (or higher g force), as discussed above. Thus, if you are lightly loaded, the airplane will stall at a lower speed when the same +3.8 g force is applied. So if you want the protection afforded by V_a against severe gusts and other forms of turbulence, you must adjust the airspeed downward. The difference is not negligible; in the Cessna 172, for example, at 700 lb under gross, V_a drops from 96 k to 80 k.

V_a at gross weight = _____

Best glide airspeed is the speed given in the Owner's Manual for maximum distance covered, power off, in the no-wind condition. It is usually very close to V_y. It is an important speed to have in mind in the event of engine failure in a single, although it will be modified according to wind conditions, as described later in chapter 11.

Best glide airspeed = _____

V_{ne}, the never-exceed speed, is shown by a red line at the top range of the airspeed indicator (ASI). This has to do with structural integrity against the increased forces on the wings and empennage.

V_{ne} = _____

V_{no}, the maximum structural cruising speed, is shown as the top of the green arc on the ASI; above this—in the yellow arc—you should not fly except in perfectly smooth air. Again, the risk to structural integrity is the reason for this airspeed limitation.

V_{no} = _____

V_{fe}, the maximum speed at which you may fly with full flaps, is shown as the top of the white arc on the ASI. Obviously, you can fly faster than that with partial flaps; the Owner's Manual usually gives maximum speeds for various flap settings. It is a common misunderstanding that **no flaps at all** can be deployed at speeds above the white arc. There are many circumstances where progressively adding the drag of flaps can help reduce airspeed. Sudden power reductions are bad for the engine because the associated rapid cooling is undesirable. For a descent from cruising altitude, therefore, lowering some flaps (just as dropping the gear in a retractable) permits a good rate of descent to be established without excessive power reduction. It is important, therefore, to learn the speed limitation associated with **each** flap setting, in order to carry out this procedure smoothly, without overstressing the flaps.

V_{fe} = _____

V_{le}, for a retractable, is the maximum speed at which the airplane may be flown with landing gear extended, and V_{lo} is the maximum speed at which the landing gear may be operated. In some airplanes, V_{le} and V_{lo} are the same; in others V_{le} may be as high as V_{ne}, while V_{lo} is much lower because of the vulnerability of the gear doors to the force of the airstream. Landing gear can be used effectively—even more effectively than flaps—as drag devices (see above), but you must not exceed the allowable speeds.

$$V_{le} = \underline{\hspace{3cm}}$$
$$V_{lo} = \underline{\hspace{3cm}}$$

V_{mc} is the minimum control speed in a twin with the critical engine inoperative. If you fly a twin, you already have learned the life-and-death importance of this number. It determines, absolutely and unforgivingly, if you can fly or not when an engine fails. It applies to the case where the inoperative engine has been feathered, the flaps are retracted, and a bank of exactly 5° into the operating engine is being maintained. If any one of these favorable conditions has not been achieved, the actual minimum control speed will be **very much higher**. A red line on the ASI indicates V_{mc}. No one but a professional pilot with regular proficiency training can safely depend on Vmc in a real engine-out emergency. Some higher speed should be adopted as a practical personal minimum, depending on your own training, experience, and current proficiency. For a detailed analysis of V_{mc} and its alternatives, see Chapter 3 in my book FLYING OUT OF DANGER (Airguide Publications Inc., Long Beach, California, 90801).

$$V_{mc} = \underline{\hspace{3cm}}$$

Fuel. In addition to the V numbers, you need to know how much fuel and oil your airplane carries, how much of the fuel is usable, and the fuel consumption in gal (or lb) per hour at normal cruise. Thus, you should be able to answer the key question: How long and how far can you fly with full tanks? You also need a reliable method of partially loading the fuel tanks so that you can measure exactly how much fuel you are carrying before you set out for a crosscountry flight. Fuel gauges are notoriously inaccurate; you should not depend on them at all, but rather should use a calibrated dipstick. The **only** value of a fuel gauge is to warn you of leakage during flight, as from an unsecured fuel cap; you should definitely be concerned if the fuel quantity seems to be going down faster than it should. On the other hand, you should **never**, under any circumstances, use a fuel gauge reading to estimate how much flight time remains. That is an invitation to disaster. Your conservatively calculated **fuel-exhausted time** should have been written down at takeoff, as explained in Chapter 5.

Density Altitude. You must understand how to read the performance charts in the Owner's Manual, and how to apply the corrections for temperature and altitude, so that you can know the required takeoff distance, climb performance, and landing roll needed under all conditions. The critical computation is for takeoff (with or without an obstacle to clear) at a high altitude field on a hot day. Density altitude determines performance;

it is what the wings "feel," namely, the amount of air flowing past, which generates the lift (see Chapter 14 for further discussion). The higher the altitude, the less dense the air, as reflected by the lower atmospheric pressure and the lower oxygen content. In addition, air becomes less dense when it warms up, because it expands. Low air density affects aircraft performance in two ways. First, with a normally aspirated engine, it reduces the maximum available power because there is less oxygen for combustion. Second—and this applies equally to a turbocharged engine—it reduces lift because fewer air molecules are flowing over the wing, and thus a higher angle of attack is required for any given flight condition.

Density altitude is what the **equivalent** altitude would be at a standard temperature. For example, at a field elevation of 5,000' on a hot summer day at 100° F., the density altitude is about 8,500'. This means that your airplane will behave just as though it were at 8,500' at 29° F, the temperature normally expected for that altitude. The effect is a big one. It may require twice the takeoff roll that you needed at sea level, and then your climb capability may be very poor indeed, perhaps no better than a couple of hundred feet per minute. This may not sound alarming because you are used to setting up a climb when you are cruising at high altitudes (and cool temperatures!), when you don't really mind if you gain altitude slowly. But think how different the situation is when you are trying to clear trees or buildings in your takeoff path!

It is true that there are small differences in the critical airspeeds given in your Owner's Manual for different altitudes, and you should learn about those. But the most important rule in takeoffs and landings at high density altitude is to fly the airplane exactly as you normally do. Your **indicated** airspeeds will accurately reflect performance, just as at sea level. The pitot tube tells you how many air molecules are bombarding it, and with what force. Thus, when the airspeed indicator reads 65 k (e.g., on final approach), the airplane will behave, in all respects, as it does for an indicated airspeed of 65 k at sea level. Likewise, the stall speeds (indicated) are the same, so your indicated airspeed as you touch down and stop flying will also be the same as you are accustomed to.

What will be very different, however, is your true airspeed (which you can't see) and your groundspeed (which you can). These will be **much faster** than at sea level. For the example given above, where the density altitude is 8,500', if you cross the threshold of 65 k indicated, your groundspeed will be 74 k—a considerable increase, meaning a longer landing roll, harder braking, and so on. The key point in all this is that you must fly the airplane according to the airspeed indicator. If you let outside references confuse you, there is a real chance of stalling inadvertently, because you will sense that you are going too fast, and you will try to compensate by slowing the airplane.

Weight and Balance. Weight and balance are critically important for the safe operation of an airplane. Every aircraft is built to carry a certain maximum load. The weight of the loaded airplane is called the **gross weight**, and the airplane is certified to fly at a certain maximum gross weight. Performance depends on the available power in relation to this weight. Exceeding the maximum certificated gross weight compromises performance, because more of the available power is needed just to sustain the extra weight against the force of gravity, leaving less to be converted to speed or climb. This means a higher rotation speed for takeoff (so more runway required), poorer climbout over obstacles, poorer rate of climb subsequently, and decreased service ceiling. Operational range is reduced, because speed at a given fuel consumption is decreased. More serious is the increase of the stall speed, much as occurs with increased g forces in a bank, because increased g is, in effect, the same thing as increased weight. This may be associated with maneuverability and controllability problems. Most serious of all, an over-gross condition threatens the structural integrity of the aircraft in turbulence or in maneuvers that produce abrupt g forces. A typical general aviation aircraft is built to withstand a flight load factor of about 3.8 g at maximum gross weight. If the aircraft is over gross, this g force will be exceeded at a degree of turbulence or abrupt control inputs that would otherwise have been within design limits. Then there is a real danger of breaking the wings or empennage.

Balance is even more critical than weight. Balance concerns the distribution of weight, which determines where the **center of gravity** (C.G.) is located. Every aircraft has a forward and rear limit for the C.G., and the flight characteristics are altered radically outside those limits. With C.G. beyond the forward limit, the aircraft is nose-heavy, so that even full up elevator can not compensate. This means trouble in rotation for takeoff, and very serious trouble in flaring for landing. With C.G. beyond the aft limit, the aircraft is tail-heavy, and the longitudinal stability is affected. Logitudinal stability requires a certain degree of nose-heaviness, which also guarantees automatic recovery from a stall. You can feel this yourself as you reduce speed for slow flight; the nose drops more and more as the speed falls off, and you need to keep adding elevator up-trim. Finally, at the stall break, the nose drops sharply, and the airplane picks up speed and begins to fly again. One of the real dangers of exceeding the aft G.C. limit is the interference with stall recovery or—even worse—spin recovery.

The weight and balance information for your airplane is contained on separate sheets—not usually in the Owner's Manual—that are required to be updated every time a piece of equipment is added or removed. Thus, the most up-to-date entry will tell you the **basic empty weight** of the airplane with all its present equipment, and also the actual C.G. and the total **moment** (explained later).

About the weight: The empty weight includes unusable fuel, undrainable oil,* and hydraulic fluids. It is the irreducible minimum weight. If this weight is subtracted from the maximum gross weight, the result is called the **useful load**. The simplest first computation is to add up all the fuel, people, and baggage you propose to take (not exceeding the maximum placarded capacities of each baggage compartment), and make sure the useful load is not exceeded. In all the examples presented here, for weight and later for balance, the essential information is presented first, so that you can carry out the computation yourself, as a practice exercise, and then compare your result with mine.

The first thing to note is that the actual empty weight of your airplane is likely to be considerably greater than the empty weight assumed in the Owner's Manual, depending, of course, on what optional equipment and avionics are installed. Thus, the useful load is likely to be less than the manufacturer advertises. As an example, the Owner's Manual for the 1980 Model N Cessna 172 Skyhawk gives 1,454 (all weights are in pounds) as the empty weight for the purpose of illustrative weight and balance calculations. Since gross weight is 2,300, this makes a useful load of 2,300 − 1,454 = 846. The club I instruct with has four of these popular aircraft, without any very remarkable equipment, and their actual basic empty weights are 1,475, 1,494, 1,495, and 1,503. Thus, the **real** useful load, instead of 846, is at best 825 and at worst 797. These are by no means negligible differences.

This brings us to another important point. Most general aviation aircraft are built for flexibility of use, so that more seats are provided than can be filled safely if the tanks are full. The pilot can leave the tanks partially filled and take a full load of passengers on a short flight, or fill the tanks and carry fewer people on a long flight. So every flight may involve some juggling of fuel loading, people loading, and baggage loading to remain within the useful load. This is where weight and balance relate directly to the flight plan, for in order to carry more people you must carry less fuel, thus shortening the legs of the flight. However, if you bear in mind that passengers find more than an hour or two of sitting in the typical cabin

---

*Most manufacturers now include full oil in the basic empty weight; you should check this point for your own aircraft to see on what basis the empty weight is calculated. At 7.5 lb/gal, the difference between the two methods of calculation could amount to around 15 lb in a single, as much as 50 lb in some twins.

of a small airplane rather trying, and if you also consider the needs of the human bladder, you will plan short flight legs anyway.

People who fly the Cessna 172 are often shocked to discover that when they fill the tanks it is no longer a four-place airplane. Consider the average useful load of my club's Skyhawks: 2,300 − 1,492 = 808. Standard tanks hold 40 gal of usable fuel, or 240 lb, leaving 568 for people and baggage. This means **three** FAA-sized standard adults of 170 lb each, with 58 lb remaining for baggage. Four people would overload the airplane, even without any baggage at all. Moreover, if the aircraft has long-range tanks (50 gal usable), and they are filled, the useful load is reduced by another 60 lb, barely allowing three people to be carried without baggage.

With standard tanks, the pilot and two passengers in this aircraft can cruise at 65% power at 6,000′ and make 113 k TAS, burning 7.4 gph, for a total flight time of 5.4 hr and a total distance of 610 NM to fuel exhaustion (no reserve). Allowing a reasonable 45 min reserve (which is actually required at night), and making allowance for the additional fuel needed for taxiing and for climbing to altitude, the realistic range is about 500 NM.

We can look at this problem differently. Suppose you do wish to load four standard-sized people and 120 lb baggage (the maximum allowable), how much fuel can you carry, and how far can you fly? The people weigh 680, the baggage weighs 120, for a total of 800. With a useful load of 808, you could carry just 8 lb of fuel, or 1.3 gal. Well, you wouldn't take off with that amount of fuel, even if you had a way to carry exactly 1.3 gal—which you don't! So if this airplane carries four people, there must be absolutely no baggage aboard. Then you can fill the tanks half full, and safely plan a 2-hr trip with some reserve.

With regard to useful load, there's nothing very special about the Cessna 172. I chose it for illustration because it demonstrates the great flexibility you usually have in choosing to carry people or baggage or fuel. But it also illustrates the potential dangers, if you are one of those happy-go-lucky pilots who just loads up and flies. Like most things that affect flight safety, you can get away with quite a lot—until some day, in a particular set of circumstances, it does you in.

In general, the more complex an airplane is, the more one has to worry about the details of weight and balance. Consider, for example, the popular Seneca II light twin. Maximum gross is 4,570, standard empty weight is about 2,840. As aircraft become more sophisticated, the optional equipment becomes heavier. A typical Seneca II that I flew had optional equipment weighing 308, for a basic empty weight of 3,148. Thus, the useful load for this aircraft was 4,570 − 3,148 = 1,422.

Many twins, like this one, have a "zero fuel weight" limitation. This means that you may not carry more than a certain weight in people and baggage, regardless of how little fuel you are willing to have aboard. In the Seneca II, the allowable zero fuel weight is 4,000. The maximum weight in people and baggage is therefore 4,000 − 3,148 = 852. The remainder of the 1,422-lb useful load (1,422 − 852 = 570) could be carried as fuel. Full standard tanks in this aircraft hold 98 gal, of which 93 are usable, so a practical loading might look like this:

Basic empty weight	3,148
Pilot + four "standard" passengers	850
Zero fuel weight (4,000 maximum)	3,998
Fuel, 93 gal usable	558
Subtotal	4,556
Allowable baggage	14
Maximum gross	4,570

You can see that to carry a reasonable amount of baggage, you could only accommodate three passengers instead of four, leaving two seats empty; or your fuel tanks would have to be less full. In the loading proposed above, full standard tanks would take you about 700 NM at 167 k, burning 20.5 gph at cruise with 65% power at 10,000'. This includes taxi and maximum power climb, but allows no reserve. Even a daytime VFR flight legally requires a 30-min reserve, and a night flight requires a 45-min reserve, which reduces the range to 575 NM.

About the balance: Here we are concerned with the position of the C.G. The C.G. is the point (called the **fulcrum**) on which the airplane would balance in a level attitude if it were possible to suspend it at that point. The airplane should be thought of as a seesaw; the downward force on each side of the fulcrum is equal to the weight times the distance from the fulcrum. The distance from the fulcrum is called the **arm**, and the product of the weight in pounds by the arm in inches is called the **moment**, measured in pound-inches. For the seesaw to balance, the moments on the two sides of the fulcrum have to be equal.

The concept makes good sense. If you put a 100-lb person forward of the C.G. at an arm of 10' (120 inches), the forward moment is 12,000 lb-inches. You can balance this force with a 50-lb person aft of the C.G. at an arm of 240 inches, or a 200-lb person at an arm of 60 inches, or a person of any other weight at an arm such that the weight times the arm equals an aft moment of 12,000 lb-inches. The C.G. of an empty airplane is about at the position of the wings, usually just at or behind the pilot's seat. Adding weight forward or aft of the C.G. moves the C.G. forward or aft accordingly. The problem is to determine if the C.G. is within the safe limits as specified by the manufacturer.

Since the position of the C.G. is somewhat different for each individual airplane of the same model, it would be inconvenient to compute arms forward and aft of the actual C.G. Instead, to simplify the computations, all measurements are made relative to an arbitrary chosen point called the **datum**. This can be located anywhere, but it is usually at an obvious place like the tip of the spinner, or the firewall. In the Cessna 172, for example, the datum is at the front face of the firewall.

The C.G. of a new empty airplane is determined at the factory by actually weighing and balancing. It is expressed as inches aft of the datum. Each piece of equipment placed in the airplane has a known weight and a specified position in inches from the datum. Thus, each item added—and eventually fuel, people, and baggage—has a certain moment, which is its weight multiplied by its arm in inches from the datum. For illustration, we are going to consider a Cessna 172 with basic empty weight (including equipment) of 1,454. Its C.G. is stated to be 39.6 inches aft of the datum, for a moment of $1{,}454 \times 39.6 = 57{,}578$ lb-inches. Moments are usually expressed, for convenience, after dividing by 1,000—thus 57.6 in this case. I shall follow that convention; just remember that if you need the actual moment, in lb-inches, you will have to multiply these smaller numbers by 1,000.

The weights and the moments of all the added items—fuel, occupants, and baggage—are added to the weight and moment for the empty airplane. Then the total moment and total weight can be located on a diagram, provided in the Owner's Manual, to see if the result falls within the acceptable envelope. This is just a shortcut for seeing if the C.G. is within limits, without actually computing the C.G. Alternatively, as I recommend, one can actually compute the C.G. in inches aft of the datum, and see if it falls within limits specified for the gross weight at which the aircraft is to fly. Since total weight times arm equals total moment, it follows that the C.G. (which is the total arm, in inches aft of the datum) is the total moment (in actual lb-inches) divided by the total weight. To simplify the job still further, a loading graph is provided. This permits one quickly to determine the moment for each given weight placed in a typical position in the airplane, such as the fuel tanks, the front seats, the rear seats, or the baggage compartments.

Now let's go through the steps for computing weight and balance in a Cessna 172, using the table and graphs furnished in the Owner's Manual and reproduced here by permission. Fig. 1-7 shows the loading arrangements, and gives the arm for each position in the aircraft. The front seats occupy positions between 34 and 46 inches aft of the datum, with 37 inches used as a representative average arm. The moment for a 170-lb pilot using the seat in an average position would be 170 × 37 = 6,290 lb-inches, or 6.3 lb-inches/1000. Note that a small pilot (say 110 lb) using the seat in a full forward position would contribute a moment of only 110 × 34/1000 = 3.7. At the other extreme, a tall and heavy pilot (say 220 lb) with the seat at its aft limit would contribute 220 × 46/1000 = 10.1. These are big differences, which could affect whether or not the airplane is within C.G. limits. Note 1 on the figure tells us that the arm for fuel is 48 (i.e., the fuel tanks are centered at a position just behind the pilot's seat), and the rest of the diagram gives arms for the rear seats and for various baggage placements.

Fig. 1-8 illustrates how a typical loading problem is worked. The basic empty weight will be different for each particular Cessna 172; the one shown here happens to weigh 1,454 lb empty and to have its C.G. at 39.6 inches aft of the datum. Thus, using a pocket calculator, we find 1,454 × 39.6/1000 = 57.6, the moment shown in the table. Suppose we are going

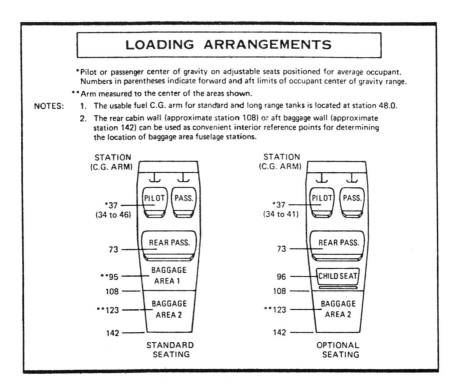

Fig. 1-7. Loading arrangements, Cessna 172.

to carry 30 gal (= 180 lb) of fuel. This weight times 48 (see above) gives a fuel moment of 8.6. On Fig. 1-8 we fill in, next to fuel, 180 under Weight, and 8.6 under Moment.

Let's have a 140-lb pilot sit alone in front, with the seat all the way forward. Fig. 1-7 tells us that the arm is 37 inches, so the moment is 37 × 140 = 5,180, which is 5.2 lb-inches/1000, and we fill this in on Fig. 1-8.

Now let's put two heavy passengers, 200 lb each, in the rear seats. This makes 400 and 29.2 on the next line of the table. Finally, we'll put the maximum allowable 120 lb of baggage in baggage area #1, for a moment of 11.4, and fill these numbers in on the fifth line. Adding all the weights gives 1,454 + 180 + 140 + 400 + 120 = 2,294, just under maximum gross. So far, so good!

Adding moments gives 57.6 + 8.6 + 5.2 + 29.2 + 11.4 = 112.0. To find the new C.G., we have only to divide the new total moment by the new total weight—112,000/2,294 = 48.8 inches aft of the datum. Is this within limits? Fig. 1-9 tells us that the farthest aft C.G. that is permissible in this aircraft is 47.3 inches. Unless something is done to move the C.G. forward, this airplane is not safe to fly, even though its total weight is under maximum gross. Calculation will show that moving one of the heavy passengers into the copilot seat would rectify the situation.

SAMPLE LOADING PROBLEM	SAMPLE AIRPLANE		YOUR AIRPLANE	
	Weight (lbs.)	Moment (lb.-ins. /1000)	Weight (lbs.)	Moment (lb.-ins. /1000)
1. Basic Empty Weight (Use the data pertaining to your airplane as it is presently equipped. Includes unusable fuel and full oil)	1454	57.6		
2. Usable Fuel (At 6 Lbs./Gal.) Standard Tanks (40 Gal. Maximum)	240	11.5		
Long Range Tanks (50 Gal. Maximum)				
3. Pilot and Front Passenger (Station 34 to 46)	340	12.6		
4. Rear Passengers	170	12.4		
5. *Baggage Area 1 or Passenger on Child's Seat (Station 82 to 108, 120 Lbs. Max.)	103	9.8		
6. *Baggage Area 2 (Station 108 to 142, 50 Lbs. Max.)				
7. RAMP WEIGHT AND MOMENT	2307	103.9		
8. Fuel allowance for engine start, taxi, and runup	-7	-.3		
9. TAKEOFF WEIGHT AND MOMENT (Subtract Step 8 from Step 7)	2300	103.6		
10. Locate this point (2300 at 103.6) on the Center of Gravity Moment Envelope, and since this point falls within the envelope, the loading is acceptable.				

* The maximum allowable combined weight capacity for baggage areas 1 and 2 is 120 lbs.

Fig. 1-8. Sample Loading, Cessna 172.

For some aircraft a diagram like that in Fig. 1-7 is not available. Instead, a Loading Graph (Fig. 1-10) is provided, from which one can obtain the moments. Finally, instead of actually calculating the C.G. position, one can find out directly on a Moment Envelope (Fig. 1-11) if the total moment is within acceptable limits for the loaded weight of the aircraft. I strongly recommend the actual computation of C.G., which is what we really want to know.

In some airplanes the balance problem is extremely tricky. In the Seneca II, for example, the Owner's Manual devotes an entire page to "General Loading Recommendations." Eight different situations are postulated, for each of which specific recommendations are made concerning baggage loading and fuel loading. With pilot only, for example: "Load rear baggage compartment to capacity first. Without aft baggage, fuel load may be limited by forward envelope..." With five occupants—one in front, two in middle, two in rear: "Load forward baggage to capacity first. Rear baggage and/or fuel load may be limited by aft envelope." This is definitely not an airplane you just load up and fly!

Now try a few problems. By actually working them out, by the exact method using a calculator, if possible, you will become thoroughly familiar with the process, as it applies to any aircraft. Answers are at the end of the chapter, starting on page 1-39.

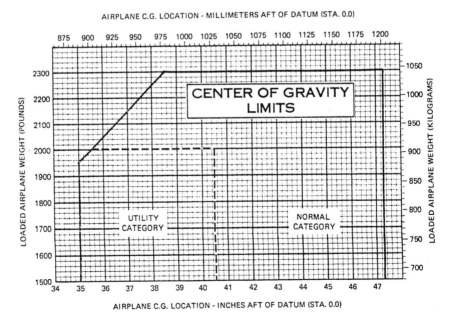

Fig. 1-9. Center of Gravity Limits, Cessna 172.

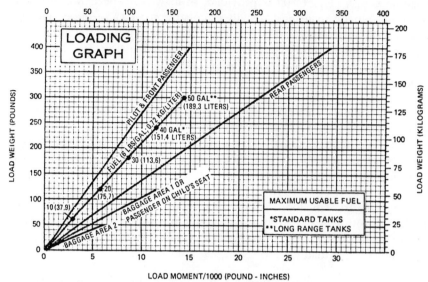

Fig. 1-10. Loading Graph, Cessna 172.

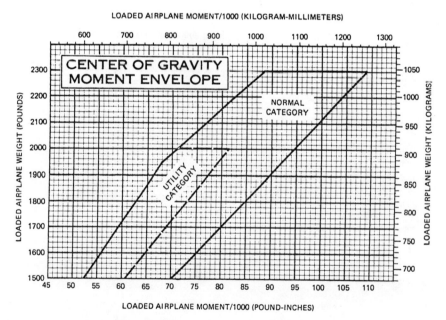

Fig. 1-11. Center of Gravity Moment Envelope, Cessna 172.

Problem 1. Referring to the Cessna 172 for which information is given in the table and figures, if you load the pilot (140 lb), a co-pilot (180 lb), one passenger (170 lb), and baggage (50 lb), how much usable fuel can you carry, and how far can you fly legally, VFR, at night. Assume the aircraft will burn 7.2 gph at 114 k.

Problem 2. The following information applies to a Cessna 152 trainer: Basic empty weight 1,136, C.G. 29.9 inches aft of datum; fuel capacity 24.5 gal usable at arm 40.0; seats, arm 39.0; baggage area #1, 120 lb maximum, arm 64.0; baggage area #2, 40 lb maximum, arm 84.0. At maximum gross (1,670) the C.G. limits are from 32.6 to 36.5 inches aft of datum.

(a) What is the total moment for the empty airplane?

(b) With full tanks, a 195-lb pilot, and a 200-lb instructur, will the airplane be within weight-and-balance limits? If not, is the problem with weight or with balance or both, and is there any solution?

(c) What is the maximum amount of baggage that a 165-lb solo pilot could carry, and can it all be placed in baggage area #1 just behind the seats?

Problem 3. Here's a tough one. Suppose the Cessna 172 described earlier (see Figs. 1.7–1.9) has long-range tanks (50 gal usable) and they are full. You are the pilot, you weigh 180 lb, and you like your seat in its full aft position. There are no passengers, but you want to carry boxes of electronic equipment weighing 30 lb each. How many can you carry, and what is the best loading arrangement? The baggage areas are each limited to 120 lb. Assume you can secure the boxes firmly on the floor or in the seats, and that you would like to keep the C.G. as near as possible to the center of the permissible range, for a good margin of safety.

D. CROSS-COUNTRY FLIGHT PLANNING

---

1. **Objective.** To determine that the applicant:
   a. Exhibits adequate knowledge by planning, within 30 minutes, a VFR cross-country flight of a duration near the range of the airplane considering fuel and loading.
   b. Selects and uses current and appropriate aeronautical charts.
   c. Plots a course for the intended route of flight with fuel stops, if necessary.
   d. Selects prominent en route check points.
   e. Computes the flight time, headings, and fuel requirements.
   f. Selects appropriate radio navigation aids and communication facilities.
   g. Identifies airspaces, obstructions, and alternate airports.

h. Extracts pertinent information from the Airport/Facility Directory and other flight publications, including NOTAM'S.

i. Completes a navigation log.

j. Completes and files a VFR flight plan.

2. Action. The examiner will:

a. Ask the applicant to plan, within 30 minutes, a VFR cross-country flight of a duration near the range of the airplane considering fuel and loading.

b. Ask the applicant to explain cross-country planning procedures, and determine that the applicant's performance meets the objective.

c. Place emphasis on the applicant's knowledge and accuracy in planning the cross-country flight.

There are various ways of plotting your VFR course on the sectional charts. I find that the best way is to draw the course line, and to tick off regular 10-NM marks on it, all the way. Of course, you should use nautical miles and knots for all your flying, even if your aircraft is an older model with airspeeds given in miles per hour. If the distance is written next to the course line every 50 NM, any intermediate distance can be read off from the tick marks at a glance. Prominent enroute checkpoints should be circled or otherwise highlighted along your course line. These could be towns, cities, intersections of major highways, bridges, railroads, airports, power lines, or other manmade structures. Beware of purely natural features like streams, hills, and valleys, because so many of them look alike. And roads in open countryside all look the same. An ideal checkpoint combines natural and manmade features—e.g., where a railway bridge crosses a river, and the railroad tracks then enter a town on the east bank of the river. If you study carefully the exact relationships between several elements, you can obtain an unmistakable checkpoint.

A **navigation log** is essential to every well organized flight. If you follow my suggestion of 10-NM legs, the log might well be arranged for 50-NM segments, or about 25–30 minutes flying time. Several pre-printed standard flight log forms are for sale, but the exact format is not important. There should be room to fill in, for every flight segment, the estimated time enroute (ETE) for that segment, the computed ground speed (GS), the estimated time of arrival (ETA) at the next fix, and the actual time of arrival (ATA) at that fix. The purpose of the log is to establish a systematic monitoring of the flight, so GS estimates can be revised continually, ETA at destination can be updated, and early diversion to an alternate can be considered if you fall significantly behind your plan.

A useful trick is to mark on the course line the point at which you will begin your descent to the destination. Do this by computing how much you have to descend from your cruising altitude to the pattern altitude, and plan the descent for 500 feet per minute (fpm). With a flying speed of about 2 NM per minute, this means that the descent should be started 2 NM out for every 500' of descent. A common error of inexperienced pilots is to delay the descent too long and then find themselves a few thousand feet above their destination airport. On the other hand, there is much to be said for planning deliberately to overfly the destination at 3000' AGL, above the airport traffic area (ATA), in order to view the whole unfamiliar situation from above, before descending to enter the traffic pattern. I very strongly recommend this procedure for night arrivals as a matter of safety (see Chapter 10). Whichever way you plan the descent, you may be surprised at how far out you have to begin. For example, to descend from cruise at 10,500' to 1,000' you will have to start down fully 37 NM from the destination. It's a good idea, too, to make a mark on the chart at the point where you plan to call the tower, FSS, or Unicom, about 15 NM out.

Once your course is plotted and measured, you will have to compute your total time enroute, based on the climbout to cruising altitude at climb airspeed, followed by cruise airspeed for the remainder of the trip. Apply wind corrections conservatively, i.e., subtract forecast headwinds from your estimated groundspeed, but don't add forecast tailwinds. Make sure you have enough fuel aboard to reach your destination with 30 minutes fuel to spare (45 minutes at night), as required by the FAR's. If the weather suggests that you may actually have to divert to an alternate, make sure you allow enough fuel for that, too.

The **Airport/Facility Directory** is one of the most useful reference publications for VFR flight. It provides a wealth of information about every airport and navaid—far more than you can obtain from the sectional chart. Unfortunately, the government has not seen fit to make it easily affordable, so many pilots do without it. At the very least, you should find a place where you can consult a current copy in preparation for every flight, or you should purchase one volume for the area where you fly most, even if you can't afford the whole subscription. Single volumes and subscriptions are available from the National Ocean Survey (NOS).

Fig. 1-12 is a typical extract—this one for the Elk City Municipal Airport in Oklahoma. The best way to illustrate how much information the Directory contains is to go through this entry with you, line by line. Starting at the upper left, the scroll symbol means that Notam service is provided concerning conditions at this airport. The airport name is followed by its three-letter identifier (ELK), then its distance in nautical miles and its location relative to the city it serves. Next comes the local time relative to Greenwich Mean Time (Coordinated Universal Time, "Zulu time"). The

· geographic coordinates of the airport are of increasing importance as Loran navigation comes into wider use. At the extreme right of the first line is the name of the sectional chart on which the airport can be found.

The second line, from left to right, gives the airport elevation, the presence (letter "B") of a rotary beacon, the extent of the repair services available ("S4" means major airframe and powerplant repairs), fuel availability and type, oxygen availability (none here), traffic pattern altitude (MSL and AGL). Airport of entry with customs service would be shown next by "AOE," then the type of certificated airport (coded to show firefighting and rescue equipment), and whether or not the airport is inspected by FAA; these positions on the second line are blank here, so none of these apply at Elk City Muni. Finally, at the far right, are the relevant IFR enroute charts for this location.

The third and fourth lines give data about the runways. Here we see that runway 17-35 is hard-surfaced ("H") and 4,400' long by 75' wide, of concrete. "S-4" means that the weight-bearing capacity is 4,000 lb. "MIRL" signifies medium-intensity runway lights. Special cautions, such as power lines, fences, or dikes are given on the next line; here there are roads at both ends of the runway.

Under **Airport Remarks** are very useful bits of information. Here we see that the airport is attended only during the daytime; and—extremely important if you arrive at night—that you need to key your mike a certain way on the Unicom frequency to bring on the runway lights.

Communications informtion is given next. There is no tower at this airport, and Unicom frequency is 122.8. With several Unicom frequencies now in use, it could be a real game of trial-and-error if you arrived at an unfamiliar airport without knowing the common traffic advisory fre-

---

§   **ELK CITY MUNI**   (ELK)   .9 NE   GMT−6(−5DT)   35°25'40"N 99°23'35"W   DALLAS-FT. WORTH
    1983   B   S4   FUEL 100LL, JET A   TPA− 2983(1000)   L-6G, 13B
    RWY 17-35: H4400X75 (CONC)   S-4   MIRL   IAP
      RWY 17: Road.   RWY 35: Road.
    AIRPORT REMARKS: Attended 1300Zt-dusk. For rwy lights, key 122.8 5 times in 5 seconds for medium, 7 times in 5
      seconds for high intensity.
    COMMUNICATIONS: UNICOM 122.8
      OKLAHOMA CITY FSS (OKC) Toll free call dial 1-800-522-3325.
      CLINTON-SHERMAN APP CON 126.3 Opr 1400-0200Zt Mon-Fri except Holidays, other times ctc FORT WORTH
        CENTER APP/DEP CON 128.4.
    RADIO AIDS TO NAVIGATION:
      SAYRE (L) VORTAC 115.2   SYO   Chan 99   35°20'42"N 99°38'06"W   057° 12.9 NM to fld. 1990/10E.
        Unmonitored and without voice when HOBART FSS clsd.
      NDB (MHW) 241   EZY   35°25'33"N 99°23'52"W   at fld

Fig. 1-12. Sample extract from Airport/Facility Directory.

quency (CTAF). The numbers you need to call FSS by phone or the Air Traffic Control facilities by radio are given next. Finally come the listings of navaids and their locations relative to the airport. Here the Sayre VORTAC (Class L, usable only to 40 NM below 18,000'), operating on 115.2 with identifier SYO, is 12.9 NM away at 1990' MSL, and the airport is on the 057° radial. The "10E" at far right of this line is the magnetic variation at this location. We see on the last line that there is also a non-directional radiobeacon right on the field, with frequency 241 and identifier EZY. The "MHW" means it is a low-powered homing beacon, usable only to 25 NM, and without voice capability. The translations of all coded abbreviations are given in seven pages of outstandingly clear explanation at the beginning of the Directory.

If Elk City Muni were your destination, and especially if you had never been there before, you can see how thorough study of the Airport/Facility Directory would familiarize you in advance with many important things about the airport. I find this publication indispensable, and I never fly without it. Many are the times it has spared me anxiety or even saved me from serious trouble, especially when I've had to divert unexpectedly to a totally unfamiliar airport. Although there is no explicit regulation that this publication must be consulted or caried aboard the aircraft, it would be a virtual necessity in order to comply fully with FAR 91.5: "Each pilot in command shall, before beginning a flight, familiarize himself with all available information concerning that flight."

The filing of a VFR flight plan is the culminating step of the preflight preparations. To make it go quickly and smoothly, follow the specified format, don't invent your own. **Write down** the items in the order in which you will read them to the FSS; this is especially important for filing by radio when you are airborne, so you don't clutter the frequency with back and forth repeats. Here is the specified format:

(1) Type of flight plan.

(2) Aircraft identification.

(3) Aircraft type/special equipment code.

(4) True airspeed (knots).

(5) Point of departure.

(6) Departure time proposed (Z).

(7) Initial cruising altitude.

(8) Route of flight.

(9) Destination (airport and city).

(10) Remarks.

(11) Estimated time enroute (hours + minutes).

(12) Fuel on board (hours + minutes).

(13) Alternate airport(s).

(14) Pilot's name.

(15) Pilot's address/telephone number.

(16) No. of persons aboard.

(17) Color of aircraft.

Here is an example of how you might read out your notes to file a flight plan for San Jose to Red Bluff, California,departing at 8:00 a.m. local standard time. The FSS knows the format, so you don't need to read the headings, just the information. Speak slowly and clearly, use the phonetic alphabet, and spell if necessary.

> "This is a VFR flight plan for November seven one niner Alpha Golf, Cessna one eighty-two slash Alpha, one three five knots, departing San Jose at sixteen hundred Zulu, six thousand five hundred, San Jose Victor three three four Sacramento, Victor twenty-three Red Bluff, destination, one plus one five enroute, four plus three zero aboard, no alternate, John Smith, San Jose; telephone four zero eight three two niner six six one two, three aboard, green and white."

Evaluate your own abilities by planning and plotting imaginary flights, and getting **actual weather briefings** for them. Calling FSS for an occasional proposed flight is no sin, even though you don't intend to fly it; the facilities that you pay for as a taxpayer are intended for training as well as for the real thing. Use the score sheet to rate yourself. It's a cheap way to fly, and you'll learn a lot about the sectional charts as you plot out different trips.

E. AIRPLANE SYSTEMS

---

1. **Objective.** To determine that the applicant exhibits adequte knowledge by explaining the airplane systems and their operation including:
    a. Primary flight controls and trim.
    b. Wing flaps, leading edge devices, and spoilers.
    c. Flight instruments.

   d. Landing gear -
      (1) retraction system.
      (2) indication system.
      (3) brakes and tires.
      (4) nosewheel steering.
   e. Engine -
      (1) controls and indicators.
      (2) induction, carburetion, and injection.
      (3) exhaust and turbocharging.
      (4) fire detection.
   f. Propeller.
   g. Fuel system -
      (1) tanks, pumps, controls, and indicators.
      (2) fueling procedures.
      (3) normal operation.
   h. Hydraulic system -
      (1) controls and indicators.
      (2) pumps and regulators.
      (3) normal operation.
   i. Electrical system -
      (1) controls and indicators.
      (2) alternators or generators.
      (3) battery, ground power.
      (4) normal operation.
   j. Environmental system -
      (1) heating.
      (2) cooling and ventilation.
      (3) controls and indicators.
      (4) pressurization.
   k. Ice prevention and elimination.
   l. Navigation and communication.
   m. Vacuum system.

2. **Action.** The examiner will:
   a. Ask the applicant to explain the airplane systems and their operation, and determine that the applicant's performance meets the objective.
   b. Place emphasis on the applicant's knowledge of the airplane systems' operation.

When these Practical Test Standards were published, in May 1984, there seemed to be a glaring omission. Not a word was said about airplane systems, even though it has always been understood that a pilot must be completely familiar with every working part of the airplane. Nor was there any explicit list of systems (like the one above) in the still earlier FAA

Flight Test Guide. Then finally, as one of many revisions issued in September 1985, this new Section E was added. It remedies a long-standing error of omission.

To be a safe pilot, prepared for any system malfunction, you have to know how everything works, where everything is, how you can recognize every possible malfunction, and what (if anything) you can do about it. The lack of standardization among aircraft means that if you fly several models, you must be sure not to become confused.

Example: In some models the gear lever and the flap lever are interchanged from their usual arrangement. Will you reach out for the wrong one as you complete your landing roll?

Example: You naturally expect that under all circumstances you will be able to extend the gear manually, if necessary. Not so! In the Cessna 337 there is a little solenoid that operates a valve in the hydraulic system. When this solenoid overheats and sticks (as it is prone to do), the hydraulic pressure can not be routed to lower the gear, and pumping manually is useless. If you fly this aircraft, you should know where the little culprit is located and how to deal with it. The expensive alternative is a belly landing.

Example: Do you know if you have an alternator or a generator, and does it matter? It certainly matters if the battery dies. An alternator requires a field voltage in order to start up after a shutdown, so you could easily produce a complete electrical failure if, in the course of trying to figure out what was wrong, you turned off the alternator switch.

Example: Do you understand the operation of the pitot-static system well enough so you can recognize the signs of a blocked static port or an insect in the pitot tube? Do you know how much difference it makes, if any, and what you can do about it?

Example: Do you know how the vacuum pump operates the gyro instruments, and which ones they are, and which back-ups you have for each? Usually, the attitude indicator and heading indicator operate on the vacuum pump, the turn indicator electrically; but these arrangements may differ in different aircraft. It matters, because you need to know in advance which instruments will still be functional after a vacuum pump failure, on the one hand, or complete electrical failure on the other.

Example: Is there an audio panel to which both COM radios are routed, so that a malfunction there ends all communications, or is the audio panel by-passed by an earphone jack? Experimenting to find the answer **after**

you have a problem is a poor idea, with the potential to turn a trivial problem into a big one.

So the message of this section is: Know your airplane and everything in it. Have a lively imagination and anticipate every malfunction. A good exercise is to walk around the airplane, touching each component part, and asking yourself, "What will happen **if**? What will I do **if**?" Then sit in the cockpit, touch every control, every instrument, every fuse and circuit breaker, every light-bulb—and ask the same two questions. A safe pilot is a pilot prepared!

Solutions to problems on weight and balance.

These problems are solved by the exact method, using a hand-held calculator. You should get essentially the same answers (though probably not precisely the same) in Problem 1 and Problem 3 by using the graphs in Figs. 1.10 and 1.11. Problem 2 must be done by the exact method, since no graphs were furnished.

Problem 1.

	Weight	Moment/1000
Basic empty weight	1,454	57.6
Fuel	240	11.5
Pilot (seat full forward)	140	4.8
Front passenger (seat full aft)	180	8.3
Rear passener	170	12.4
Baggage, area #1	50	4.8
	2,234	99.4

So the weight is under maximum gross. Dividing 99,400 by 2,234 gives 44.5 for the C.G., and Fig. 1-9 shows that this is within the allowable limits for this gross weight. The fuel aboard will give 5.56 hr at 114 k, and allowing 45 minutes for the required reserve leaves 4.81 hr, for a range of 4.81 × 114 = 548 NM.

Problem 2.

(a) 1,136 × 29.9/1000 = 34.0

(b)

	Weight	Arm	Moment/1000
Basic empty weight	1,136	29.9	34.0
Fuel, 24.5 gal	147	40.0	5.9
Seats	395	39.0	15.4
	1,678		

Since 1,678 exceeds the maximum gross of 1,670, no further calculation should be done until the weight excess of 8 lb. is dealt with. If you do add up all the moments, you will get 55.3, and dividing 55,300 by 1,678 would give 33.0 inches aft of datum for the C.G., which is within limits and toward the forward end of the allowable range of 32.6–36.5. We may as well admit that many pilots, in this situation, would fly, figuring that the weight is less than 1% over gross, and the C.G. is well within limits and amply forward. Some would even argue that 1% is within the error of weighing the airplane and its contents, and therefore, that it might even be technically legal. Moreover, the 8-lb excess, even if it is real, represents only 1.3 gal of fuel, some of which will burn off during taxiing.

I write this way to recognize reality, not to advocate flirting with illegality or potential danger. The main problem with this approach is that if you step over the line in one area, you are likely to do it again in another. In this way you abandon the protections carefully worked out for you, which help to make flying safe. It is like an IFR pilot who ducks "just a few feet" below minimums on an IFR approach. If you **never** bend the rules, you will **never** come to grief in any aspect of flying in which the rules protect you. If you **ever** do, you have embarked on an uncharted sea, and some day, in some particular set of circumstances, your infractions could make you a statistic in the NTSB accident reports. For many instructive examples, I urge you to read my book FLYING OUT OF DANGER (Airguide Publications Inc., Long Beach, California, 1984).

(c)

	Weight	Arm	Moment/1000
Basic empty weight	1,136	29.9	34.0
Fuel, 24.5 gal	147	40.0	5.9
Seats	165	39.0	6.4
	1,448		
Maximum gross	1,670		
Available capacity	222		

Thus, 222 lb of baggage can be carried. Now we have to consult the placarded limit for each baggage area: #1, 120 lb; #2, 40 lb. This leaves 62 lb to be strapped securely into the right seat. It remains to check the balance for this new loading:

Basic empty weight	1,136	29.9	34.0
Fuel, 24.5 gal	147	40.0	5.9
Seats, 165 + 62	227	39.0	8.9
Baggage area #1	120	64.0	7.7
Baggage area # 2	40	84.0	3.4
	1,670		59.9

C.G. = 59,900/1,670 = ... 35.9

So the C.G., at 35.9 inches aft of datum, is within the allowable limits (32.6–36.5), but rather near the aft limit. On the principle that aft C.G. is more dangerous than forward C.G. (see page 1-23), it would obviously be a good idea to move more of the baggage, if pratical, into the right seat.

Because the baggage areas have such long arms, whereas the seats are quite near the C.G., even 40 lb moved forward from baggage area #2 would make a big difference. We would then have:

Basic empty weight	1,136	29.9	34.0
Fuel, 24.5 gal	147	40.0	5.9
Seats, 165 + 102	267	39.0	10.4
Baggage area #1	120	64.0	7.7
Total	1,670		58.0

C.G. = 58,000/1,670 = ... 34.7

Now the C.G. is nearly 2 inches forward of the aft limit, right in the center of the allowable C.G. range.

Problem 3.

Basic empty weight	1,454	39.6	57.6
Fuel, 50 gal	300	48.0	14.4
Pilot	180	46.0	8.3
	1,934		
Maximum gross	2,300		
Available capacity	366		

366/30 = 12 boxes, with 6 lb useful load not utilized.

Maximum, baggage area # 1,
    four boxes   120   95.0   11.4

So we can put four boxes in baggage area #1. Baggage area #2 has a capacity of only 50 lb, so it will take only one box, leaving for the rear seats 360 − 120 − 30 = 210 lb, or seven boxes. Let's try it that way. Then, in addition to the empty weight, fuel, and pilot (tabulated above), we have:

Baggage area #2, one box	30	123.0	3.7
Rear seats, seven boxes	210	73.0	15.3
Total	2,294		110.7

C.G. = 110,700/2,294 = ... 48.3

This C.G. is well aft of the aft C.G. limit of 47.3. The solution is to move boxes forward. The problem did not specify how many boxes could be strapped securely into the right front seat; let's assume two, for a total of 60 lb. We'll get these from as far aft as possible, thus one from baggage area #2 and one from baggage area #1. Then we have:

Rear seats, seven boxes	210	73.0	15.3
Baggage area #1, three boxes	90	95.0	8.6
Baggage area #2	—	—	—
Right front seat, two boxes	60	34.0	2.0
Total	2,294		106.2

C.G. = 106,200/2,294 = ... 46.3

The C.G. now is well within limits, a full inch forward of the aft limit. If it were practical to move more boxes into the seats, the C.G. could be brought still farther toward the center of the allowable range by transferring boxes from baggage area #1 into the rear seats, and from the rear seats into the right front seat.

Score Sheet: 1. Preflight Preparation

Date											
Knowing where to find and how to interpret all certificates, documents, and logbooks.											
Obtaining, reading, and analyzing weather information, including sequence reports and forecasts, and weather charts.											
Knowing critical airspeeds.											
Obtaining information from the performance charts.											
Understanding density altitude and how to compute it, and knowing its effect on performance.											
Knowing fuel capacity and consumption, duration of flight, and range.											
Understanding weight and balance, and ability to compute weight and balance.											
Planning cross-country flight and plotting course line with check points.											
Computing heading from winds aloft.											

Score Sheet: 1. Preflight Preparation (continued)

Date									
Computing fuel requirement to destination and from destination to alternate.									
Getting airport information for destination and en route airports, using the Airport/Facility Directory.									
Getting all applicable SIGMETS, AIRMETS, NOTAMS, and PIREPS.									
Computing estimated time enroute to destination and from destination to alternate.									
Completing a navigation log.									
Preparing and filing a VFR flight plan.									
Familiarity with all airplane systems.									
TOTAL SCORE									
Divide by 16 = AVERAGE SCORE									

2

GROUND OPERATIONS

A. VISUAL INSPECTION

---

1. **Objective.** To determine that the applicant:
   a. Exhibits adequate knowledge of airplane visual inspection by explaining the reasons for checking the items.
   b. Inspects the airplane by following the checklist.
   c. Determines that the airplane is in condition for safe flight emphasizing-
      (1) fuel quantity, grade, and type.
      (2) fuel contamination safeguards.
      (3) fuel venting.
      (4) oil quantity, grade, and type.
      (5) fuel, oil, and hydraulic leaks.
      (6) flight controls.
      (7) structural damage including exhaust system.
      (8) tiedown, control lock, and wheel chock removal.
      (9) ice and frost removal.
      (10) security of baggage, cargo, and equipment.
   d. Notes any discrepancy and determines whether the airplane is safe for flight or requires maintenance.

2. **Action.** The examiner will:
   a. Ask the applicant to explain the reasons for checking the item during a visual inspection.
   b. Observe the applicant's visual inspection procedure, and determine that the applicant's performance meets the objective.
   c. Place emphasis on soundness of the applicant's judgment regarding the airplane's condition.

The first thing looked for by an examiner on your check ride or by an instructor on your biennial flight review is **checklist discipline**. Flying without a **written** checklist is—sooner or later—an invitation to disaster. If you think you can dispense with a checklist because your memory is so good, you should read the morbidly fascinating and amazing National Transportation Safety Board investigations of air carrier accidents. Here we are observing (often post-mortem) the behavior of seasoned airline veterans, pilots with thousands of hours, who certainly should be able to dispense with checklists if anyone could. **Example:** An airliner took off from an icy field in Alaska with an external elevator lock in place, and crashed, of course, since no climb could possibly be initiated. "Controls free?" Could that crew have used their checklist? **Example:** Airliner checklists require the copilot to call out altitudes during the approach to landing. But repeatedly, airliners have been flown into the ground at night or in IFR conditions, under perfect control and carrying power. Could the approach-to-landing checklist have been followed? **Example:** A bystander was cut to ribbons by the propeller of a small plane when the engine was started. "Clear?" On the checklist, but was the checklist being used?

Some have argued that a written checklist is not required for the preflight inspection because the whole checklist is in front of you, physically, as you walk around the airplane. Starting at the pilot's door, and ending at the pilot's door, you will check everything in the order in which you come to it. The thoroughness of the check depends upon the discipline you have established on the many occasions you have gone through it before, so that you never omit a thing. And yet, even here, pilots have been known to miss a bird's nest in the cowling, a cover on the pitot tube, a tiedown rope, or even an external gust lock in place. The FAA guidelines are quite clear that a **checklist** provided by the manufacturer should be used for the external inspection.

Fuel and oil are critically important for the safety of a proposed flight. During the preflight inspection it is essential to confirm visually that the tanks are full, or if not, to establish with a calibrated dipstick exactly how much fuel is aboard. Then you will have the added security of knowing you have secured the fuel tank caps yourself. Would you trust your life and the lives of your passengers to the driver of a fuel truck, whom you may not even know? That has been the cause of accidents due to fuel exhaustion because a loose cap permitted the fuel to be lost overboard during flight. It is also essential to drain samples from all fuel sumps, and to inspect them for contamination with water or debris, and also to make sure their color corresponds to the octane requirements of your engine. The adequacy of the oil supply must be checked, too, and the security of the oil cap verified. In addition, thorough inspection of the oil dipstick requires that you rub the oil between your fingers to make sure there are no gritty or metallic particles.

Some pilots wait until they are in the cockpit to check operation of the flaps and elevator. This is a mistake, because no adequate inspection of the flap attachments can be made unless the flaps are fully extended. And the structural integrity of the elevator can not be checked unless the gustlock is removed so the elevator can be manipulated up and down by hand. The only correct preflight procedure, therefore, is to enter the cockpit **first**, turn on the master switch, lower the flaps fully, remove the gustlock, and turn on pitot heat. Then go and feel the pitot tube carefully to make sure it is warm to the touch. Pitot heat is of primary concern to the IFR rather than the VFR pilot, but even so, if you have a heated pitot, why not make sure it is working? I once trusted to a movement of the ammeter when I turned on the pitot heat from the left seat, and took off on a long IFR flight. As things turned out, there was unpredicted icing in the clouds, my pitot heat failed to operate, and I watched with fascination as the pitot head iced over. I completed the flight safely despite having no airspeed indication whatsoever, but the lesson was clear. Ironically—as so often happens—the very reason it didn't work was the same reason it gave me an ammeter reading, namely, a partial short circuit in the system.

The point of the above story is that everything worth checking is worth checking **right**. Check the pitot heat by feeling it (sometimes it's very hot, don't burn your fingers!). Check the fuel by looking at it and putting a dipstick in, not by reading a fuel gauge. Check for structural integrity by shaking the vertical stabilizer and moving the wings up and down. Check the propeller by feeling the edge and looking carefully for hairline cracks. Check for water in the fuel by taking samples from the sumps, and then—especially with some airplanes—rocking the wings and taking another sample. Check the tires and brakes by getting down and looking closely. Check for the beginnings of an oil leak by looking for oil streaking on the belly. If your aircraft gives you access to the engine compartment, don't be content with a fleeting glance; feel for the security of all magneto leads and fuel lines and every other component you can get your hands on. Check for bird nests in the engine air intake, behind the cowl flaps, and in the gear wells. Check the exhaust stack and the plumbing that leads to it. Check the battery to be sure it is firmly secured and that there is no obvious acid corrosion nearby.

Ice and frost present special problems. The most insidious condition is a seemingly thin dusting of frost over the whole airplane. It looks so innocuous! But adequate lift depends upon the **smooth** flow of air over the wings. A remarkably small amount of frost can interfere significantly; it must be removed completely before takeoff. You may be well aware of the fact that aircraft flying in IFR conditions sometimes experience rime icing or even clear icing, yet they manage to fly despite it. Knowing that, you may be inclined to minimize the danger of a little frost. What you forget is the enormous difference in the amount of lift required for takeoff and climbout, as compared with what is needed for level flight or descending flight. All the engine's power and all the lift obtainable from the wings are needed to overcome the force of gravity and produce a climb. In this situation any reduction of lift could be critical. At high density altitude and at gross weight, you can barely get off the ground anyway, and climb performance is almost nil, as you have discovered if you've done any flying from high-altitude fields. In that kind of marginal situation, even the slightest amount of frost can be disastrous.

The proper stowing of baggage and other cargo is of great importance. Turbulence can not be antiticipated. Nothing could be more dangerous in flight than to have some heavy object thrown into the air and strike a passenger or even the pilot. A cargo flight into Washington National Airport a few years ago was carrying unsecured heavy boxes. On final approach, the nosedown pitch and some moderate turbulence combined to make the boxes slide forward, thus shifting the C.G. well beyond the forward limit. As a result, even full back yoke could not lift the nose. The airplane was unable to flare, and it was destroyed in a nose-down crash on the runway. Everything aboard an aircraft must be securely lashed down!

B. COCKPIT MANAGEMENT

---

1. **Objective.** To determine that the applicant:
   a. Exhibits adequate knowledge of cockpit management by explaining related safety and efficiency factors.
   b. Organizes and arranges the material and equipment in a manner that makes them readily available.
   c. Ensures that the safety belts and shoulder harnesses are fastened.
   d. Adjusts and locks the foot pedals or pilot's seat to a safe position and ensures full control movement.
   e. Briefs the occupants on the use of safety belts and emergency procedures.

2. **Action.** The examiner will:
   a. Ask the applicant to explain cockpit management procedures.
   b. Observe the applicant's cockpit management procedures, and determine that the applicant's performance meets the objective.
   c. Place emphasis on safety items related to good cockpit management.

How a pilot gets settled in the left seat tells a lot about their sense of organization, which has so much to do with piloting skills. First of all, every pilot should have some kind of flight bag, in which all the necessities are kept, each in its own place so they can be found instantly and without groping around. Nothing is more disruptive of good cockpit management than having to look for things: "Where did that sectional chart go to, I thought it was in the glove compartment?" "I can't seem to find a pencil, this one's point is broken." "The ground control frequency here? It's in the Airport/Facility Directory, but I must have left that home." My own flight bag is ready to go at all times; I only need to pick it up—I know that nothing is missing, ever.

Several years ago a Lockheed Electra lost all its electrical power at 12,000′ out of Salt Lake City on a pitch-black night. In the two minutes it took to find a flashlight, the aircraft had entered a graveyard spiral, from which it never recovered. Think about it; could that happen to you? No electrical power is needed to fly the airplane, nor do you need any of the instruments that operate electrically. But if you can't **see** your attitude indicator, you have no way to keep the wings level. In that situation, sooner or later, you're dead! So can you reach your flashlight, without advance warning, any time, instantly, because you know just where it is? And will the batteries and bulb be working when you need it? In my opinion anyone who flies at night without **two** working flashlights is a suicidal gambler. And you can never know when a flight may turn into a night flight. It's not just a question of deciding you'll be at your destination before nightfall. A repair might be needed at an intermediate stop, or an unexpected delay anywhere could postpone a departure until after dark. What this means, then, is that working flashlights must **always** be aboard.

Remember that you, as pilot in command, are responsible to see that all passengers secure their seat belts and shoulder harnesses. One of the real absurdities of our regulatory system is that while so many nit-picking and useless rules are imposed, the FAA has never mandated retrofitting of shoulder harnesses. This despite the fact—proved again and again—that they prevent head injuries, which are so common a cause of death in aircraft accidents.

You might not think that checking the seat lock is a life-and-death matter, but it is. Cessna learned that lesson at a cost of several million dollars in damages, when their flimsy seat locking mechanism failed, and a crash resulted; as the seat slid back suddenly at takeoff, the pilot pulled the yoke back with him, stalling the aircraft. Needless to add, the right seat is even more vulnerable because the passenger may not know how to lock it. A passenger sliding back could cause a stall the same way, so make it your job to prevent that from happening.

Develop and use your own reassuring way of preparing passengers for the need to exit the aircraft rapidly in an emergency. Point out the suitable methods of escape, should you be disabled in a crash. Most accidents in light aircraft are survivable, but survivors must escape and get well clear, in case of fire. Therefore make it your business to brief each passenger on how to release the buckle of the seat belt, as well as on how to secure it.

Finally, as you take the left seat, review your own **personal** checklist. Is there any reason you should not be flying at this moment? Numerous studies of the human factors behind accidents show the importance of the pilot's physical condition and state of mind. No-go items: Fatigued. Headache. Coming down with a virus. Upset stomach. Angry at the boss. Argument with a spouse or lover. Serious financial problems. In other words, is **anything** going on in your life that will distract your attention from the demands of flying, or that will make you irritable enough to take chances you wouldn't take otherwise?

And when was your last intake of alcohol or some other mind-altering drug? The rule of eight hours from bottle to throttle is an absolute minimum; it doesn't take into account that a **lot** of drinking eight hours ago will leave you in no condition to fly now. And don't make the mistake of thinking that one beer or one glass of wine a few hours ago doesn't matter. It does! Blood alcohol levels well below those defined as intoxicating for highway purposes—e.g., 0.05–0.10%—interfere with the fine three-dimensional control and the split-second judgments needed in flying.

Above all, listen carefully to yourself and to your passengers. If someone says, "Are you sure you're feeling OK to fly?," you are probably not. **Something** about your behavior made them ask. You may hear your own voice (or your inner voice) saying things like this: "Everything will be OK, we've planned this trip for a long time, they're expecting us and we don't want to disappoint them." Watch out! They will be much more disappointed if you start out and never arrive.

C. STARTING ENGINE

---

1. **Objective.** To determine that the applicant:
   a. Exhibits adequate knowledge by explaining engine starting procedures, including starting under various atmospheric conditions.
   b. Performs all the items on the before-starting and starting checklist.
   c. Accomplishes a safe starting procedure with emphasis on -
      (1) positioning the airplane to avoid creating hazards.
      (2) determining that the area is clear.
      (3) adjusting the engine controls.
      (4) setting the brakes.
      (5) preventing undesirable airplane movement after engine start.
      (6) avoiding excessive engine RPM and temperatures.
      (7) checking the engine instruments after engine start.

2. **Action.** The examiner will:
   a. Ask the applicant to explain starting procedures including starting under various atmospheric conditions.
   b. Observe the applicant's engine starting procedures, and determine that the applicant's performance meets the objective.
   c. Place emphasis on safe starting procedures.

With the preflight walk-around completed, you will be following a checklist for starting the engine. Remember, first, that if shoulder harnesses are provided, they are required to be used, and that the pilot is responsible to see that the passengers comply and use both seat belts and shoulder harnesses. Don't shout "clear" in a perfunctory way—I have even seen people hit the starter first, and then shout "clear." **Look around first.** Make sure a child or an animal isn't out of easy sight, under the nose of the airplane. Make sure no one is walking toward you at just this moment. Remember that an airplane makes a lot of noise when the engine is running, but spinning propellers are invisible—people have walked right into them. Finally, when you see that everything really **is** clear, shout "clear" anyway, and then look again before you hit the starter.

Every type of aircraft engine has its own best method for starting, which is described by the manufacturer. The procedure should always be followed precisely. There are a few general principles that apply to starting all engines. First, if everything is in good order, and the preliminaries are carried out correctly, the engine should start the moment the starter is activated. If not, something requires attention—battery, spark plugs, magnetos, carburetor or fuel injector, or whatever. Of course, you are going to keep on cranking in the hope of getting it to start, but that could be a mistake. An aircraft battery does not store a great deal more electricity than an automobile battery, yet the drain in turning over an aircraft engine is enormously greater than that required to turn over an automobile engine. So, in general, if it won't start very soon, don't keep trying, but do something different.

There are three principal reasons why an aircraft engine won't start. First and commonest is a weak battery; if your generator is keeping the battery charged, and the airplane doesn't sit around for long periods without flying, and if there are no partial shortcircuits draining away electricity, and if the battery is not too old to hold a charge, you should have no trouble getting a vigorous start. Of course, the starter motor itself must be up to speed. The second cause of trouble is cold weather. Here it is just a question of adequate preheating, the main purpose of which is to uncongeal the oil—otherwise all the moving parts are literally frozen in position. The third reason an engine has difficulty starting is exactly the opposite—it is too hot. A hot engine promotes fuel vaporization, giving the equivalent of an over-rich mixture, and it also promotes vapor lock that interrupts the fuel flow in the lines running to the engine. The correct way to start a hot engine—or any engine on a very hot day—is to leave the mixture at idle cutoff, and open the throttle to a moderate extent. Sometimes, with this configuration of the power controls, a boost from the fuel pump is helpful. The basic idea is to lean out the vapor in the cylinders to the point where the mixture is just right for ignition, and at the same time to clear the fuel lines of any vapor lock. The whole trick in this procedure is to be ready to advance the mixture quickly and retard the throttle the instant the engine fires up. Of course, the same procedure would be used if fruitless attempts to start, under any circumstances, had flooded the engine.

Immediately after you start the engine, turn on the rotating beacon. High up on the tail, it will serve as a warning that your airplane is alive. This will be especially useful when you start taxiing and you begin to move among the many other aircraft parked on the field. If there is a control tower, the beacon will show the ground controller where you are, so you can be guided more knowledgeably. Do not turn on strobes until you are ready for takeoff; these can be disconcerting to other pilots while you are taxiing.

D. TAXIING

---

1. **Objective.** To determine that the applicant:
   a. Exhibits adequate knowledge by explaining safe taxi procedures.
   b. Adheres to signals and clearances and follows the proper taxi route.
   c. Performs a brake check immediately after the airplane begins moving.
   d. Controls taxi speed without excessive use of brakes.
   e. Recognizes and avoids hazards.
   f. Positions the controls for the existing wind conditions.
   g. Avoids creating hazards to persons or property.

2. **Action.** The examiner will:
   a. Ask the applicant to explain safe taxi procedures.
   b. Observe the applicant's taxi procedures, and determine that the applicant's performance meets the objective.
   c. Place emphasis on correct airplane control, taxi speed, and avoidance of hazards.

In taxiing to the active runway, the principal error made by many pilots is not to move slowly enough. An airplane should taxi no faster than would be safe without brakes—just in case the brakes do fail. Usually this means a walking pace, but it depends a lot on the circumstances, such as how many other aircraft are nearby, and the length and width of the taxiway. You will certainly not taxi at a walk if a DC-10 is following on your tail on the same taxiway! If you are cleared to taxi to a certain runway, you are automatically cleared to cross any intervening runway. This automatic rule makes me uncomfortable, because ground control and local tower control are usually different positions—i.e., different people. There is a chance, therefore, for human error. Not a fanciful worry, this; it really does happen, and every year sees several "incidents" of this kind investigated by FAA. Typically, the ground controller clears aircraft A to cross an active runway, not noticing that aircraft B has been cleared to land or take off on the same runway. I never cross a runway without questioning verbally if it is all right, even if this occasionally makes a controller think I don't know the rules. I'd rather be sure—and I use my eyes, too! Certain items can only be checked during taxi, and since you won't want to be distracted by a list when you should have your eyes out front, you should incorporate these into your regular taxi procedure. One is to check the operation of those **instruments that should operate in a turn**. These are the needle (or turn coordinator), the gyroscopic heading indicator, and the magnetic compass. All three should be checked (a glance is sufficient) during a right turn and again during a left turn, to make sure they are operative. Before any IFR flight this is an absolute essential, but it is the mark of a good pilot to do it routinely. When you do, say out loud: "Right turn, one, two, three OK," and "Left turn, one, two, three, OK."

Two purposes are served by speaking out loud when checking things. The most important has to do with your psychology. When you get used to the sound of your own voice saying these things, you will notice the silence if you become distracted and forget. This same important principle governs the all-important "Gear down" call-out that will be discussed in a later chapter. The second purpose has to do with an examiner's or instructor's psychology. It lets them hear, loud and clear, that you are a safe pilot, that you know what you're doing.

The other item to check during taxi—as soon as the airplane starts moving—is the **brakes**. You won't have another chance until your landing roll, and that is no time to discover they don't work! So as soon as taxiing begins, bring the aircraft to a near-stop with the brakes, so you'll know they are working and feel all right. And say out loud: "Brakes OK," as you do this.

Take seriously the techniques for taxiing in a crosswind. Keeping up-aileron into the wind will require movements of the yoke every time you make a turn. Smooth technique requires that you coordinate these yoke movements with the changing directions of the airplane on the taxiways.

Holding the yoke forward or back will have to be coordinated with the aileron movements, since you want the wind to hold your tail down at all times. Facing the wind, you hold the yoke back, putting the elevator up into the wind, so the wind pressure pushes the tail down. With the wind behind you, the opposite is needed; make the elevator droop down, so the wind can again push the tail down.

The strongest winds you will ever experience on the ground are the jet blasts of heavy aircraft, so the same techniques have to be used. Just consider the large aircraft to be the source of the wind—yoke back if the jet blast is coming from in front, yoke forward if it is from behind. The purpose is to keep from being lifted and flipped over. The main precaution, you should remember, is to remain well clear—keep your distance from such monsters at all times, and refuse any controller instructions that place you in jeopardy.

E. PRE-TAKEOFF CHECK

1. **Objective.** To determine that the applicant:
   a. Exhibits adequate knowledge of the pre-takeoff check by explaining the reasons for checking the items.
   b. Positions the airplane to avoid creating hazards.
   c. Divides attention inside and outside of the cockpit.
   d. Ensures that the engine temperature is suitable for runup and takeoff.
   e. Follows the checklist.
   f. Touches control or switch, or adjusts it to the prescribed position after identifying a checklist item.
   g. States the instrument reading, when appropriate, after identifying a checklist item.
   h. Ensures that the airplane is in safe operating condition emphasizing -
      (1) flight controls and instruments.
      (2) engine and propeller operation.
      (3) seat adjustment and lock.
      (4) safety belts and shoulder harnesses fastened and adjusted.
      (5) doors and windows secured.
   i. Recognizes any discrepancy and determines if the airplane is safe for flight or requires maintenance.
   j. Reviews the critial takeoff performance airspeeds and distances.
   k. Describes takeoff emergency procedures.
   l. Obtains and interprets takeoff and departure clearances.
   m. Notes takeoff time.

2. **Action.** The examiner will:

    a. Ask the applicant to explain reasons for checking items on the pre-takeoff check.

    b. Observe the pre-takeoff check, and determine that the applicant's performance meets the objective.

    c. Place emphasis on the applicant's ability to recognize discrepancies and to use sound judgment in making decisions related to the flight.

The most critical time for a checklist is at run-up and just before takeoff. To use a checklist properly requires **checklist discipline**. It is amazingly easy to skip an item on a checklist. It is a normal trick of the human eye to skip over a line. It probably happens to you often when you are reading a book or a newspaper. But then you know it at once, because what you are reading suddenly doesn't make sense. In fact, your brain can even pick up the nonsense and send your eyes back a line or two without your being aware of what happened. Unfortunately, a checklist makes just as much sense if you skip a line as when you do it right. How, then, can you overcome this skipping tendency? The secret is to use your **finger** as a pointer, and to verify the item you have just checked—again, out loud—before going on to the next one. Once this technique is learned, you will have a sure method of covering everything, without omissions.

Let's take a typical example of items to be checked at the run-up. **Throttle 1700 RPM**. Set the throttle, check the RPM indicator, then return to the same item—Throttle 1700 RPM. It's done. **Now** move your finger down to the next item—**Carb heat**. Do it. Done. And so on. A real advantage of this discipline becomes evident when—as often happens—your checklist is interrupted. When you resume, you automatically go back to the last thing you **know you completed**. If the interruption did not require you to use your pointer finger, it should still be on the previous item. Then move your finger to the next item, and continue. This method may sound tedious, but it is just as fast and a great deal more reliable than a haphazard one.

I have found, from years of instructing, that checklist discipline is a serious problem for many pilots. I am not sure why, but I would guess it is because most people never have to organize themselves in such a strict way in the course of their ordinary lives. You have heard, no doubt, how piloting skills spill over into other parts of life. It is true; many people, as they learn the tight organization and control of behavior that is needed to fly an airplane, find that they are better organized in everything else they do, too. Many a time have I sat in the right seat and watched in wonder as a 200-hour pilot with checklist in hand conducted a completely disorganized pre-takeoff check, actually missing important items on the list. So work on this if it is a problem for you; it will pay off in flight safety, I guarantee you.

Again I urge you not to be silent. Pretend you are an air carrier captain, reading every item out loud so your co-pilot can respond. If you actually have another pilot with you in the front seat, do it as call-outs and responses. If you are solely responsible, call each item out anyway, check the item, then give your own vocal response. The spoken word impresses your auditory memory that an item is completed and thus provides additional protection in case the checklist is interrupted—as it frequently is.

Checking the instrument panel is a very special case. Listing a few instruments—as on many manufacturer's checklists—creates a false sense of security, because the truth is that **all** the instruments have to be checked. Therefore, I strongly advocate having only a single entry, **instrument panel**, for this part of the written checklist. I begin at the upper left of the panel, and physically touching each instrument with my finger (and adjusting it if necessary), I verify that it is in working order, insofar as that can be done before flight. I move across the panel on the top row, all the way from left to right, then down one row and repeat, then down another row, and so on, down to the switches, fuses, and circuit breakers.

During the panel check, you should check your NAV radios when you come to them, especially if there is a VOR within range. And check for an audible verification of the station identifier, so you will know your NAV audio is working. If you wait until you need the navaid and then can't hear an identifier, you won't know if the trouble is with the station or with your equipment. Consider a NAV radio to be a single unit with two parts—one part on which you tune the frequency and listen to the identifier, another part that displays your position by movement of the needle when you rotate the omni bearing selector (OBS). Never touch one part without also touching the other. Thus, when you are tuning a VOR and listening for the identifier, center the needle with FROM showing, and check the radial you are on. If this can be done as part of your pre-takeoff check in the run-up area, so much the better—you will learn if the radial displayed on the OBS is the same as it ought to be according to the sectional chart or the Airport/Facility Directory.

If you have two COM radios, make it a habit to alternate them. This has two advantages. First, if you talk to ground control on one and to tower on the other, you'll take off knowing that both are working. Second, should you—some time later, in flight—be unable to get an answer on a frequency you have just shifted to, the old frequency (that you know is working) will still be set on the other radio.

Finally, a special kind of checklist is needed just prior to takeoff. You will already be taxiing toward the double yellow line, either after the run-up or after a taxi-back, so you won't want to consult a written checklist at this time. Yet there are **ten items** that absolutely must be checked, every time you roll up to that line, before you enter the active runway for takeoff. I use and recommend a special memory aid for these ten crucial items: COMPLETE TAKEOFF CHECKLIST FOR FLIGHT, DEPART WITH SAFETY, TAKE CARE. The first letters of these ten words stand for the items to be checked:

COMPLETE	=	C	=	CONTROLS
TAKEOFF	=	T	=	TRIM
CHECKLIST	=	C	=	COWLFLAPS
FOR	=	F	=	FLAPS
FLIGHT	=	F	=	FUELPUMP
DEPART	=	D	=	DOORS
WITH	=	W	=	WINDOWS
SAFETY	=	S	=	SEAT/SHOULDERBELTS
TAKE	=	T	=	TRANSPONDER
CARE	=	C	=	CARBHEAT

These ten items are in a special category for good reason, and they are grouped according to the order in which they are most conveniently checked. They are all important to a safe takeoff, and moreover, they may well have been left undone—especially after a taxi-back—until the last moment. Let us consider each one in turn. CONTROLS should certainly be verified free before each and every takeoff, without exception. TRIM may not have been set to the neutral range after the last landing. COWL-FLAPS could well have been left closed; unless they are opened, the engine will be damaged during application of takeoff power. FLAPS might not have been retracted after landing, and the drag created by full flaps can prevent an airplane from taking off successfully. FUELPUMP, if required in your airplane, might well have been turned off routinely during a taxi-back. Moreover, it **should** have been off during the routine taxiing from tiedown to run-up area, in order to make sure that the engine-driven fuel pump is working. DOORS and WINDOWS are frequently opened on the ground, for ventilation, especially in hot weather. Passengers may have unbuckled their SEATBELTS and SHOULDERBELTS prematurely, for comfort, or may never have buckled them up at all. The pilot in command is responsible, according to the FARs, and your insurance company will surely take that position! The TRANSPONDER should be at standby until just before takeoff, when you cross the double yellow line onto the active runway. CARBHEAT, on a wet day, is properly used during idling of the engine on the ground, but it must be removed just before the takeoff roll begins, in order to obtain maximum power.

An examiner's or instructor's judgment of your piloting ability is very largely made before you ever fly. The way you go about the preflight procedures tells what kind of pilot you are, and most important, how careful and safe a pilot you are. By the time you take the active runway for takeoff, a preliminary favorable or unfavorable opinion about you has already been formed. You're obviously off to a better start if it's favorable. You might even be forgiven for some imperfections in your flying maneuvers, if it is perfectly clear from the start that you're a safe pilot.

Score Sheet: 2. Ground Operations.

Date								
Thoroughness of external inspection.								
Organization in the cockpit.								
Knowing where to find everything that may be needed.								
Working flashlights available.								
Checking seat belts, shoulder harnesses, and seat locks.								
Clearing the area before engine start.								
Engine starting procedures.								
Checking brakes and turn instruments.								
Taxi speed.								

Score Sheet: 2. Ground Operations (continued).

Date										
Yoke position to compensate for wind.										
Following pre-takeoff written checklist.										
Briefing passengers on emergency procedures.										
The ten critical items to be checked immediately before takeoff—Can you recite them all from memory?										
Noting takeoff time.										

3
AIRPORT AND TRAFFIC PATTERN OPERATIONS

A. RADIO COMMUNICATIONS AND ATC LIGHT SIGNALS

1. **Objective.** To determine that the applicant:
   a. Exhibits adequate knowledge by explaining radio communication, ATC light signals, and prescribed procedures for radio failure.
   b. Selects the appropriate frequencies for the facilities to be used.
   c. Transmits requests and reports using the recommended standard phraseology.
   d. Receives, acknowledges, and complies with radio communication.

2. **Action.** The examiner will:
   a. Ask the applicant to explain radio communication procedures, phraseology, prescribed procedures for radio failure, and ATC light signals.
   b. Observe the applicant's communication procedures, and determine that the applicant's performance meets the objective.
   c. Place emphasis on the applicant's phraseology, clarity, and use of appropriate frequencies.

The way you use the radio tells an examiner or instructor a good deal about your general abilities as a pilot. Good communications are crisp. Rehearse what you are going to say before you press the mike key, say it as briefly as possible, using standard terminology, and immediately release the mike key. On crowded frequencies this is absolutely essential, otherwise the controller can't handle other aircraft expediously. Speak in a natural tone of voice, lips close to the mike, and don't shout. It is not necessary to speak in full sentences. Just say the essentials. The aim is to communicate the message, not to deliver a speech. Always listen first, before you transmit, so you will not break into someone else's communication. If an exchange of transmissions is already going on, listen to it, because most of the time the information you want is being transmitted to someone else.

Just listen, some day, to the ground control or tower frequency at a controlled airport. You will hear the same information being given again and again and again, to one pilot after another. If you get the information first by listening, you can call in "with the numbers" and save a lot of time. You can carry the same principle even farther. Suppose you are inbound to a controlled airport. At about 20 miles out, start listening to the tower frequency. If there's a fair amount of activity at the airport, you'll know everything in a couple of minutes—ceiling, visibility, wind, altimeter, active runway, traffic pattern, and anything else of importance. Then, at 15 miles out, you can call: "Metro Tower, Cessna 1234 Xray." Tower will reply: "Cessna 1234 Xray, Metro Tower." Your next transmission could say it all: "34 Xray 15 miles northeast with the numbers, will report right downwind." Tower will reply, "34 Xray that's approved," and a smooth, efficient exchange has been completed.

Use the phonetic alphabet for clarity in your communications. Say "niner" to distinguish clearly from "five," even if it sounds silly; under difficult communications conditions this habit will make a big difference. Likewise, use the standard terms "affirmative," "negative," and "say again." Don't be afraid to request "speak slowly"; it's a lot faster, in the long run, than having to ask for repeats until finally you're too embarrassed to get the information at all. Besides, the real problem may be with the controller, as some controllers seem to cultivate a machine-gun delivery that actually slows down rather than expedites communication.

Tower frequencies are shown on the sectional charts, but ground control frequencies are not. The latter are given in the **Airport/Facility Directory**, but there's no great problem if you don't know the ground control frequency, because the tower controller will tell you.

When there is an automatic terminal information service (ATIS), it will be shown, with its frequency, on the sectional chart. The typical format of an ATIS broadcast is presented in the **Airman's Information Manual.** If you are parked at such an airport, you must listen to ATIS before calling ground control for your taxi clearance, when you will then indicate, by saying "with Bravo" (or whatever the current identifier is), that you have the current information. Just saying "with ATIS" or "with the numbers" is not correct, since the controller needs to be sure you have the most current information.

When you are parked at a very busy major airport, you may be required to contact **clearance delivery** on a special frequency after you have the ATIS and before contacting ground control. State your intentions, such as "Cessna 1234 Xray with Romeo, departing VFR to the east." You will be given a VFR clearance for your departure, containing instructions for headings and altitudes after takeoff, and a discrete transponder code other than 1200. You should **write down** the clearance, then read it back for verification. When you call ground control, you should say "Metro Ground, Cessna 1234 Xray at Smith's Flying Service, with clearance." Note that calls to Ground Control must always tell where you are on the airport, so the controller can issue sensible taxi instructions and also locate you visually from the control position in the tower cab. On the other hand, in this instance, saying you want to taxi to the active runway for takeoff would serve no useful purpose because the fact that you have departure clearance makes it obvious.

Avoiding useless and redundant conversation is a mark of the experienced pilot. When you call Ground Control to taxi, the single word "taxi" tells the whole story. When you call the tower for landing, the single word "landing" is sufficient. Regulations do require that you preface every transmission with the name of the facility you are talking to, and include in every transmission the last three characters of your aircraft identification, and acknowledge every single transmission. **On a check ride, you'd better do just that**, but common sense dictates many exceptions, and good pilots use common sense. On the initial call-up you should say "Metro Ground" to establish that you are talking to the right facility on the right frequency. But once communications are established, it makes no sense to say "Metro Ground" again. The ground controller knows you are one of their clients, and you know you are in touch with Metro Ground. On the other hand, **every single transmission you make**—there are no exceptions—should include your abbreviated identification. The controller must know who you are, without engaging in a voice-guessing game. You can see how hazardous it could be if a traffic warning or a clearance or other specific instruction were acknowledged by the wrong pilot, without the controller being aware of the confusion.

Some transmissions from a controller do not really require acknowledgement at all. That is the case whenever your action is perfectly obvious, and there's no possibility of error. For example, when you are already on final and you are "cleared to land," repeating the clearance is pointless; the controller knows you're going to land, and you should be giving full attention to the airplane. On the other hand, "Taxi into position and hold" should be repeated back, because otherwise the controller can not be sure, when you taxi onto the runway, that you won't start a takeoff roll. The terrible disaster at Tenerife, when a KLM jumbo jet accelerated down the runway into a Pan Am jumbo jet, was the result of just such a misunderstanding. "Taxi to runway three zero" should be acknowledged, if only to reassure the ground controller that you know where you are going on the airport.

At fields with a flight service station but no tower, you will communicate with FSS on the airport advisory frequency 123.6 to get information about airport conditions and traffic, and to advise your intentions. FSS, of course, has no traffic control functions.

For uncontrolled fields with Unicom and no FSS, the **Airport/Facility Directory** will indicate which frequency (122.7, 122.8, or 123.0) is applicable. At controlled airports, Unicom operates on 122.95. At an uncontrolled field without Unicom or FSS, communication is on 122.9. When a tower operates only part-time, the proper frequency to use when the tower is closed is the tower frequency. These **common traffic advisory frequencies** (CTAF) are for listening and self-announcing, especially to tell other pilots you are taking the active runway or that you are entering the traffic pattern. One other frequency that may be of interest to you is 122.75, used for air-to-air communications.

You should be thoroughly familiar with obtaining airport advisory information on Unicom, and you should anticipate extreme congestion on the frequency because of the large number of airports sharing each frequency. Here again, listening for a while may get you all the information you need, without your contributing to the noise.

Unicom serves a very important function in the traffic pattern at uncontrolled fields. Use Unicom frequency to announce your position on the 45-degree entry to the downwind, and your turn to base leg. These are the spots in the pattern at which the most hazardous potential traffic conflicts are just ahead (entering downwind, turning final). At uncontrolled fields without Unicom, 122.9 is used for the same purpose in the pattern. Remember, since several airports within radio distance may be using the same frequency, you must preface each transmission with the name of the field you are at. Thus, "Boondocks traffic, Cessna 1234 Xray on the 45 for left downwind runway 14."

Approach and departure control are primarily IFR facilities, but they can perform a useful traffic advisory service for the VFR pilot. You will be obliged to use their services if you enter a TCA or ARSA; the appropriate frequencies for this are shown on the appropriate chart. Or you can obtain the frequency by calling a FSS. Before you contact approach control, you should be prepared to give your position, either with reference to a clear terrain feature ("Cessna 1234 Xray over Middletown") or to VOR radials ("Cessna 1234 Xray, 22 miles from Linden VORTAC on the 221 radial"). Advisory service is given on a work-load permitting basis, and it requires that you be within range of a radar antenna (often a problem at low attitudes). If the controller agrees to provide the service, you will be given a discrete transponder code, you may be asked to IDENT, and you will be told you are in "radar contact." If your relationship to the controller is voluntary, you can terminate it at any time with the phrase "Cessna 1234

Xray, frequency change," to which the controller will reply, "34 Xray, frequency change approved, squawk 1200, good day."

Light signals are used routinely, by pre-arrangement, when aircraft not equipped with radio use a controlled airport. For all other aircraft they are used in the event of radio failure, so you have to be prepared to deal with them. If your radios are working but you don't have the tower frequency (maybe that part of your sectional chart is illegible), try the various ground control frequencies—121.6, .7, .8, .9, and 125.0. If that doesn't work, call the nearest FSS, if you can; or try 121.5 to establish communications. However, the best solution to this sort of problem is to carry the Airport/ Facility Directory with you at all times. In the event you have an actual radio failure, it is a good idea to have the meanings of the light signals on a special card kept in a specific emergency packet, along with checklists for various kinds of equipment malfunction. For a check ride, you'll have to memorize the signals (see the Airman's Information Manual). Actually, the ones you may have directed at you when you are approaching the airport traffic pattern are fairly obvious: steady green (cleared to land), steady red (don't proceed into the pattern, give way to other traffic, circle and wait), and flashing red (airport unsafe, do not land). Following takeoff, flashing green means "return to land." Alternating red and green (use extreme caution) is rather vague and mysterious; you'll just have to be alert to whatever the problem may turn out to be.

Light signals on the ground are as obvious as in the air: steady green (cleared for takeoff), flashing green (cleared to taxi), steady red (stop), flashing red (taxi clear of runway in use), flashing white (return to starting point on airport).

B. TRAFFIC PATTERN OPERATIONS

---

1. **Objective.** To determine that the applicant:

   a. Exhibits adequate knowledge by explaining traffic pattern procedures at controlled and non-controlled airports including collision avoidance.

   b. Follows the established traffic pattern procedures consistent with instructions or rules.

   c. Corrects for wind drift to follow the appropriate ground track.

   d. Maintains adequate spacing from other traffic.

   e. Maintains the traffic pattern altitude, ± 100 feet.

   f. Maintains the desired airspeed, ± 10 knots.

   g. Completes the pre-landing cockpit checklist.

   h. Maintains orientation with the runway in use.

   i. Completes a turn to final approach at least one-fourth mile from the approach end of the runway.

2. Action. The examiner will:

   a. Ask the applicant to explain airport traffic pattern operations.

   b. Observe the applicant's ability to conform with the established traffic pattern procedures, and determine that the applicant's performance meets the objective.

   c. Place emphasis on the applicant's planning and division of attention in relation to collision avoidance.

Many otherwise proficient students and licensed pilots fly a sloppy pattern. Compared with the fun of high and low maneuvers, cross-country, and landings, the pattern is rather dull most of the time. When it's not dull it can be so hectic that there's little time to worry about polished technique; your whole attention is on looking out for your traffic and trying to understand what the harried voice in the tower is telling you to do. But when smooth pattern technique becomes second nature, everything else becomes easier too. The airplane won't need much conscious effort at all, so you can direct all your attention outside the cabin in a relaxed and self-assured way.

Little things can make it easy. For example, the microphone should be in your lap, the cable across your leg, to keep the mike from falling onto the floor. The last thing you need in a busy situation is to grope for it and then grope again trying to hang it up. It may seem trivial to say so, but laying it in your lap **face down** (if you're right handed) lets you pick it up naturally, with the push-to-talk button where your right thumb is. When this becomes routine, you no longer need to make sure if you're talking into the front or the back of the mike each time you use it.

When you reach 500 feet in your climbout, look over to the left, then make a clean square turn, neither too shallow nor too steep—a 20° bank is just right. Roll out level on the crosswind leg, momentarily, so you can adequately scan the downwind leg ahead of you. Then make another square turn onto downwind. All this time you'll be monitoring your altitude. At pattern altitude, no matter what else you're doing at that moment, push forward on the yoke, lowering the nose to the position below the horizon that you have become accustomed to in flying the pattern, reduce power, and trim to relieve the pressure on the yoke. A mark of the good pilot is flying an exact pattern altitude—800 feet AGL (or whatever it is at your airport), not 820 or 780. This close a tolerance is not required for the private pilot check ride, but why be satisfied with less? The usual error is not to correct altitude decisively. For small deviations, raise or lower the nose appropriately. But if you are more than 50 feet high or low, climb or descend by increasing or decreasing power, and **do it now**.

You have surely discovered for yourself and have often read that a good landing (or a bad one) begins on the downwind leg. You have to change from level flight at, say, 90 k on downwind without flaps to, say, 52 k with full flaps at touchdown. This is accomplished in small steps for maximum smoothness. There are three segments of the landing approach, each with its own airspeed, altitude, and configuration.

Segment 1 is from opposite the point of intended landing to the place where you turn base. When you are abeam the numbers on downwind, smartly reduce power to a definite new setting. In a small trainer, you might have carried 2300 RPM on downwind, and you'll now reduce to 1700 RPM. Remember carb heat if it is needed in your ship. Lower flaps 10° (one notch, if you have a manual control). Applying flaps, in some aircraft, produces a strong nose-up tendency; you'll need to oppose that with forward yoke pressure, and then trim, if needed. Usually, however, if the immediate pitch-up is prevented, little if any trim adjustment will be needed. Reduced power will allow the nose to drop and a descent to begin, and the increased drag will slow the aircraft. By the time you are ready to turn base, you should have lost about 200 feet. The flaps will have added enough drag to slow you down by about 10 k, say from 90 to 80.

Now for **segment 2**. As you turn base, add another 10° of flaps (another notch), and again prevent the nose from rising. The additional drag will slow you another 10 k (say to 70). Now you start to control your descent carefully with throttle—more power if you're too low, less if you're too high.

Segment 3 starts with the turn from base to final, as you apply full flaps. Try to lead this turn neatly, taking the wind into account, so you roll out exactly in line with the runway. Many stall-spin accidents happen during this turn, as you have been warned. If you never exceed a 20° bank, and if you keep the nose down at all times, it is virtually impossible to stall the airplane at approach airspeeds. It's as simple as that. But you could be distracted—by traffic, a passenger, or dropping the mike. Then, if you're not well trimmed for a nose-down attitude, as soon as you relax your pressure on the yoke, the nose goes up, the airpseed falls off, and especially if you are in a steep bank (higher stall speed), you are suddenly in trouble—maybe your last trouble!

If you do things right, you apply full flaps as you turn final, you **keep the nose down**, you trim for nose-down, and you use whatever power is necessary to control the descent. Your right hand should be on the throttle continuously from the moment you turn final until you taxi off the active. And your eyes, the whole time, should be looking over the nose. If you can't see the ground over the nose, you are in big trouble because your nose is too high and your airspeed is too low. Occasionally, you should glance at the airspeed indicator out of the corner of your eye. The extra drag of full flaps should slow you down nicely to, say, 65 k on long final, and you'll lift the nose very slightly to 60 k on short final, ready for the flare. (Airspeeds cited here are typical of small trainers, but the numbers will be different for different models of aircraft.)

If your airplane has retractable gear, something very special has to be done every time you line up with the runway on final approach. You should look at the gear lights and say, **out loud**, "Gear lights green." This may sound rather fussy and pedantic, but there's a reason for it. Sooner or later, you've heard, every pilot will land gear up. But this is nonsense. The ones who will never have a gear-up landing are those who build in a fool-proof system to prevent one. If you get into the habit recommended here, you can never land gear-up, because every landing must be preceded by a final approach. And this **final approach situation** is what you have conditioned yourself to recognize as requiring a gear-down check. Why say it out loud? Won't the passengers think it's silly? What the passengers think now is much less important than what they'll think of a belly landing. The reason for actually saying it out loud is psychological—to establish a conditioned association, as I explained in Chapter 2. If you hear yourself saying something, you know an expected event has occurred, and if you don't hear it, you know something is wrong. If you do it all in your head, this necessary event vs. no-event check is missing; you can simply forget.

Since you undoubtedly performed your GUMP procedure (Gas, Undercarriage, Mixture, Props) well before entering the pattern, you may wonder why we need this redundancy about the gear. It is to avoid any remote possibility of altered procedures resulting in the gear being retracted at touchdown. For example, you are all set to land, when you are instructed to go around. Of course, you retract the gear, and a lot of other things keep you busy as you come around again to land. This is a perfect time for a gear-up landing, unless you use the out-loud check procedure as you line up on final.

Another likely situation that can lead to a gear-up landing is a long straight-in approach. Of course, you should lower the gear in ample time, but it is remarkably easy to find yourself on short final with the gear still retracted. Here is where the short-final, runway-in-sight-straight-ahead, out-loud check procedure pays off.

Gear-up landings are very common in twins that have lost an engine enroute. Here the pilot is operating under maximum stress, and is worried (rightly so) about an overshoot that would force a single-engine go-around—one of the most hazardous operations in all of aviation. With all that on their mind, they simply skip the gear-down check.

The psychology of human error is fascinating. It is quite possible to say "Gear lights green" in an unthinking, mechanical way, and not notice that the lights are **not** green, and go right ahead to a belly landing. This can happen if the phrase itself has been incorporated into a routine procedure, without anything to trigger it. The key to the gear-down check is therefore not the spoken phrase, but actually touching the green light with a finger, as part of a real check. Then the phrase, spoken out loud, becomes a **confirmation** that the gear is down. This may seem a trivial point, but it is the difference between an actual check and the mere appearance of a check. This principle, of course, applies to all aspects of checklist procedures, not only to the landing gear. Gear-up accidents are especially frequent because fatigue, maximum work load, distraction, and sometimes anxiety are all greatest at the end of a flight, and these are exactly the factors that increase the chance of human error.

The single **most** important thing to attend to on base and on final is the nose attitude. Keeping the nose down (i.e., keeping the angle of attack low) is the central safety rule in flying. To the extent that any instrument is important in the landing approach, that instrument is the airspeed indicator. With sufficient airspeed you can't go far wrong.

The **least** important thing to attend to, once you have turned final, is communication with the tower. Flying the airplane deserves all your attention, and there is nothing important to say to the tower anyway. "Cessna 1234 Xray cleared to land." Don't acknowledge. The tower controller sees you, or you wouldn't have been cleared. And you're obviously going to land—that's what you're there for. If you are suddenly told "Cessna 1234 Xray go around," just do it, don't acknowledge. In a go-around, there's plenty to do—and fast—without carrying on a conversation.

Finally, a few words are in order about departing the pattern. Some kind of checklist is needed here to make sure that flaps are up, fuel tanks are switched, and fuel pump is turned off. In aircraft that use some flaps for takeoff, it is surprisingly easy to go cruising with flaps, and then wonder why your cruising airspeed isn't up to what it should be. Why switch tanks (assuming you don't have crossfeed)? Because if there is any block to the fuel flow from the other tank, now is the time to find it out, not halfway to your destination. And finally, if there is a fuel pump, you left it on in the pattern, but now you'll want it off before climbing out on course. I find it easy to remember "Three F's" leaving the pattern—**Flaps, Fuel-tanks, Fuel-pump** (Fig. 3-1).

You should be aware that the traffic pattern is a dangerous place from the standpoint of collision hazard, and you should know just where the problems are likely to occur. One place is where inbound traffic enters downwind on a 45-degree angle. You should be craning your neck and scanning the whole area as you turn from crosswind to downwind, and as you proceed downwind. Another point of traffic conflict is in the area of base leg and long final. Very frequently, while you are on downwind, you will be told to follow a particular aircraft turning base or already on final. If you can't see it, you might ask the tower to "call base" for you, i.e., tell you when to turn base leg so that you'll be clear of the traffic. At a tower-controlled airport, you will receive traffic advisories, telling you where to look ("over to your left," "on a wide downwind ahead of you," "at your 10 o'clock position," and so on). Acknowledge every such advisory by telling the tower that you **see the traffic**, or you are **looking for the traffic**, or you **do not see the traffic** ("negative contact, 34 Xray").

A special danger in the traffic pattern at large airports—especially on the approach and departure paths and the runway itself—is **wake turbulence**. Wake turbulence from large aircraft, especially jets, is a killer. The

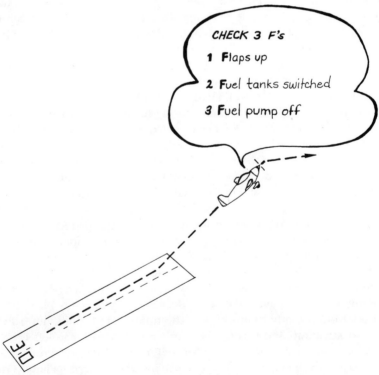

Fig. 3-1 Leaving-the-pattern checklist: The three F's.

rapid and powerful cyclone movement streaming down from the wing tips when lift is being generated can easily invert a small trainer and break it apart. The point, therefore, is to avoid wake turbulence at all costs.

If you are crossing the flight path of a large aircraft during cruise, either cross above it, or delay your crossing until two minutes or more have passed. This will allow the most dangerous force of the cyclones to die down. A standard-rate 360 should take care of most situations pretty well, even though you may still get a jolt or two passing through.

The heavier and the slower the jet, the greater is the wake turbulence hazard. Therefore, the most serious problems you can encounter are near the ground, in takeoffs and landings behind a large aircraft—precisely the location where the recovery from an upset is least likely. Nearly all accidents due to wake turbulence have occurred on airports and on landing approaches.

If a large aircraft takes off just before you, the controller will say "Cessna 1234 Xray, caution wake turbulence from the 727 just departed, cleared for takeoff." Your response should be "34 Xray will wait two minutes." Time two full minutes. Don't let yourself be rushed. If someone wants to take off before you, let them go. Since wake turbulence from a jet has killed many a small plane pilot, why risk testing out your technique when, at the cost of a couple of minutes, you can let the hazard largely dissipate? As the jet departed, you should have noted its point of rotation down the runway. Wake turbulence is generated only when there is lift, so the portion of the runway between you and the rotation point will be safe, if there is no wind. Your aim will be to lift off well before the jet's lift-off point, to remain above its flight path as you climb, and to turn away as soon as possible. If there is wind, the wake turbulence will be carried down the runway toward you, and possibly to one side or the other. The stronger the wind, the faster the wake turbulence will move, but at the same time, the more quickly is it broken up. Therefore, the most dangerous conditions are those in which the wind is light or absent. The worst case is a crosswind of about 5 k, because the turbulence spreads laterally at about 5 k, so this will be just the right wind to keep the vortexes from one wing right on the runway.

It remains to discuss the procedures when landing after a large aircraft. In order to remain above its flight path all the way to touchdown, you have to observe the jet as it comes down the glide slope. Then make your own approach higher. Also note where the jet touched down on the runway, and make sure you touch down beyond that point. You have to be careful in the same way even if the jet has landed on a parallel runway. The wake turbulence spreads out forcefully as it strikes the ground, and a real tornado rolls along the surface, perpendicular to the landing runway. As noted earlier, the worst case is with light wind or no wind, because then this spreading force may be just enough to move the turbulence over to the parallel runway. With a strong wind, even if it is blowing from the jet's runway over to yours, there is the compensating factor that strong wind, itself, will break up the rotating mass of the turbulence.

The remaining case concerns landing after a jet has taken off. If you observe the point of rotation, you can plan to land very short, so that your rollout is complete before you reach that point on the runway. In any case, if you are ever concerned about a wake turbulence situation, tell the tower controller you will make a 360 to delay your landing, or follow the tower's instructions for delaying your landing in some other manner.

C. AIRPORT AND RUNWAY MARKING AND LIGHTING

1. **Objective.** To determine that the applicant:
   a. Exhibits adequate knowledge by explaining airport and runway markings and lighting aids.
   b. Identifies and interprets airport, runway, and taxiway marking aids.
   c. Identifies and interprets airport lighting aids.

2. **Action.** The examiner will:
   a. Ask the applicant to explain the meaning of various airport and runway markings and lighting aids.
   b. Ask the applicant to identify the various airport and runway markings and lighting aids, and determine that the applicant's performance meets the objective.
   c. Place emphasis on the applicant's ability to explain how markings and lighting aids relate to safe operations.

At tower-controlled airports the wind and traffic pattern information is given by the tower. Nevertheless, the wind cone, wind sock, or wind tee closest to the approach end of the runway should be observed during final approach. It will reflect most accurately the wind conditions you will encounter near touchdown, and the instruments used by the tower controller may well be located elsewhere. Nevertheless, useful additional information can be obtained by requesting "wind check" while on final approach, especially if the wind has been gusty and shifting.

At uncontrolled airports a segmented circle outlines the wind indicator. Wind cones and wind socks give an approximate indication of the wind velocity as well as the direction. The wind tee tells direction only; it is shaped with its crosspiece corresponding to the wings of an airplane, and it faces into the wind in the same way an airplane would when landing. A tetrahedron tells nothing about the wind; it is set in a fixed position so that its small pointed end points to the direction of landing or takeoff.

Flanking the segmented circle are landing runway indicators, and further indicators to show the direction of the traffic pattern for each runway if other than standard left traffic. At some fields there is an amber light near the center of the segmented circle, which can flash to show that a right traffic pattern is in effect. However, absence of such a flashing light obviously cannot be taken to mean that a standard pattern is in effect, and actual traffic, actual wind conditions, and the traffic pattern indicators flanking the segmented circle should all be considered.

You must be thoroughly aware of all runway markings in order to comply with airport procedures. A closed runway or taxiway is marked with an X, and airports closed to the public are also shown on sectional charts with an R enclosed in a circle, and additionally by the notation "Pvt." A displaced threshold marks the start of that part of the runway that is available for landing. The threshold itself is indicated by a prominent line across the runway, and arrows along the centerline lead up to it. The portion of the runway containing the arrows may be used for all purposes except for landing; the restriction on landing is due to lack of a full-strength pavement.

Taxiways are marked with yellow centerlines, and often with double yellow edge lines. It is most important to recognize the significance of the taxiway holding lines. These are double yellow lines across a taxiway at the entrance to a runway. An aircraft is clear of the runway only when all parts of its structure are clear of the holding lines.

The Visual Approach Slope Indicator (VASI) functions both in daytime and in nighttime to provide a safe glideslope to the approach end of the runway. There are various systems, but they are identical in function. The principle is so simple, it is difficult to understand why there is so much confusion about it. In the usual two-color system, two beams are projected upward from the runway—a higher beam that is white, and a lower beam that is red. The typical two-bar system has identical units very close to the runway threshold and somewhat farther down the runway. An ideal glide slope will bring you down between the two, thus you should be high with respect to the nearest bar and low with respect to the farthest one. Therefore you should see white and red all the way down. If you drop below the glide slope, the near bar will turn red, so you will see both bars red, as a warning you are too low. If you go above the glide slope, both bars will be white, telling you that you are too high. In a three-bar system you can use the nearest two or the farthest two bars in exactly the same manner as for a two-bar system. So-called "tri-color VASI's" show a green central beam, which turns yellow if you go too high or red if you go too low. Unfortunately, the transition between green and red also looks yellow. FAA says "pilots should be aware . . . that this anomalous yellow signal could cause confusion." They would do better to abolish this idiotic arrangement entirely!

Airport beacons, obstruction lights, taxiway and runway lights, and other lighting used primarily at night will be discussed in Chapter 10.

Score Sheet: 3A. Radio Communications and ATC Light Signals

Date									
Crisp communication technique									
Consistent use of phonetic alphabet and standard terminology									
Listening before speaking									
Use of ATIS									
Use of FSS Airport Advisory Service									
Use of Unicom									
Use of approach or departure control									
Knowledge of light signals									
TOTAL SCORE									
Divide by number of items attempted = AVERAGE SCORE									

Score Sheet: 3B. Traffic Pattern Operations

Date									
Understanding runway markings and lighting									
Understanding and flying the VASI									
Taxiing procedures, wind compensation, large aircraft avoidance									
Pattern: Square turns									
Pattern: Altitude control (± 100 ft)									
Pattern: Airspeed control (± 10 k)									
Pattern: Vigilance for traffic									
Pattern: Nose down on base and final									
Pattern: Smooth transition in the three segments of the landing approach									
Pattern: Correct responses to traffic advisories									
Pattern: Wake turbulence avoidance									
TOTAL SCORE									
Divide by number of items attempted = AVERAGE SCORE									

Score Sheet: 3C. Airport and Runway Marking and Lighting

Date									
Interpretation of wind sock, wind cone, wind tee, and tetrahedron.									
Understanding the segmented circle.									
Identifying restricted airports on sectional chart.									
Understanding runway markings and displaced thresholds.									
Recognizing taxiway markings and taxiway holding lines.									
Use of the VASI.									
TOTAL SCORE									
Divide by 6 = AVERAGE SCORE									

4

TAKEOFFS AND CLIMBS

A. NORMAL TAKEOFF AND CLIMB

1. **Objective.** To determine that the applicant:

   a. Exhibits adequate knowledge by explaining the elements of a normal takeoff and climb including airspeeds, configurations, and emergency procedures.

   b. Aligns the airplane on the runway centerline.

   c. Advances the throttle smoothly to maximum allowable power.

   d. Checks the engine instruments.

   e. Maintains directional control on runway centerline.

   f. Rotates at the recommended[1] airspeed and accelerates to V_y.

   g. Establishes the pitch attitude for V_y and maintains V_y, $\pm$ 5 knots.

   h. Retracts the wing flaps as recommended or at a safe altitude.

   i. Retracts the landing gear, if retractable, after a positive rate of climb has been established and a landing can no longer be accomplished on the remaining runway.

   j. Maintains takeoff power to a safe maneuvering altitude.

   k. Maintains a straight track over the extended runway centerline until a turn is required.

   l. Completes after-takeoff checklist.

2. **Action.** The examiner will:

   a. Ask the applicant to explain the elements of a normal takeoff and climb including related safety factors.

   b. Ask the applicant to perform a normal takeoff and climb, and determine that the applicant's performance meets the objective.

   c. Place emphasis on the applicant's demonstration of correct airspeed, pitch, and heading control.

---

[1]The term "recommended" as used in this standard refers to the manufacturer's recommendation. If the manufacturer's recommendation is not available, the description contained in AC 61–21 will be used.

A normal takeoff, as you already know from experience, is a trivial exercise. When the airplane reaches flying speed, it will fly. You can delay the takeoff a little by holding the nose down, but you would have to really fight with the airplane to keep it from flying as it picked up enough airspeed. What happens during the minute or so after lift-off distinguishes the experienced pilot from the novice.

The point is to set up a maximum rate of climb, smoothly and efficiently. Every airplane has a definite airspeed, V_y, which you know already for your airplane. Usually this is about 1.6 times the no-flaps stall speed, but whatever it is, you will find it specified in your Owner's Manual. Let's assume it is 70 k. Rotation will usually be at a somewhat slower airspeed, perhaps 55 k. Clearly, then, the first thing you have to do in order to set up your maximum rate of climb is to build up the airspeed. This is why the first step in a normal takeoff, the instant you leave the ground, is to lower the nose just a little, to fly level in ground effect, while the airspeed increases. If, on the contrary, you immediately establish the nose-up pitch for V_y, the effect may be just the opposite—your airspeed may fall off. Indeed, this would be just what you did when you practiced takeoff and departure stalls!

When the airspeed has climbed to V_y while you fly along just above the runway, the next step is to establish the correct pitch attitude for maintaining exactly that speed during the climbout. You need to know, in advance, just what that pitch attitude looks like—how the cowl looks in relation to the horizon, and how the little airplane looks on the attitude indicator. Establish that pitch and hold it.

If you understand the function of elevator trim (trim wheel or crank), you can make this whole procedure easy and automatic. If not, you will spend a lot of time fooling around with different pitch attitudes and chasing the airspeed needle.

When you adjust elevator trim, you are essentially setting up the airplane to fly **at a certain airspeed**, hands off. This function of elevator trim is discussed exhaustively in Langewiesche's classic text, STICK AND RUDDER. If an airplane is trimmed for—let us say—70 k in level flight, it will maintain very nearly the same airspeed, not varying more than a few knots higher or lower, regardless of the power setting. With full climb power, the nose will automatically rise, the airplane will climb, and the airspeed will remain quite close to 70 k. If power is reduced to idle, the nose will drop, the airplane will descend, and the airspeed will still not vary much from 70 k. If you don't believe this, go up to a safe altitude and try it for yourself. A thorough analytical explanation of this fundamental principle of flying will be found in Chapter 14.

What all this means for takeoff is that if you know the trim setting that corresponds to V_y, you can set it up in advance. In order to lift off when you reach adequate flying speed, you will have to exert some pull on the yoke, i.e., you will have to rotate by a positive action. Then you will have to press forward just a little to fly level in ground effect. Finally, as you reach V_y, you will only need to release all pressure, and the airplane will climb out at the right airspeed without any further action on your part. The final phase of a takeoff, after climbing to about 500 feet, is to lower the nose, to continue the climb at cruise-climb airspeed for better visibility and better engine cooling.

When to retract the gear is a tricky question. The key rule is to be sure you are safely airborne first. In some aircraft, the opening and closing of gear doors creates more drag than the wheels themselves. In that case the pilot who flips the gear handle right after rotation is in for a nasty surprise some day—an unwanted touchdown with no wheels to cushion the blow! Timing of gear retraction is more critical in a twin, because in case of engine failure the airplane will only climb if it is in a clean configuration (and not too well even then!). This fact dictates retracting the gear as soon as a landing on the runway is no longer possible, no sooner, no later. Flaps should be retracted immediately after the gear; takeoff flaps—20° or less—cause less drag than the extended gear.

B. CROSSWIND TAKEOFF AND CLIMB

---

1. **Objective.** To determine that the applicant -
   a. Exhibits adequate knowledge by explaining the elements of a crosswind takeoff and climb including airspeeds, configurations, and emergency procedures.
   b. Verifies the wind direction.
   c. Aligns the airplane on the runway centerline.
   d. Applies full aileron deflection in proper direction.
   e. Advances the throttle smoothly to maximum allowable power.
   f. Checks the engine instruments.
   g. Maintains directional control on the runway centerline.
   h. Adjusts aileron deflection during acceleration.
   i. Rotates at the recommended airspeed, accelerates to V_y, and establishes wind-drift correction.
   j. Establishes the pitch attitude for V_y and maintains V_y, ± 5 knots.
   k. Retracts the wing flaps as recommended or at a safe altitude.
   l. Retracts the landing gear, if retractable, after a positive rate of climb has been established and a landing can no longer be accomplished on the remaining runway.
   m. Maintains takeoff power to a safe maneuvering altitude.

   n. Maintains a straight track over the extended runway centerline until a
      turn is required.

   o. Completes after-takeoff checklist.

2. Action. The examiner will:

   a. Ask the applicant to explain the elements of a crosswind takeoff and
      climb including related safety factors.

   b. Ask the applicant to perform a crosswind takeoff and climb, and deter-
      mine that the applicant's performance meets the objective. (NOTE: if
      a crosswind condition does not exist, the applicant's knowledge of the
      TASK will be evaluated through oral questioning.)

   c. Place emphasis on the applicant's demonstration of correct airspeed,
      pitch, heading, and drift control.

The first thing to consider about **crosswind and gusty-wind takeoffs** is
whether or not it is safe to practice at all. You can easily get off the ground
in a stronger crosswind than will permit you to land safely again. The only
crosswind your airplane feels is the crosswind **component** of whatever
wind is blowing. If the wind direction is perpendicular (90°) to the runway,
the entire wind velocity is crosswind. But at lesser wind angles, the crosswind component naturally is smaller. In small trainer aircraft, crosswind
components in excess of 20 k are, in general, not safe. The computation
involves trigonometry, but a few simple guidelines can be stated here. If a
90-degree crosswind of 20 k is within your capabilities, you will be able
to manage 23 k from a 60-degree angle, and 28 k from a 45-degree angle.
A 40 k wind from a 30-degree angle will give you the same 20 k crosswind
component, and if the wind is stronger than 40 k you probably shouldn't
be flying anyway, whichever direction it's coming from. Try another day.

The wind tends to make you ground loop by blowing on the surface of
the vertical stabilizer, but this is not usually a problem with tricycle gear
aircraft. Your normal technique of steering the nosewheel straight down
the centerline will work perfectly well. The important thing is to hold a
wing down into the wind, to keep the upwind wing from being lifted—
something that can happen quite easily in a gusty crosswind. The aim is
to lift off cleanly and without the slightest settling. As soon as your wheels
leave the ground, even momentarily, the airplane will start to move with
the wind, sideways on the runway. If the wheels should then touch down
again, they will be subjected to severe sideways forces that may overstress
the gear.

The technique is relatively simple, once you understand what you are
trying to accomplish. As you move onto the runway for takeoff, you should
be holding aileron into the wind anyway, just as you should have been
doing when you were taxiing. Hold aileron into the wind as you start the

takeoff roll, and keep it there until you are airborne. Steer with rudder in the usual way. Hold forward yoke pressure in order to actively **prevent the aircraft from flying off** until it is well above the usual takeoff speed. For example, if you normally let it fly off smoothly, by itself, at 52 k, hold it on until the airspeed climbs to around 70 k. Then bring the yoke back decisively to lift off. As you do that, neutralize the ailerons, and then, once airborne, set up a wings-level crab into the wind, so that you move straight out along the runway heading.

C. SHORT-FIELD TAKEOFF AND CLIMB

1. **Objective.** To determine that the applicant:

   a. Exhibits adequate knowledge by explaining the elements of a short-field takeoff and climb including the significance of appropriate airspeeds and configurations, emergency procedures, and the expected performance for existing operating conditions.

   b. Selects the recommended wing flap setting.

   c. Positions the airplane at the beginning of the takeoff runway aligned on the runway centerline.

   d. Advances the throttle smoothly to maximum allowable power.

   e. Adjusts the pitch attitude to attain maximum rate of acceleration.

   f. Maintains directional control on the runway centerline.

   g. Rotates at the recommended airspeed and acclerates to V_x.

   h. Climbs at V_x or recommended airspeed, $+ 5, - 0$ knots until obstacle is cleared, or until at least 50 feet above the surface, then accelerates to V_y and maintains V_y, $\pm$ 5 knots.

   i. Retracts the wing flaps as recommended or at a safe altitude.

   j. Retracts the landing gear, if retractable, after a positive rate of climb has been established and a safe landing can no longer be accomplished on the remaining runway.

   k. Maintains takeoff power to a safe maneuvering altitude.

   l. Maintains a straight track over the extended runway centerline until a turn is required.

   m. Completes after-takeoff checklist.

2. **Action.** The examiner will:

   a. Ask the applicant to explain the elements of a short-field takeoff and climb including the significance of appropriate airspeeds and configurations.

   b. Ask the applicant to perform a short-field takeoff and climb, and determine that the applicant's performance meets the objective.

   c. Place emphasis on the applicant's demonstration of correct airspeed control.

In a short-field takeoff it is assumed not only that the runway is short, but that there are obstacles (trees, for example) at the end of the runway. A 50-foot obstacle is usually assumed.

The takeoff is conducted in three distinct phases (Fig. 4-1). First, you want to accelerate as rapidly as possible, by applying full throttle rapidly, yet smoothly. You must know the best angle of climb airspeed (V_x) for your airplane. As soon as this speed is reached, smoothly pull back the yoke, maintaining V_x as you lift the nose to the pitch attitude (rather steep) that you know corresponds to a climb at this airspeed at full power. The common error is not to rotate to a steep enough attitude, so that the airspeed soon increases. You should find out by practice how the cowling has to look in relation to the horizon when you are climbing at V_x, and you should back this up by knowing how the little airplane in your attitude indicator should look in relation to its artificial horizon.

In the second phase you have to maintain V_x, within $+5$ k. This is easy if you concentrate on pitch attitude. Don't try to fly the airspeed indicator, just glance at it occasionally to verify that you are holding the correct airspeed. The idea of maintaining V_x is to get the maximum gain in altitude for the least distance travelled, in order to clear the obstacles. Every airplane has a specified airspeed that will give this best angle climb. Slower than that, you'll mush along, too close to the stall, and you won't gain enough altitude. That is why the FAA does not allow you plus or minus 5 k in this maneuver, but only 5 k on the fast side. Faster than V_x, you'll gain altitude quickly, but at too shallow an angle, possibly taking you right

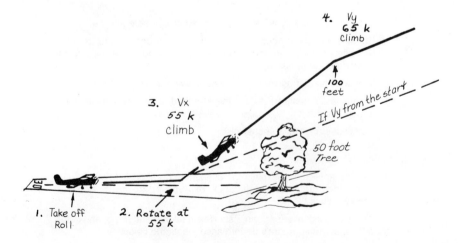

Fig. 4-1 Short-field takeoff over an obstacle.

through the trees (Fig. 4-1). Best angle of climb airspeed is usually about midway between the noflaps stall speed and the speed for best rate of climb. Another way to figure it is at about 1.3 times V_{so}. In a small trainer this may be about 55 k, but the exact value will be found in your Owner's Manual.

In the third phase, when the obstacles are well cleared (say, when you have gained 100 feet of altitude), gently lower the nose to the usual attitude for best angle of climb airspeed (V_y). If your trim was set for this airspeed in the first place, as suggested earlier, you have only to relax altogether on the yoke, and V_y (say 70 k) will establish itself automatically. The mark of a good pilot is that the three phases will be very distinct, with a definite change, at just the right time, from one to the other.

The most important part of a short-field takeoff happens before you start the takeoff roll. It is the decision whether or not to do it. Again and again, inexperienced pilots attempt the impossible. There are fields and conditions where you **cannot** take off safely, even with perfect short-field technique. Four factors determine, for any given airplane, whether or not a safe departure is possible. (1) **The length of the runway and the obstacles to be cleared.** (2) **The altitude.** Climb capability diminishes with increasing field elevation, because as the air becomes less dense, performance deteriorates. You can no longer develop the same power at full throttle that you could at sea level. Moreover it takes a higher groundspeed (therefore a longer takeoff run) to get the same lift in thin air that you could in the denser air at sea level. (3) **The temperature.** Higher temperature means lower air density, so temperature has the same effect as altitude in ruining your takeoff performance. Koch charts and computers let you compute the **density altitude** from the altitude above sea level and the temperature. Remember, the density altitude is what your wings "feel," it determines what lift you can get. To take an extreme example, nothing could be more ridiculous than trying to take off in an airplane with a service ceiling of 13,000 feet on a hot summer day at a high altitude field. The density altitude can be nearly 13,000 feet. Not only won't you get over the trees, you won't even get off the ground! (4) **The aircraft weight.** This is pretty obvious—the lighter the load, the easier you can make it. Fortunately, your Owner's Manual gives you information for calculating in advance the necessary takeoff roll for clearing a 50-foot obstacle at various density altitudes and aircraft weights. Familiarize yourself with these charts, including the corrections for field elevation and temperature. If the numbers don't work out with plenty to spare, don't try it. Wait for a cooler time of day, or reduce your load, or both.

D. SOFT-FIELD TAKEOFF AND CLIMB

1. **Objective.** To determine that the applicant:

   a. Exhibits adequate knowledge by explaining the elements of a soft-field takeoff and climb including the significance of appropriate airspeeds and configurations, emergency procedures, and hazards associated with climbing at an airspeed less than V_x.

   b. Selects the recommended wing flap setting.

   c. Taxies onto the takeoff surface at a speed consistent with safety.

   d. Aligns the airplane on takeoff path without stopping and advances the throttle smoothly to maximum allowable power.

   e. Adjusts and maintains a pitch attitude which transfers the weight from the wheels to the wings as rapidly as possible.

   f. Maintains directional control on the center of the takeoff path.

   g. Lifts off at the lowest possible airspeed and remains in ground effect while accelerating.

   h. Accelerates to and maintains V_x + 5, − 0 knots, if obstructions must be cleared, otherwise to V_Y, ± 5 knots.

   i. Retracts the wing flaps as recommended or at a safe altitude.

   j. Retracts the landing gear, if retractable, after a positive rate of climb has been established and a landing can no longer be accomplished on the remaining runway.

   k. Maintains takeoff power to a safe maneuvering altitude.

   l. Maintains a straight track over the center of the extended takeoff path until a turn is required.

   m. Completes after-takeoff checklist.

2. **Action.** The examiner will:

   a. Ask the applicant to explain the elements of a soft-field takeoff and climb including the significance of appropriate airspeeds and configurations.

   b. Ask the applicant to perform a soft-field takeoff and climb, and determine that the applicant's performance meets the objective.

   c. Place emphasis on the applicant's demonstration of correct airplane control and remaining in ground effect while accelerating to climb airspeed.

The whole point of a soft-field takeoff is to get the nose-wheel up out of the mud, grass or snow, at the earliest possible moment. The reason is obvious: You don't want to nose over as the airplane develops power. The central principle is stated well in Objective **e** above: "... which transfers the weight from the wheels to the wings as rapidly as possible."

The technique is simple in principle, but difficult to execute in practice. It begins with a rolling takeoff as you taxi onto the runway; it is assumed that if you stop, your wheels may sink into the mud or swampy grass. And from the moment you enter the runway, the yoke must be **full back**, right against the stop. As the roll begins, within a very few feet, as you pick up speed, the nose will, of course, pitch up very sharply, since you are holding a ridiculously high angle of attack—well above what would produce a stall. The trick is to relax the back pressure at such a rate that the nosewheel stays just off the ground. This will happen when the cowling stays just on the horizon, as you watch it from the pilot's seat, sitting tall (a certain amount above the horizon, if you are short). Perfectly done, this is an elegantly smooth maneuver, with the cowling remaining in a fixed position on the horizon, while you gradually let the yoke come forward, until finally you are flying.

Once off the ground, the nose is lowered slightly, to allow the airplane to pick up speed in ground effect. Then, when best rate of climb airspeed is reached (or best angle of climb, if there are obstacles), you set up a normal climb. The inexperienced pilot over-controls, pulls the nose up too high, then lowers it too low, and thus the airplane porpoises its way onward and upward. With really bad overcontrolling, the nose wheel will slam down on the runway again—with possibly disastrous outcome on an actual soft field. Getting the right coordination between the relaxation of back pressure and the increasing airspeed (with increasing pitch-up tendency) is the whole trick. A common error is caused by timidity. For fear of letting the nose pitch up, you don't really hold the nosewheel off the ground at all. It's a lot easier that way, but that's not the maneuver.

It takes a lot of practice to do a good soft-field takeoff. Spend a whole session on it, and perfect it. Do it five or ten times or more, to get the feel of the errors and how to correct them. This is a maneuver that will benefit a great deal more from 10 trials in a single hour than from one trial a week for 10 weeks. You need to fine-tune the coordination between your eyes and arm muscles. For this kind of learning, immediate rehearsal of small corrections is essential.

Score Sheet: 4A. Normal Takeoff and Climb

Date									
Directional control down runway									
Smooth lift-off, then level in ground effect									
Smooth transition to climb at V_y									
Airspeed control at V_y (± 5 k)									
Track aligned with runway during climbout									
Smooth transition to cruise climb									
Ball centered at all times									
TOTAL SCORE									
Divide by 7 = AVERAGE SCORE									

Score Sheet: 4B. Crosswind Takeoff and Climb

Date									
Ailerons and elevators into wind during taxi									
Aileron into wind during takeoff roll									
Directional control down runway									
Holding on runway for lift-off at increased airspeed									
Decisive lift-off, neutralization of ailerons, and setting up crab angle									
Climbout at V_y (± 5 k)									
Track aligned with runway during climbout									
Smooth transition to cruise climb									
Ball centered at all times									
TOTAL SCORE									
Divide by 9 = AVERAGE SCORE									

Score Sheet: 4C. Short-Field Takeoff and Climb

Fill in the numbers from your Owner's Manual: $V_x =$ _____

$V_y =$ _____

Date										
Computing Density Altitude										
Using the Takeoff charts in the Owner's Manual										
Rapid and smooth application of full power to initiate takeoff roll										
Smooth liftoff at V_x										
Establishing and maintaining climb at $V_x + 5$ k										
Smooth transition to V_y after clearing the obstacles										
Continued climb at $V_y \pm 5$ k										
TOTAL SCORE										
Divide by 7 = AVERAGE SCORE										

Score Sheet: 4D. Soft-Field Takeoff and Climb

Date																
Yoke full back against the stop initially																
Throttle advanced smoothly and rapidly to full power																
Nosewheel off the ground (high pitch attitude) very early in takeoff roll																
Smooth relaxation of back pressure to hold nose in fixed position on horizon																
No porpoising before airborne																
Directional control, straight down runway																
Level Attitude in ground effect when airborne																
Rotation to appropriate pitch attitude to maintain V_y (or V_x for obstacle clearance)																
Climb-out at v_y(orV_x) $\pm$ 5 k (or $+$ 5 k)																
TOTAL SCORE																
Divide by 9 = AVERAGE SCORE																

5
CROSS-COUNTRY FLYING

A. PILOTAGE AND DEAD RECKONING

1. **Objective.** To determine that the applicant:
   a. Exhibits adequate knowledge by explaining pilotage and dead reckoning techniques and procedures.
   b. Follows the pre-planned course solely by visual reference to landmarks.
   c. Identifies landmarks by relating the surface features to chart symbols.
   d. Navigates by means of precomputed headings, groundspeed, and elapsed time.
   e. Combines pilotage and dead reckoning.
   f. Verifies the airplane's position within 3 nautical miles at all times.
   g. Arrives at the en route checkpoints ± 5 minutes of the initial or revised ETA and estimates the destination, ± 10 minutes.
   h. Computes the remaining fuel.
   i. Corrects for, and records, the differences between preflight groundspeed and heading calculations and those determined en route.
   j. Maintains the selected altitudes, within ± 200 feet.
   k. Maintains the appropriate power setting for the desired airspeed.
   l. Maintains the desired heading, ± 10°.
   m. Follows the climb, cruise, and descent checklists.

2. **Action.** The examiner will:
   a. Ask the applicant to explain navigation by pilotage and dead reckoning.
   b. Ask the applicant to navigate by pilotage and dead reckoning, and determine that the applicant's performance meets the objective.
   c. Place emphasis on the applicant's ability to locate the airplane's position at all times, and to estimate ETA's and fuel consumption accurately.

Filing a flight plan is good insurance. The moment you open your flight plan (usually after takeoff), you must do something to avoid forgetting to close it. It is amazing how easy it is to forget, if you leave it to your unaided memory. Some pilots put the flight plan form in the door, so they can't leave the airplane without seeing it. I use a simple and effective technique. Whenever I open a flight plan, I move my wrist watch to the opposite wrist. When I close a flight plan, I return it to its normal position. If you wear a wrist watch, you will find you can't be at your destination very long without noticing if it's on the wrong wrist.

Noting the time of takeoff is very important, and it is easy to forget. When you are cleared for takeoff, take a few seconds **before** you start the takeoff roll to write down the time. All fuel computations for your flight depend on knowing when you started. Estimating headwinds also requires that you know the starting time, so you can compute groundspeed along your course. This is important because the sooner you discover an unantici-pated strong headwind, the better you will be able to alter your plans to be on the safe side with respect to fuel. Another very important point is to know with certainty how much fuel you started with. Usually this means filling the tanks completely, because you know your total usable fuel. If the tanks aren't full, the gauges are not accurate enough to give you an exact figure, and you wind up with uncertainty about how much fuel remains. Toward the end of a long flight with unexpectedly low ground-speed, that kind of uncertainty is something you can do without.

You should add your estimated time en route to the takeoff time, to obtain an estimated time of arrival (ETA) at destination, and also an ETA at the first checkpoint. The most important ETA will be the first one you compute after leveling off in cruising flight, because you will then be making your maximum speed, so you can see how closely you are adhering to your flight plan.

Once the aircraft has been trimmed for cruising flight, with the proper power setting, you should recheck all systems. Were both tanks operated, so you are sure they both feed fuel properly? Was the fuel pump shut off when you departed the pattern? Are the flaps fully retracted? Are the cowl flaps closed? Have you leaned for best mixture? Is your heading indicator in agreement with the magnetic compass? Are the navigation radios oper-ative? Are you relaxed and comfortable? Then you can give your attention to navigation for the rest of the trip.

As soon as convenient after establishing stable cruising flight, find a def-inite fix on your course line—by terrain reference or by a VOR radial—and note that position and the time on your sectional chart. It is a good idea to make a large prominent mark (I use a triangle) with the time noted beside it. These position marks are the keys to a smooth and successful flight. In wild and desolate country, especially where there are few VOR stations, these marks can be life savers.

Establishing your groundspeed, and checking it periodically, is essential. This is simply a question of timing between position marks on your course line, measuring the distance, then dividing the distance by the elapsed time on your computer. Note your indicated airspeed, altitude, and outside air temperature, and compute your true airspeed. The difference between true airspeed and groundspeed gives your headwind or tailwind component. If your groundspeed is surprisingly low, start to think about fuel requirements and alternate airports. Stopping to refuel may lose you a half hour, but it's a lot better than running the tanks dry half a minute from your destination runway.

It is a very good idea to report your position regularly to a FSS. Transmit on 122.1 and listen on every VOR you pass. If you run into real trouble and don't arrive at your destination, search and rescue will be able to concentrate on the area beyond your last reported position, rather than having to comb your entire route of flight. Another advantage of position reports is that you will receive fresh altimeter settings and also new weather developments. Between VOR stations, stay in contact with Flight-watch, on 122.0, for up-to-date information and pilot reports. The pilot who is travelling your route 10 minutes ahead of you knows a lot more about flight conditions than any report you got during your preflight briefing.

Finally, it is very useful to stay in touch with air traffic control during your flight. Although this service is primarily intended for IFR flights, the controllers will gladly give you **flight following** service, with traffic advisories, if their workload permits. You can ask FSS for the "discrete sector frequency" for the area in which you are flying, tune that frequency, and state your request: "Salt Lake Center (or whatever), Cessna 1234 Xray, VFR 9,500, by the Carbondale VOR, destination Phoenix, request advisories." When you leave the sector, you will be "handed off" to the next controller. You will be given a new frequency, and the new controller will be expecting you even before you call. Once you have been identified on their radar, you will receive traffic advisories, by the "clock-face system." Here 12 o'clock means straight ahead, 3 o'clock means out to the right side, and so on. What you have to grasp is that all these directions are relative to your flight path, not to the airplane. The radar controller will have no idea how much you are crabbing into a wind; you have to apply crab angles to the traffic advisories. If you are crabbing 15 degrees to the right, it follows that 12 o'clock will be 15 degrees to the left of the airplane's nose, and all other positions will be 15 degrees ("one hour") counter-clockwise from what the advisory says. Depending upon whether you are crabbing to the right or to the left, therefore, and upon the amount of the crab angle, you should always have in mind where you really need to look for traffic. The whole value of the system is to allow you to concentrate your scan in that sector where the traffic is, until you spot it. Most of the time the traffic will be at an entirely different altitude from where you are, and you'll never spot it. But occasionally the advisory may save your life by directing your attention to a real collision hazard.

A big safety advantage of flight following is that you always have a "hot line" to a controller. In case of trouble, you only have to hit the mike button, and help is at hand. Sometimes you will be flying too low to be picked up on the controller's radar screen. His tendency will be to drop you, saying "Radar service terminated, frequency change approved." Ask to remain on the frequency anyway, even without radar service. Ask when you might come into another controller's radar range. If communications are about to be lost because you are too low, ask for the next sector frequency, and for advice as to when you should be in range for communication. Controllers are extraordinarily helpful, except when they are very busy with IFR traffic. You are paying for the service. Take advantage of it.

The point at which you should start your descent will already be marked on your chart, as described earlier. Remember that whenever you begin a descent from cruising altitude, you will have to begin enriching the mixture. If you have an exhaust temperature gauge, you can do this quite accurately, adjusting it every thousand feet or so. Otherwise, you have to do it by guesswork; always err on the rich side. On a cross-country flight, you will be interested in maintaining a good speed. In the descent, you can make up most of the groundspeed you lost during the climb, by leaving the power alone and just lowering the nose. The speed will pick up considerably, but don't let it get into the yellow range if there is turbulence. Apply whatever nose-down trim is needed to stabilize the new airspeed.

The biggest problem at an unfamiliar destination is finding the airport. As you have certainly experienced, the lower you are, the harder it is to spot a runway. For this reason, with uncontrolled fields, unless very good landmarks are available, or there is a VOR on the field (to which you can track directly),plan to overfly the airport at about 2000' AGL. This will add a few minutes, but it allows you to complete your flight in a relaxed manner. Whether or not you take this easy way, study the chart very carefully to form a mental image of how the airport is positioned in relation to prominent terrain features. The best thing to find is a "bracket"—for example, a major highway on the right of the airport, a railroad track on the left of it, a town just this side of it, a lake just beyond it. You may actually be able to follow a highway, railroad, or river directly to the airport.

If the airport has a control tower, you will have called in about 15 miles out, and you will know the altimeter setting, the wind, and what runway is in use. If an ATIS frequency is shown on your chart, listen to the information first, before you call the tower. Then you can report that you have

"Information Bravo" (or whatever) on your first call-up. If the destination airport has no tower but has a flight service station on the field, the procedure is identical, except that you will not be given clearances, you'll be on your own to enter the pattern and land.

Special techniques are required at fields without a control tower or FSS. Your sectional chart tells you if there is a Unicom. Call Unicom from 15 miles out and get all the information you need. At such a field you should announce your presence on the 45 degree entry to downwind. Using the Unicom frequency, call "Boondocks traffic, Cessna 1234 Xray entering left downwind for runway 32." This alerts traffic in the pattern at a potential point of conflict. Also announce turning base: "Boondocks traffic, Cessna 1234 Xray turning left base for 32." This alerts anyone who may be attempting a straight-in or who may, through some confusion, be turning base opposite you.

At uncontrolled fields without Unicom, use frequency 122.9 to make all the same announcements. Here, however, you can't know what runway is in use, or what the wind is, or whether the traffic pattern is right or left, unless you overfly the field first, at 1500'–2000', to see for yourself. The windsock, the segmented circle, and any traffic will give you the information you need. Then you can fly out past the field, make a wide descending turn, and enter the traffic pattern appropriately and at the usual 800' altitude.

Don't let your pleasure at finding the field make you forget the usual pre-landing checklist (Fig. 5-1). The GUMP memory aid works well: Gas (full-

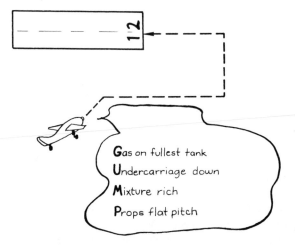

Gas on fullest tank
Undercarriage down
Mixture rich
Props flat pitch

Fig. 5-1 Pre-landing checklist: GUMP.

est tank), Undercarriage (gear down), Mixture (full rich), Props (flat pitch, full forward). All this should be done and checked before you enter downwind. And a final reminder: **Close your flight plan.** The best procedure is to close it from the air as soon as the destination airport is in sight for certain. It's easy to forget to make that telephone call after you land!

B. RADIO NAVIGATION

---

1. Objective. To determine that the applicant:

a. Exhibits adequate knowledge by explaining radio navigation, equipment, procedures, and limitations.

b. Selects and identifies the desired radio facility.

c. Locates the airplane's position relative to the radio navigation facility.

d. Intercepts and tracks a given radial or bearing.

e. Locates the airplane's position using cross bearings.

f. Recognizes or describes the indication of station passage.

g. Recognizes signal loss and takes appropriate action.

h. Maintains the appropriate altitude, ± 200 feet, and desired airspeed, ± 5 knots.

2. Action. The examiner will:

a. Ask the applicant to explain the procedures used for radio navigation.

b. Ask the applicant to intercept and track a given radial or bearing, and determine that the applicant's performance meets the objective.

c. Place emphasis on the applicant's ability to identify a navigation signal and to track a radial.

VOR navigation is so simple that it is remarkable how many pilots don't really understand it. The VOR radials extend out in all directions, and they are named for their magnetic courses outward from the VOR. If you are on the 090° radial, you are due East of the VOR; a line **from** the VOR to you is a magnetic course of 090° from the VOR. It makes no difference which way you are heading, or whether you are in the air or on the ground, you are still on the 090 radial. If you tune the VOR and center the needle with FROM showing in the TO-FROM box, your omni bearing indicator will show 090°. If your position is unknown, you can find out quickly what radial you are on by tuning the VOR, centering the needle with FROM showing, and reading the number of the radial from the omni bearing indicator. If you draw a line on your sectional chart corresponding to that radial, your position must be somewhere on that line. If you do the same thing with another VOR, the two lines will intersect at your position (Fig. 5-2).

To fly outbound along a desired VOR radial, as you would do in following an airway, set the omni bearing indicator to the desired radial. The TO-FROM indicator should show FROM. If it doesn't, something is wrong; either you are tuned to the wrong VOR, or the radial you want is on the other side of the VOR. Once you have set the bearing and verified the FROM indication, the position of the needle tells you which way to go. Always fly toward the needle. If the needle is to the right, the radial you want is to your right. The only question remaining is what heading to fly in order to intercept the radial. Obviously, the fastest way to get there is to take up a heading at 90° toward the radial. At a great distance from the VOR, this might actually be the best thing to do. But usually, a smaller intercept angle is more efficient, because you can fly in the general direction you are trying to go, and also avoid overshooting the radial. A common intercept angle is 30°, but you will learn to judge what is appropriate as you gain experience.

Let's suppose you want to intercept and fly outbound the 135° radial (Fig. 5-3). You turn the omni bearing selector to 135, and verify the FROM indication. Let's say the needle is to your right. Then you want a heading that is 30° to the right of 135, or 165°. After a few minutes, the needle should begin to move in toward the center. If it doesn't, increase the intercept angle by 10°, changing your heading to 175°. Every few minutes, if the needle doesn't move, increase your intercept angle, but remember

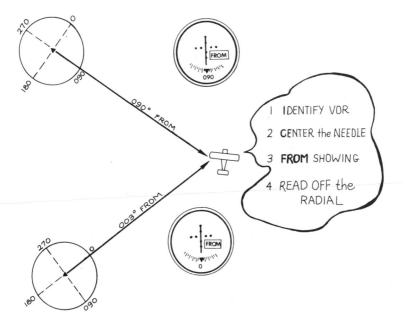

Fig. 5-2 Finding position by intersection of VOR radials.

not to exceed a 90° intercept (in this example, 135 plus 90 = 225°), or you will be heading backward toward the VOR. As the needle moves toward the center, begin a rollout, trying to keep pace with the needle, so that when the needle has centered, your heading will be 135°. Now you are on the desired radial. The only problem is to stay on it. This means watching the needle from time to time, and compensating your heading to stop the needle drift (really your crosswind drift). Suppose the needle moves just a little to the left. Change your heading 10° to the left, and watch. If this doesn't stop the needle movement, correct another 10° to the left, and so on. Once the needle has been stopped, you know what heading will just compensate for your drift. Note it, because you will want to come back to it. Now add another 10° toward the needle, wait for it to center again, then return to the heading that stopped the needle.

Thus, flying on a radial is a matter of constant trial-and-error correction, never letting the needle get far from the center. Flying a radial outbound is an easy exercise, because the farther you get from the VOR, the less sensitive is the needle to small heading changes. This is because the radials deviate as they get farther from the VOR. The distance between the 135° and 136° radials at 60 miles from the station is a full mile, whereas a mile from the station it is only about 100 feet.

The importance of identifying the VOR by its code or voice signal cannot be overemphasized. It is all too easy to tune the wrong frequency and fly off into the wilds, dumb and happy because the needle stays centered (you might not even notice the OFF flag). More important, the VOR signal may actually be on the air, but give incorrect indications because the station is being serviced. At such times the identifier is taken off the air. Therefore, never use a VOR for navigation unless you can identify it positively.

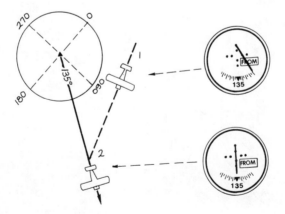

Fig. 5-3 Intercepting and flying outbound on a VOR radial.

If you seem to require a great deal of crab angle to stay on course, you may, of course, be fighting a strong crosswind. The usual cause, however, is that you have forgotten to reset your heading indicator after a long period of precession. In that case, you are actually flying the right heading, as long as you keep the needle centered, even though your heading indicator says something else.

The other navigation procedure using a VOR is flying directly to the station. You may be on an airway, and you have just switched over from the VOR you left behind to the next one ahead. Or you may be off the airways and simply want to fly directly to a VOR. The procedure is exactly the same as before, in that the omni bearing indicator will show your required course. Here you center the needle with the TO indication showing. The omni bearing indicator tells you the heading to fly to the station, and you make corrections toward the needle, as before. If you want to intercept a certain radial and fly it to the station, set the **reciprocal** of that radial with the omni bearing selector, since this will be your desired **course**. Then follow the usual interception procedure (Fig. 5-4). Many pilots become confused by this, so let's take an example. Suppose there is an airway on the 255 radial and you want to fly on that radial, **inbound** to the station. Your inbound course will be 255 minus 180, or 075°. So set 075 with the omni bearing selector. The TO-FROM indictor should show TO, or something is wrong. Then, if the needle is to the right, fly heading 075 plus 030, or 105° to intercept. If the needle is to the left, fly 075 minus 030, or 045°.

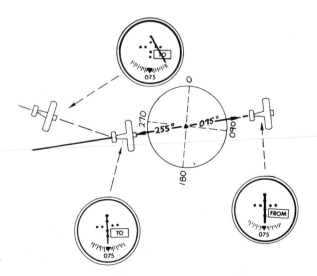

Fig. 5-4 Intercepting and flying inbound on a VOR radial.

Observe that the two procedures described here are basically the same. If you want to fly on a certain inbound course to the VOR, you set that course with the omni bearing selector, and the TO indication is automatic, unless you have the wrong VOR or the course you want to fly is on the other side of the VOR. However, if you simply want to fly directly to the station, you don't know what course is needed. You could center the needle at either of two settings of the omni bearing selector—one showing TO, the other (the reciprocal heading) showing FROM. Here you definitely choose the TO indication in order to fly to the station.

Tracking a radial inbound to a VOR is an exacting maneuver. It is satisfying to do correctly, because it is the basis of instrument approaches, and therefore it is good training for more advanced flying skills. The maneuver starts out easy, and you have no great trouble keeping the needle centered. But as you approach the station, the needle becomes increasingly sensitive, for the reason explained earlier. This means that corrections have to be smaller and smaller as you get closer. When you are within a few miles of the station, heading corrections need to be as small as a degree or two, and this demands perfection in holding your heading. Above all, don't "chase" the needle, or you will surely lose it entirely by overcorrecting. Always fly a **definite heading**. If the needle moves ever so slightly, make a definite small heading correction toward it, and hold the new heading. Bring the needle back to the center, then take out part (say half) of the correction. Finally, as you come very close to the station, the needle will begin to swing rapidly, one way, then the other. Don't worry about this, but simply hold your last heading, until finally the TO-FROM indicator flips from TO to FROM, and the needle settles down again. You have crossed the station, and if you keep the needle centered, you will now be flying outbound (FROM) on the radial that is the reciprocal of the one you flew inbound on. Nothing changes except the TO-FROM indication.

A DME is a tremendous aid to VOR navigation. You don't need intersections of radials from two different VORs to find your position, because the DME gives you the distance from the station. Knowing the radial and the distance tells you your exact position. The DME is also helpful in flying inbound to a station. By telling you how far out you are, it guides you in choosing appropriate heading corrections when the needle deviates from center. Remember, however, that near the station, you are probably a mile or two closer than the DME says you are, depending upon your altitude. At 12,000 feet above the VOR, your DME will read two NM at station passage.

If your airplane is equipped with ADF, "homing" to the station is an elementary procedure. You turn the airplane until the needle points directly upward (straight ahead), note your heading on the heading indicator, and continue to fly that heading. If the needle begins to point to the right or left, alter your heading to center it again. Eventually you will reach the station and the needle will reverse rapidly at station passage, thereafter pointing at the tail (straight down). To use ADF most effectively, you should not only employ the non-directional radio beacons that are shown in red on the sectional charts, but also commercial radio broadcast stations, which are also shown on the charts. Note, however, that while the non-directional beacons transmit identifiers continuously, commercial broadcast stations identify themselves formally only every 15 minutes or so. If there is talk, particularly advertising, you can usually determine if the station you are listening to is in the city it is supposed to be. Without identification, you should be wary, for low-and medium-frequency signals can be heard over very long distances, especially at night.

The ADF homing procedure breaks down if there is a strong crosswind and you are quite far from the station. Suppose, for example, you are an hour away and there is a 30-k crosswind from your left. In the course of the hour, you are going to drift 30 NM to the right. In order to keep the needle straight upright, you will be changing your heading continuously to the left. Eventually, you will get to the station, but only after a rather sloppy spiral approach that gives you a real tour of the countryside.

The point, of course, is to stay on a straight course. When your crab angle into the wind is just right to keep you from drifting off course, the ADF needle will be stationary. That is the situation you want to achieve. In this example, when you crab to the left just enough to compensate for the crosswind, the needle (which always points to the station) will be pointing steadily to the right of its upright position. Start out by heading directly to the nondirectional beacon (NDB), with the needle upright. When the needle moves a few degrees to the left (because the wind is drifting you to the right), turn **toward it** and **past it**. Why "past it"? Because if you only keep bringing the needle upright, that is the homing procedure, which—as I pointed out already—is not suitable here. So continue your left turn until the needle points to the other side (to the right) by about the same amount. This maneuver is called "doubling the deviation." In our example, if you have drifted far enough to the right so that the needle points 5° to the left, turn toward it by 10°. This will put you on a 10° crab angle, and the needle will now point 5° to the right. Then watch it closely. If it moves to the left again, make a further correction to the left. If it moves farther to the right, take out some of your crab correction by turning a bit toward the right. The simple rule is to turn in the same direction as the most recent needle movement. It's all trial and error, but the aim is always the same—to **stop the needle**.

A final point is to verify that you are on the desired magnetic course, as plotted on your chart. Here it is essential to check your heading indicator for precession; ADF course tracking (though not homing) depends entirely on its accuracy. A simple bit of arithmetic is all you need to find the magnetic bearing to the NDB. Just add the readings of the two panel indicators—the **heading indicator** and the **ADF indicator**. For this purpose the straight-up position of the ADF needle is called zero. **Plus** is to the right of zero, **minus** is to the left of zero, just as you would expect. Here are a few sample problems and their solutions:

HI 230°, ADF + 15°, bearing = 245°.
HI 018°, ADF − 20°, bearing = − 2° = 358°.
HI 340°, ADF + 30°, bearing = 370° = 010°.

If the numbers don't add up to what your magnetic course should be, it will be obvious which way you have to turn to re-intercept it. The same mental arithmetic as before will tell you at what point you have intercepted and should turn toward the station, thus putting the ADF needle straight up again.

For outbound tracking of a course, the principle is the same, except that now the needle arrow is pointing down. But you should read off the plus and minus deviations exactly as before, at the top of the indicator, using the **tail** of the needle to give you the information. The only real difference in procedure here is that when you correct drift by turning toward the needle arrow, the deviation will become greater. I think the way to make sense out of all this is to visualize, constantly, where the station is; you know that the needle always points to it. Your aim will be the same as before—to stop the needle movement, and to verify you are on course with the same mental arithmetic.

Some ADF indicators are equipped with a movable outer circle, which can be positioned manually to correspond with the aircraft's heading. Then the ADF needle's arrow not only points to the station, but gives a direct readout of the bearing to the station. This works fine if you remember that every time you change heading, this gadget has to be reset to correspond. I don't like it, I don't use the one I have on my own airplane, and I strongly advocate setting the scale so zero is upright and leaving it alone. Quite different (and perfectly acceptable) is an ADF needle positioned on a radiomagnetic indicator so that the correct aircraft heading is automatically displayed.

C. DIVERSION TO ALTERNATE

---

1. **Objective.** To determine that the applicant:
   a. Exhibits adequate knowledge by explaining the procedures for diverting to an alternate airport including the recognition of conditions requiring a diversion.
   b. Selects an alternate airport and route.
   c. Proceeds toward the alternate airport promptly.
   d. Makes a reasonable estimate of heading, groundspeed, arrival time, and fuel consumption to the alternate airport.
   e. Maintains the appropriate altitude, ± 200 feet and the desired airspeed, ± 5 knots.

2. **Action.** The examiner will:
   a. Ask the applicant to explain the reasons for diverting and the procedures for selection of an alternate airport, estimating time en route, and estimating fuel consumption.
   b. Present a situation in which diversion to an alternate airport would be required, and determine that the applicant's performance meets the objective.
   c. Place emphasis on the applicant's judgment and performance in diverting to an alternate airport.

This is an exercise to see if you can respond smoothly and competently to an unexpected necessity to change your destination. This might be caused by unexpected bad weather on your course, by a mechanical malfunction of the airplane, or by pilot or passenger illness. During a check ride, the examiner will suddenly ask you to divert to an alternate, and you will be expected to do so in the most expeditious fashion.

First, and most obvious, find the new destination airport on your sectional chart. You already know your approximate position if you have been following the procedures outlined earlier in the chapter. Lay some kind of straight edge (even a pencil will do) between your present position and the new destination airport, and estimate roughly what heading you should turn to. Make sure there are no terrain problems at your altitude, and then make an immediate turn to the new heading. While you work on refining your heading and working out a new ETA, it's a great deal better to be flying in the general direction you want to go than to continue on your old course.

The simplest way to check terrain clearance is to look at the number printed in the center of each rectangle on the sectional chart. That tells you the highest terrain in the whole rectangle—actually the altitude shown would allow you to clear the highest terrain by at least 100 feet. If this terrain clearance number is below your cruising altitude, you have no problem. If not, look more closely at the highest elevations shown near your proposed new course. If terrain requires, you may have to fly a circuitous course, perhaps entirely by pilotage, following roads, railroads, or streams, to reach the alternate airport. Don't forget to make full use of radio navigation aids—VOR or ADF—if they can help you get to the alternate.

Once you are flying on a new approximate heading, you should draw a new course line, and take up an accurate heading, which you can then adjust as the flight to the alternate progresses. Also, you should measure the distance to the alternate from the point at which you changed heading. As you can understand, all estimates will depend upon your knowing the exact position at which you changed your heading, and the exact time when you were there. That position should be marked clearly on the chart, and the time written next to it.

Knowing your approximate groundspeed from the initial legs of your journey, and having some idea of the wind direction and velocity, should help you apply reasonable corrections to your airspeed on the new course. From this you can obtain an estimated time enroute, which, when added to the time when you changed heading, will give you an ETA at the alternate. Knowing your fuel consumption, you can also readily compute how much will be required, as specified in the guidelines below.

My own feeling about fuel is that at your regular cruising airspeed, fuel is time, and you don't really care about how many gallons or how many pounds you have left. What you want to know is how much **time** you have left. For this reason, I like to write down, at the moment I write down my takeoff time, another time—the **fuel-exhausted time**. This is obtained by adding the total duration of flight, for the fuel aboard, from the Owner's Manual, to the takeoff time. If you keep this time prominently in view throughout your flight, you will be unlikely to join the roster of pilots who "ran out of fuel" in the accident reports.

The exercise of diverting to an alternate will have to be practiced with another pilot in the right seat, under good VFR conditions. The whole point is surprise, to see if you can exercise good judgment under such conditions. Have your friend in the right seat throw you some curves, then score yourself on how you manage.

D. LOST PROCEDURES

1. **Objective.** To determine that the applicant:
   a. Exhibits adequate knowledge by explaining lost procedures including the following items:

(1) maintaining the original or an appropriate heading, identifying landmarks, and climbing if necessary.

(2) rechecking the calculations.

(3) proceeding to and identifying the nearest concentration of prominent landmarks.

(4) using available radio navigation aids or contacting an appropriate facility for assistance.

(5) planning a precautionary landing if deteriorating visibility and/or fuel exhaustion is imminent.

   b. Selects the best course of action when given a lost situation.

  2. Action. The examiner will:

    a. Ask the applicant to explain lost procedures for a given situation, and determine that the applicant's performance meets the objective.

    b. Place emphasis on the applicant's judgment in selecting the most appropriate procedure for a particular lost situation.

If you are ever in doubt about your position, you can measure by elapsed time (knowing your groundspeed) how far from the last known position you must have come. You may have drifted off course a bit, but an arc extending from one side of the course line to the other **must** include your approximate position. An example is shown in Fig. 5-5. You are proceeding northeasterly on the course line. At 3:21 p.m. you were just opposite Lusk airport, with the town of Lusk on your left. Now, 15 minutes later, you try without success to find the loop road and railroad that should be just ahead of you. Instead, you are about to cross a mysterious highway, and an equally mysterious river is ahead.

Feeling lost creates panic. There is a strong tendency to spot some landmark like a road, river, or small town, and decide it **must** be such-and-such a place on your chart. Be wary. One road, river, or small town looks pretty much like another. Since you are 15 minutes from your last known position, draw a 15-minute arc, computed from your known airspeed or from a recently calculated groundspeed. You must be somewhere near that arc. If the place you think you are is nowhere near the arc, you're not where you think you are. If you think about it, you'll realize that there are only two ways to not be where you should be. First, your ground speed could suddenly have changed radically. That is very very unlikely, since 15 minutes ago you knew what it was; even with a significant wind shift, you still have to be only a few miles this side or that of where you belong. The second is the more likely possibility—that your heading indicator has precessed much more than you expected, so that the heading you've been flying is not what it should be. Referring back to Fig. 5-5, you'll see that if you had been flying 30° to the right of the course, you would now be approaching a highway and a river—just what you see ahead of you.

In general, when you first think you're lost, don't make any drastic heading change. Just continue, looking for some new landmark that should come up at a certain time, according to your elapsed time calculation, and nine times out of ten, it will. In other words, you weren't really lost. The way to get truly lost is to panic, set off in some other direction, and soon have no point of reference at all. If that ever does happen, remember that by climbing you can get into receiving range of a VOR, and you can also get a wider view of the terrain, for comparison with the sectional chart.

There are reliable and unreliable landmarks. Unreliable are all roads, rivers, towns, mountains, valleys, lakes, powerlines, etc., taken by themselves, because one looks pretty much like another. A reliable landmark is a **cluster**—a unique "concentration of prominent landmarks" (as the FAA guidelines put it). This means a combination of manmade and natural features

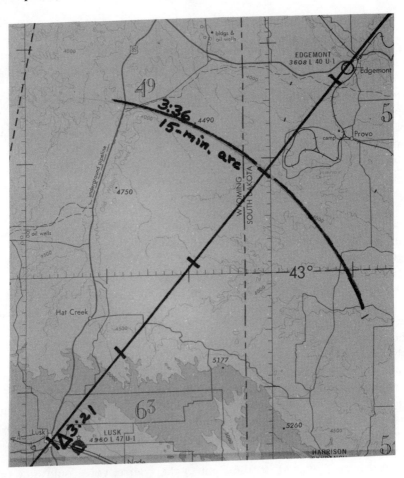

Fig. 5-5 Approximate position by timing from last fix.

that identify a certain location with certainty. An example would be a certain town set in a valley, with a large mining complex about 2 miles south, a divided highway coming from the east and turning south to enter the town, and a small airstrip tucked into the bend of the highway. Find such a cluster within a reasonable distance of where you ought to be, and it is probably where you are.

If you are really lost and can't locate yourself by reference to the terrain—perhaps you are on top of an overcast, or the visibility has deteriorated, or you have even actually blundered into clouds—it is time to get help. Fortunately, help is always available. The simplest, most direct procedure is to call on 121.5. For some reason, pilots are reluctant to use this frequency, although that is exactly what it is for. If you can get in touch with Air Traffic Control through one of their sector frequencies, or with FSS through 122.1 and listening on a VOR, or through 122.2, that's fine. But why not use 121.5 first—you have enough to keep you busy without rummaging through your flight bag looking for frequencies.

It will be helpful to tell them approximately where you are. If any VOR is in range, you can center the needle with FROM showing, and read off the radial you are on. Then if you can also give some rough estimate of how far from the station you are, that would tell them pretty well where you are. After you establish contact, you will be given a transponder code, and you will be asked to IDENT. Then, if you are high enough to be within range of their radar, they can identify you with certainty and guide you to an appropriate airport or to better VFR conditions. If you have no transponder, you will be asked to fly certain headings, so the radar controller can identify you positively on the radar screen.

If you are not in convenient radar range, you may be able to get a DF steer from a Flight Service Station. The equipment permits the flight service specialist to obtain a line of bearing to you if your radio transmitter can be heard. You will be asked to key your microphone for about 10 seconds, and then you will be given a heading to fly that will bring you directly to the location of the Flight Service Station.

To become familiar with these emergency procedures, you should practice them under the hood while a competent pilot in the right seat (or your instructor) plays the part of the radar controller or flight service specialist. A useful exercise, while under the hood, is to request a practice DF steer from a Flight Service Station, using one of the frequencies shown on the sectional chart, or 122.2 (a universal FSS frequency). Alternatively, call on 122.1 and listen on a VOR frequency. The opportunity to conduct practice DF steers is welcomed by flight service personnel.

Score Sheet: 5A. Pilotage and Dead Reckoning

Date												
Writing down time of takeoff (score 0 or 10)												
Correct computation of ETA at destination												
Computation of ground speed enroute between two checkpoints												
Estimating position by intersection of two VOR radials												
Opening flight plan												
Position reporting to FSS enroute												
Use of Flightwatch enroute												
Timely descent at destination												
Communications and pattern at destination airport												
Closing flight plan												
TOTAL SCORE												
Divide by 10 = AVERAGE SCORE												

Score Sheet: 5B. Radio Navigation

Date												
Flying to or from VOR												
Identify the VOR												
Center the needle with TO showing												
Fly the heading ($\pm$ 20°)												
Altitude control ($\pm$ 100')												
Airspeed control ($\pm$ 10 k)												
or Flying to or from NDB												
Identify the station												
Turn until needle straight up												
Fly the heading ($\pm$ 20°)												
Altitude control ($\pm$ 100')												
Airspeed control ($\pm$ 10 k)												
TOTAL SCORE												
Divide by 5 = AVERAGE SCORE												

Score Sheet: 5C. Diversion to Alternate

Date									
Immediate turn to an approximately correct heading									
Immediate notation of time and position at instant of heading change									
Judgment on terrain clearance, climb to higher altitude or circuitous course if necessary									
Accurate heading computed									
ETA at alternate computed correctly									
Fuel required computed correctly									
Use of VOR or ADF if appropriate (score 10 if not applicable)									
TOTAL SCORE									
Divide by 7 = AVERAGE SCORE									

Score Sheet: 5D. Lost Procedures

Date									
Ability to contact help by radio (simulated)									
Ability to follow instructions for radar identification (simulated)									
Ability to follow instructions for obtaining DF steer (simulated)									
Ability to fly assigned heading (± 20 degrees)									
Altitude control (± 100 ft)									
Airspeed control (± 10 k)									
TOTAL SCORE									
Divide by 6 = AVERAGE SCORE									

6
FLIGHT BY REFERENCE TO INSTRUMENTS

A. STRAIGHT-AND-LEVEL FLIGHT

1. **Objective.** To determine that the applicant:
   a. Exhibits adequate knowledge by explaining flight solely by reference to instruments as related to straight-and-level flight.
   b. Makes smooth and coordinated control applications.
   c. Maintains straight-and-level flight for at least 3 minutes.
   d. Maintains the desired heading, $\pm$ 15°.
   e. Maintains the desired altitude, $\pm$ 100 feet.
   f. Maintains the desired airspeed, $\pm$ 10 knots.

2. **Action.** The examiner will:
   a. Ask the applicant to explain flight solely by reference to instruments as related to straight-and-level flight.
   b. Ask the applicant to perform straight-and-level flight by reference to instruments, and determine that the applicant's performance meets the objective.
   c. Place emphasis on the applicant's ability to maintain altitude and heading.

Maintaining control of the airplane under instrument meteorological conditions is an essential skill for any VFR pilot. Whatever the reason may be, whether justified or unjustified, you may some day fly into marginal weather that turns worse than you anticipated. Or, despite all your careful planning, unexpected weather at your destination may trap you on top with insufficient fuel to reach a clear area where you can descend. And suddenly finding yourself IFR may happen quite readily during night flight. For these reasons you are required to demonstrate your ability to fly under the hood, both on the check ride and at the biennial flight review. You will have to maintain altitude, maintain heading, make turns to headings, and carry out climbs and descents. The key instrument is the attitude indicator (AI), which gives you guidance for the appropriate nose-up pitch for climb or nose-down pitch for descent and the wings level or banked condition. Handling the airplane is identical to what you are already used to in ordinary VFR flight.

A technique that is required in IFR flight is called "scanning." That means moving your eyes around the panel in a systematic way, so you don't fixate on a single instrument, but take in information from a number of sources at once. The all-important AI depends on the vacuum pump for the gyro action, and vacuum pumps often die. When that happens, the AI slowly and insidiously tips over on its side. If your attention is fixated there, you will roll the airplane in the opposite direction, in order to keep the wings level on the artificial horizon, and by the time you realize anything is wrong, it is too wrong to correct. So in actual instrument conditions, check the AI periodically against the turn indicator and the heading indicator— in other words, scan the panel.

The gentle touch! That's the secret of safe flying by instruments. Gentle handling of the yoke, gentle banks, gentle pitch changes, gentle power changes! To fly straight and level, do nothing, and keep only a thumb and forefinger gently on the yoke. The FAA guide says you should maintain straight-ahead flight for at least 3 minutes, and not deviate more than 15° in heading, 100' in altitude, or 10 k in airspeed. That should be easy to do—mostly by doing nothing.

B. STRAIGHT, CONSTANT AIRSPEED CLIMBS

---

1. **Objective.** To determine that the applicant:
    a. Exhibits adequate knowledge by explaining flight solely by reference to instruments as related to straight, constant airspeed climbs.
    b. Establishes the climb pitch attitude and power setting on an assigned heading.
    c. Makes smooth and coordinated control applications.
    d. Maintains the desired heading, ± 15°.
    e. Maintains the desired airspeed, ± 10 knots.
    f. Levels off at the desired altitude, ± 200 feet.

2. **Action.** The examiner will:
    a. Ask the applicant to explain flight solely by reference to instruments as related to straight, constant airspeed climbs.
    b. Ask the applicant to perform a straight, constant airspeed climb to an assigned altitude by reference to instruments, and determine that the applicant's performance meets the objective.
    c. Place emphasis on the applicant's ability to maintain heading, pitch attitude, and airspeed.

To climb by the instruments, you need do nothing at all except bring in climb power. The climb will begin automatically, and you can focus attention on the heading. If you were trimmed for cruise airspeed, do not change the trim. Again here, the aim is to disturb things as little as possible; it is a mistake to get into a confused situation in which you change all sorts of settings at once, and then you have to struggle to stabilize the airplane again. I mean this literally—your **only** control for ordinary climbs and descents is the throttle. Don't touch anything else.

Leveling off is simplicity itself—you just return snappily to cruise power when you reach the desired altitude. If you know what the power setting was when the climb began, as you should, you have only to return the RPM or MP to that same setting. It is odd that the FAA permits 200' deviation from the level-off altitude; the truth is, even a complete novice can come within 50' on the first try, if they do it the way I describe.

If you have a controllable prop, you have learned a great deal about advancing RPM before power for a climb, and reducing power before RPM for a descent. I believe, however, that when a VFR pilot finds themselves in IFR conditions, first things should come first—and worrying about the RPM comes last. This situation we are practicing for here is an emergency, in which the highest priority is to keep good control of the aircraft. That is why I advocate so strongly the method of changing **nothing** except power for climbs and descents. When and if you are comfortable in your complete control of the aircraft, then and only then make the RPM adjustments that are called for—high RPM for climb power, low RPM for the descent with low power.

C. STRAIGHT, CONSTANT AIRSPEED DESCENTS

1. **Objective.** To determine that the applicant:
   a. Exhibits adequate knowledge by explaining flight solely by reference to instruments as related to straight, constant airspeed descents.
   b. Determines the minimum safe altitude at which the descent should be terminated.
   c. Establishes the descent configuration, pitch, and power setting on the assigned heading.
   d. Makes smooth and coordinated control application.
   e. Maintains the desired heading, ± 15°.
   f. Maintains the desired airspeed, ± 10 knots.
   g. Levels off at the desired altitude, ± 200 feet.

2. **Action.** The examiner will:
   a. Ask the applicant to explain flight solely by reference to instruments as related to straight, constant airspeed descents.
   b. Ask the applicant to perform a straight, constant airspeed descent to an assigned altitude by reference to instruments, and determine that the applicant's performance meets the objective.

c. Place emphasis on the applicant's awareness of the minimum safe altitude and ability to level off within tolerance.

Following through on the same recommendations leaves me very little to say about descents. Reduce the power a little, and the descent will be under way. The only difference in technique is that you will have to lead the level-off, that is, to bring in cruise power some 50' above the desired altitude. Why is this needed here, when it wasn't required in leveling after a climb? Because of gravity and the airplane's momentum. In the climb, gravity is working to level you off as soon as you reduce the power. But in a descent, gravity is working to keep you descending, and the airplane's momentum cannot be cancelled out instantaneously.

D. TURNS TO HEADINGS

---

1. **Objective.** To determine that the applicant:
   a. Exhibits adequate knowledge by explaining flight solely by reference to instruments as related to turns to headings.
   b. Enters and maintains approximately a standard-rate turn with smooth and coordinated control applications.
   c. Maintains the desired altitude, ± 200 feet.
   d. Maintains the desired airspeed, ± 10 knots.
   e. Maintains the desired bank angle, not to exceed 25°.
   f. Rolls out at the desired heading, ± 20°.

2. **Action.** The examiner will:
   a. Ask the applicant to explain flight solely by reference to instruments as related to turns to headings.
   b. Ask the applicant to turn to a specific heading by reference to instruments, and determine that the applicant's performance meets the objective.
   c. Place emphasis on the applicant's ability to maintain a constant bank and pitch attitude to avoid an uncontrolled spiral.

The secret of turns to headings by instruments is paying attention to the bank angle on the AI and the turn rate on the turn needle (or turn coordinator). The AI is by far the most important, because if you maintain a constant small bank angle, you will turn surely and safely, even though the rate of turn would not get you through an IFR check ride. But that's not the point, is it? In most small aircraft flying at around 120 k, a standard-rate (2-minute) turn requires a bank angle of about 15°–20°. I have to disagree with FAA's guidelines about this small point. If you regard VFR flight into IFR conditions as the true emergency it is, then it is pointless to expect standard-rate turns. The real essential is to keep bank angles very small, to avoid any possibility of overbanking and losing control. What's the hurry in turning to a new heading? Does it really matter if a full 180° of turn takes exactly 1 minute (by standard rate) or 2 minutes or 3 or 4? I recommend never exceeding 10° of bank. The slow rate of turn will then make everything else easier to manage. The heading will change slowly enough so there will be no need to lead the rollout; when you get to the new heading, just level the wings. And the shallower the bank, the less will airspeed or altitude change, and no back pressure will be necessary to maintain altitude.

On the rare occasions when I really disagree with FAA, I am of two minds what to do. The easy way would be to teach and write what **they** want done, regardless of what I think and know to be right. The other way— which is the only ethical position because it promotes safety—is to say what I am convinced is right. If you learn it my way and have to take a check ride, have a thorough discussion beforehand with the examiner, to let them know **why** you are going to make less-than-standard-rate turns. Show them you have safety first and foremost on your mind. If, on the other hand, you decide to learn and practice it the FAA way, fine. But when your check ride is over, and you ever get into a tight spot where you need these skills, go back to my procedure, please, and don't take any chances. When you get your IFR rating you'll have plenty of opportunity to make standard-rate turns.

E. CRITICAL FLIGHT ATTITUDES

NOTE: Critical flight attitudes, such as a start of a power-on spiral or an approach to a climbing stall, shall not exceed 45° bank or 10° pitch from level flight.

1. **Objective.** To determine that the applicant:
   a. Exhibits adequate knowledge by explaining flight solely by reference to instruments as related to critical flight attitudes.
   b. Recognizes critical flight attitudes promptly.
   c. Interprets the instruments.
   d. Recovers to level flight by prompt, smooth, coordinated control, applied in the proper sequence.
   e. Avoids excessive load factors, airspeeds, or stalls.

2. **Action.** The examiner will:
   a. Ask the applicant to explain the instrument indications of critical flight attitudes and proper recovery procedures.

b. Maneuver the airplane into a critical flight attitude and ask the applicant to recover to straight-and-level flight, and determine that the applicant's performance meets the objective.

c. Place emphasis on the applicant's ability to interpret instruments and promptly recover avoiding excessive load factors.

The basic rule is to believe the instruments and to ignore all the evidence of your senses. No matter what you **feel** is happening, **believe** what the instruments tell you is happening. The most important single instrument for this purpose is the attitude indicator (artificial horizon), but the turn indicator, the airspeed indicator, and the VSI all serve as backups, to confirm what the attitude indicator tells you.

There are really only two essentials. **First**, you must keep the wings level except when executing turns, and even then, the bank angle should be kept very small, certainly not more than produces a standard rate turn on your turn indicator. It is instructive to fly with another pilot or with your instructor, with your eyes closed, just to find out what inevitably happens if you don't watch the instruments. Sooner or later a wing will drop. If not corrected, an increasing bank angle will develop. The loss of lift drops the nose, and the airspeed picks up. You can hear, by the sound of the engine, that you are diving, so you will pull back on the yoke. This tightens the turn, and the nose drops still further. Soon you are in what is called, for good reason, a "graveyard spiral." You cannot recover unless you level the wings and then pull out of the dive, but you cannot level the wings without reference to the instruments—you don't even know which way you are banked.

Second, you must maintain adequate airspeed at all times. If you do initiate a dive or even just attempt to deal with turbulence, pulling back on the yoke will tend to reduce the airspeed, and you may well approach a stall.

Avoiding these two catastrophes—a graveyard spiral and a stall—is the purpose of the "unusual attitudes" maneuvers. You will be under the hood with your eyes closed and your head down, while your instructor carries out maneuvers designed to induce vertigo. Then the airplane is placed in one of two situations—an approach to the stall, or a spiral dive—and you are asked to take over.

The first thing to look at is the airspeed indicator. **If the airspeed is decreasing**, you are at too high an angle of attack, essentially approaching a stall. The response is to make a normal stall recovery—yoke forward, full power, level the wings (by reference to the attitude indicator), and recover to level flight. **If the airspeed is increasing**, you are diving. The response is to kill the power, level the wings, then recover from the dive. Note that in this case the wings must be levelled before pulling back on the yoke, otherwise (as described above) you will only tighten the spiral. After return to level flight, bring in power and return to your cruising altitude.

Basic hood work should be practiced with your instructor or with a competent pilot in the right seat keeping a sharp lookout for traffic and not letting the airplane get out of hand. You should be able to maintain straight and level flight, using the attitude indicator as primary instrument, and the turn indicator, heading indicator, and airspeed indicator as back-ups. Turns to headings should be smooth, without exceeding a standard rate turn, and with rollout exactly on the assigned new heading. You should be able to initiate a climb to a new altitude, with a smooth level-off. You should be able to descend to a new altitude by appropriate power reduction, again with a smooth level-off by bringing power in to the cruise setting. All these basic maneuvers should be conducted at a safe altitude. Recoveries from unusal attitudes should be practiced only with your instructor.

F. RADIO AIDS AND RADAR SERVICES

1. **Objective.** To determine that the applicant:
   a. Exhibits adequate knowledge by explaining radio aids and radar services available for use during flight solely by reference to instruments under emergency conditions.
   b. Selects, tunes, and identifies the appropriate facility.
   c. Follows verbal instructions or radio aids for guidance.
   d. Determines the minimum safe altitude.
   e. Maintains the desired altitude, ± 200 feet.
   f. Maintains the desired heading, ± 15°.

2. **Action.** The examiner will:
   a. Ask the applicant to explain radio aids and radar services available for use during flight solely by reference to instruments under emergency conditions.
   b. Ask the applicant to use radio aids or radar services for guidance, and determine that the applicant's performance meets the ojective.
   c. Place emphasis on the applicant's knowledge of the services available and ability to follow the instructions.

Many weather-related accidents could have been avoided by exercising the rudimentary IFR skills described here. VFR pilots often embroil themselves deeper and deeper in impossibly risky situations, with marginal or zero-zero visibility, a few hundred feet above terrain, even in mountainous territory, in the vain hope of finding an airport or a safe field for an emergency landing. Because they are not IFR rated they reject the safest escape route under the circumstances. That is to make a gentle 180-degree turn, initiate a climb into the clouds, tune to 121.5, declare an emergency, and get effective help. True, you will have a lot of explaining to do after you have landed, but FAA will not assess a death penalty against you. I am not advocating illegal procedures, and you should never have to resort to this extreme measure if you have planned and conducted your flight properly. But if you **do** find yourself in a desperate situation—and attempting to maintain VFR in instrument meteorological conditions is flirting with death—don't hesitate to use the skills you learned (and practiced) under the hood.

The material under these guidelines has been covered thoroughly already in Chapter 5, Section D (Lost Procedures). The only difference between being lost in VFR conditions and being unexpectedly (and illegally) in the clouds, is that when you are VFR—whether lost or not—you can see the terrain and avoid it. When you inadvertently lose visual contact, get your priorities straight! Priority number one is to fly the airplane, keep the wings level, and initiate an immediate climb. A glance at the sectional chart will tell you the minimum safe altitude where you are—that is the prominent number denoting thousands of feet and the smaller number denoting hundreds of feet, right in the center of the grid square. If you are certain which way to turn to avoid high terrain, initiate such a turn as soon as you start the climb. Make the turn gentle, as I advised above, unless you know that dangerously high terrain is close ahead of you. If you do have to turn quickly, watch your AI very closely and do not under any circumstances exceed a 30° bank.

When you reach a safe altitude, call on 121.5 and get the help you need. It may even happen that you reach VFR on top in the course of your climb. All the better. When you do communicate, confess the situation exactly, don't make up a story to justify the position you got yourself into. Don't lie. The more they know about your actual situation, the better they can help you. An emergency like this is no time to worry about how angry the FAA will be, or how they'll penalize you. Deal with that later, your life and your passengers' lives are on the line right now.

You may think you would never do anything so stupid as to blunder into the clouds and then destroy your airplane, yourself, and everyone with you. But it happens all the time. Why? Pride, that's why! Let me tell you a true story about a member of my flying club who planned a flight of about 300 NM to a large airport in the Los Angeles basin. With him were his wife, his daughter, and his son-in-law. The young couple had left their two small children with friends. This pilot had several hundred hours experience, and he was IFR-rated, but he was not current (and therefore not legal) for IFR. Nor was he current (therefore not legal) for a night flight. A cold front with extremely poor weather associated with a Pacific storm system was right across his route, and his destination was marginal VFR. A ground fog had shut down all but IFR takeoffs at the departure airport, so he waited dutifully but increasingly impatiently all day long. Then at about sunset, the fog lifted, and he chose to depart. He knew he would encounter bad weather, and he knew he would arrive at his destination after nightfall, so there was no way he could complete the trip legally. And he surely understood that he was running a significant risk. But you know how it is—a promised trip, pressure to go, pride in his piloting abilities.

Three hours after takeoff, at a small uncontrolled airport in the Los Angeles basin, with a ceiling of about 100′ in rain, in darkness, the aircraft was observed to make a low pass, then come around onto final at a very low altitude, and fly into the ground well short of the runway. The aircraft was destroyed, and all the occupants were killed.

There is nothing novel about this story. It is typical of more than half of all general aviation accidents. "VFR pilot continued flight into IFR conditions." Admittedly, this pilot's decision to depart in the first place was a bad one. But then, when the chips were down and he flew into deteriorating weather, he was too proud to make a 180, too proud to ask for help. The tragedy here is compounded by the fact that a major international airport at Ontario was only a few miles away. By getting assistance from the radar controllers, he could have been brought down safely onto the long and wide runways there, with glide slope guidance all the way by a VASI system and by verbal instructions. He preferred to gamble his life away at a small, unknown, uncontrolled airport in the rain and the dark, below VFR minimums, and with insufficient night experience to manage the task, especially at the end of what must have been a harrowing flight.

What is my point? Just this. This pilot was not an idiot or a bungler. He was like any of us, human. His fatal mistake was poor judgment made worse by false pride. Think about it! Don't let it happen to you!

Score Sheet: 6A–D. Flight By Reference To Instruments: Basic Maneuvers

Date											
Straight and level flight											
Turns of at least 180° to a heading (± 15°)											
Climbs to new altitude (± 200')											
Descents to new altitude (± 200')											
General smoothness and coordination											
TOTAL SCORE											
Divide by 5 = AVERAGE SCORE											

Score Sheet: 6E. Flight by Reference to Instruments: Recovery From Critical Flight Attitudes

Practice only with instructor

Date												
Approach to stall												
Prompt recognition, immediate stall recovery (yoke and throttle forward)												
Level the wings												
Return to level pitch												
Climbout to initial altitude												
Resume cruising flight on original heading												
or Spiral dive												
Prompt recognition, immediate power reduction												
Level the wings												
Pull smoothly out of dive												
Add climb power, return to initial altitude												
Resume cruising flight on original heading												
TOTAL SCORE												
Divide by 5 = AVERAGE SCORE												

7

FLIGHT AT CRITICALLY SLOW AIRSPEEDS

A. FULL STALLS—POWER OFF

1. **Objective.** To determine that the applicant:

   a. Exhibits adequate knowledge by explaining the aerodynamic factors and flight situations that may result in full stalls—power off, including proper recovery procedures and hazards of stalling during uncoordinated flight.

   b. Selects an entry altitude that will allow the recoveries to be completed no lower than 1,500 feet AGL.

   c. Establishes the normal approach or landing configuration and airspeed with the throttle closed or at a reduced power setting.

   d. Establishes a straight glide or a gliding turn with a bank angle of 30°, ± 10°, in coordinated flight.

   e. Establishes and maintains a landing pitch attitude that will induce a full stall.

   f. Recognizes the indications of a full stall and promptly recovers by decreasing the angle of attack, leveling the wings, and adjusting the power as necessary to regain normal flight attitude.

   g. Retracts the wing flaps and landing gear (if retractable) and establishes straight-and-level flight or climb.

   h. Avoids secondary stalls, excessive airspeed, excessive altitude loss, spins, or flight below 1,500 feet AGL.

2. **Action.** The examiner will:

   a. Ask the applicant to explain the aerodynamic factors associated with, and the flight situations that may result in, full stalls—power off.

   b. Ask the applicant to perform full stalls—power off, in normal approach or landing configuration from straight glides and gliding turns, and determine that the applicant's performance meets the objective.

   c. Place emphasis on the applicant's ability to promptly recognize and recover from the stall.

There are two reasons for practicing stalls. The most important is to learn recognition of an imminent stall, so an actual stall can be prevented. The second reason is to learn stall recovery technique, in case one ever does occur unexpectedly.

The leading killers in general aviation are flying into weather beyond the pilot's ability to handle, and stall-spin accidents. Inadvertent stalls happen through lack of attention to airspeed, especially during maneuvers in the traffic pattern. The unmistakable sensations and sounds of an airplane approaching the stall, and the heavy feel of the controls as they lose their effectiveness should produce an instant response in every pilot—like a warning bell or the stall warner itself: **Both hands forward**, one on the yoke, the other on the throttle. This reaction has to become instinctive, so that it is carried out under all circumstances, and no matter how near the ground. The natural tendency to pull the yoke back when the nose pitches down a few hundred feet from the ground must be overcome, since holding the yoke back ensures a continued stall all the way to ground contact. The place to practice all this, of course, is at safe altitude and after thorough clearing turns have been made.

The difference between practicing imminent stalls and full stalls is simply a matter of when recovery is initiated. In imminent stalls, you recover at the very first sign of that special vibration called "burbling," caused by the disturbed airflow over the wings, or at the first slight tendency of the nose to oscillate up and down. Smooth recovery by lowering the nose and adding power should be possible with almost no altitude loss. In full stalls, you wait until the nose actually drops through the horizon, and then execute the same recovery procedure followed by a climb to regain the lost altitude, and appropriate coordinated use of ailerons and rudder to recover a wings-level attitude and return to the original heading. This is necessary because full stalls may be accompanied by abrupt dropping off of one wing or the other.

The simplest kind of stall is the **power-off stall without flaps**. It should be practiced first as an imminent stall, then with a full stall break. The maneuver begins in much the same way as the entry into slow flight, except that no flaps are used. After clearing the area, reduce power to idle, and apply back pressure to keep the nose on the horizon. As the airspeed falls off, the characteristic signs of the imminent stall will become evident. The controls become mushy, the airplane starts to shudder and to wallow, the normal sound of the airflow past the cabin becomes muted. The stall warning activates (unless it has been shut off). The nose may begin an oscillatory up and down motion.

As you approach a stall, aileron control will become quite ineffective, since the air flow over the trailing wing edge is so disrupted. If a wing drops and you try to raise it with opposite aileron, it will require outrageously excessive control movement. If you should then execute a stall recovery, the ailerons may come to life suddenly and produce an extreme roll. As you approach a stall, keep ailerons neutral and counteract wing-dropping tendencies, maintaining the heading, entirely with rudder, which remains reasonably effective.

Stall recovery always starts out the same, regardless of the type of stall, or whether it was an imminent stall or a full stall: yoke forward to reduce the angle of attack, and power to prevent excessive loss of altitude. It is not necessary to dive the aircraft, merely bring the nose down a bit, perhaps just to the horizon or slightly below. And in modern trainers the recovery does not really require positive forward yoke pressure but only a relaxation of back pressure. After the stall has been broken, and the airplane is flying again, climb back to the altitude at which the stall was initiated. Full power will be needed to minimize the altitude loss during recovery, and for the climb after recovery; after a stall near the ground, this could be critical.

A full stall is obtained by bringing on more and more back pressure until the nose abruptly pitches down. In some trainers, smooth and gentle application of back pressure will not produce a stall break; the yoke will be back against the stop, the stall warning horn blaring, and the airplane sinking as it mushes along. In such an airplane, a more rapid pulling up of the nose may be required. In all stalls, since angle of attack is very high, a great deal of right rudder will be required. It is important to have the ball centered throughout the stall entry to avoid a spin, which may occur if the aircraft stalls out of a skid or slip.

Some pilots are unduly alarmed by the sudden change of attitude in a full stall. The airplane seems suddenly to be pointing straight at the ground. This is an exaggerated impression, but the downward pitch angle is certainly greater than one ever experiences in ordinary flight. The most important thing to learn in stall training is that wherever the nose is pointing, the only way you can recover from a stall is with forward yoke. It is easy to imagine why inexperienced pilots might panic in a stall close to the ground (say, turning from base to final), and pull back on the yoke in desperation. **Yoke forward, break the stall; full power, climb out—** that sequence should become completely instinctive as a result of sufficient stall practice.

Stalls are among the safest of maneuvers. During the stall break, since the airplane is not really flying at all, no unusual stresses are encountered. And a prompt recovery will prevent the development of a dive.

The **power-off stall with full flaps** is also called an **approach-to-landing stall**. Its purpose is to simulate what might happen in the turn from base to final if the nose is allowed to come up inadvertently. Set up the landing configuration, with full flaps, power off, and the airspeed where it would normally be on base leg. Start a gentle banked turn (15° of bank) and simultaneously apply excessive back pressure until the stall occurs. The common error is not to pull back on the yoke sufficiently and decisively; in that case, you will be well into a 360-degree turn before you stall. The stall should occur as you **begin** the turn.

The fine points of this rather simple stall concern the recovery, as illustrated in Fig. 7-1. Since it is assumed you are dangerously near the ground (of course, all stalls are practiced at safe altitude), the point is to recover very promptly by setting up an obstacle climb, then a standard rate climb, leveling off only at or above the altitude at which you stalled. It is a stepwise procedure, as is everything else in flying. **First**, break the stall with forward yoke, and apply full power. **Second**, get rid of about half your flaps and get the gear up (if you're flying a retractable), so you'll be able to climb. **Third**, establish a climb at best-angle airspeed, and remove more flaps, leaving only about 10° of flaps. Continue the climb until you have gained 100′ and are well clear of the supposed obstacles. **Fourth**, lower the nose to best-rate airspeed, simultaneously removing all flaps, and climb out to at least the altitude at which you initially stalled. Your total climb will usually be about 300′. **Fifth**, lower the nose to the level flight position, accelerate to cruise airspeed, and reduce power to the appropriate cruise setting.

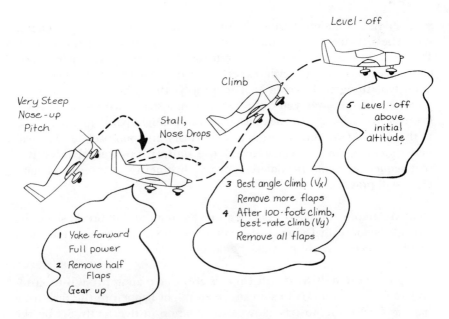

Fig. 7-1 Recovery from approach-to-landing stall.

The five-step recovery from an approach-to-landing stall is one of the most important maneuvers in flying. It is identical to the go-around procedure (cf. Chapter 12, Section C). It should be practiced to perfection, because you will need to use it often in go-arounds, and you will want to be able to do it instinctively and perfectly should you ever have the misfortune to stall at low altitude.

B. FULL STALLS—POWER ON

1. **Objective.** To determine that the applicant:
    a. Exhibits adequate knowledge by explaining the aerodynamic factors and flight situations that may result in full stalls—power on, including proper recovery procedures, and hazards of stalling during uncoordinated flight.
    b. Selects an entry altitude that will allow recoveries to be completed no lower than 1,500 feet AGL.
    c. Establishes takeoff or normal climb configuration.
    d. Establishes takeoff or climb airspeed before applying takeoff or climb power (reduced power may be used to avoid excessive pitch-up during entry only).
    e. Establishes and maintains a pitch attitude straight ahead that will induce a full stall.
    f. Establishes and maintains a pitch attitude that will induce a full stall in a turn with a bank angle of 20°, ± 10°.
    g. Applies proper control to maintain coordinated flight.
    h. Recognizes the indications of a full stall and promptly recovers by decreasing the angle of attack, leveling the wings, and adjusting the power as necessary to regain normal flight attitude.
    i. Retracts the wing flaps and landing gear (if retractable) and establishes straight-and-level flight or climb.
    j. Avoids secondary stalls, excessive airspeeds, excessive altitude loss, spins, or flight below 1,500 feet AGL.

2. **Action.** The examiner will:
    a. Ask the applicant to explain the aerodynamic factors associated with, and the flight situations that may result in, full stalls—power on.
    b. Ask the applicant to perform full stalls—power on, in a takeoff or normal climb configuration, from straight climbs and climbing turns, and determine that the applicant's performance meets the objective.
    c. Place emphasis on the applicant's ability to promptly recognize and recover from the stall.

The **power stall** is likely to be the most abrupt of the stalls. With power, the nose has to be raised to a steeper pitch angle to get the stall, and therefore the pitch-down in a full stall will be more extreme. This stall is best practiced first as an imminent stall by increasing the pitch very gradually in a climb. As the airspeed falls off well below V_X, the rate of climb will fall drastically. Finally, you are carrying full power just to maintain altitude, well on the back side of the power curve. This is a good place to convince yourself that the only way you can initiate a climb is to **lower** the nose in order to increase the airspeed. Bringing back the yoke just a bit more will produce all the signs of an imminent stall, from which you can recover by bringing yoke forward again. Repeating the maneuver, but bringing in just a little more back pressure will produce a full stall. Since you are already carrying full power, you only need to bring the yoke forward to recover, and if you do this at the very moment the nose starts to pitch down, you can minimize the altitude loss. After breaking the stall, you can level the wings (if there was a sharp drop-off to left or right) and gently pull out of the dive.

This same stall done from a gentle banked turn ($15°$) simulates the inadvertent application of excessive back pressure after takeoff, so it is called the **takeoff and departure stall**. To avoid an extremely high pitch angle at the break, followed by an excessive pitch-down, this stall is often done with something less than full power, as one might be carrying with full throttle at a high-altitude field (e.g., 2300 RPM in a light trainer). The first step is to reduce airspeed to what one might have just after lift-off, say 60 k. Then bring in power, start a gentle turn, keeping the ball centered, and simultaneously bring back the yoke. **The airspeed should not be allowed to increase at any time**; if it does, insufficient back pressure is being applied. On the contrary, if the yoke is brought back continuously, the airspeed will fall off promptly, despite the power, and a good stall will occur. The ideal smooth recovery is made by releasing back pressure the instant the nose **begins** to pitch down, rather than waiting for a complete break.

The **accelerated stall** is a maneuver to demonstrate how increased G forces in a steep turn make the airplane stall at a higher airspeed than in level flight. The maneuver is carried out at reduced power, to avoid overstressing the airplane. In a light trainer, 2000 rpm would be appropriate. The main problem encountererd by the inexperienced pilot is failing to pull back sufficiently on the yoke to get a prompt stall as soon as the $45°$ bank angle is established. The procedure is simple. Roll into the bank, and as you do so (not afterwards), bring on a lot of back pressure. If the stall doesn't occur promptly, roll out and try again, with faster application of back pressure. Don't do a full 360 trying to bring on the stall!

The accelerated stall may have some interesting surprises for you. Theoretically, if you are flying in a perfectly coordinated steep turn at the moment you stall, the nose should drop directly away from you, just as it does in level flight. However, very slight slipping or skidding makes a big difference. A stall from a slip will tend to stall the outside wing first, so there will be a sudden roll toward the outside of the turn as the stall occurs. A stall from a skid will drop the inside wing, causing the exaggerated impression that the airplane is rolling into an inverted attitude. Recovery, in any case, is absolutely routine—yoke forward, full power, level the wings, then recover smoothly and gently from the dive.

This has always been a rather difficult maneuver to do well—so much so that FAA no longer includes it in the flight test guide. Nevertheless, it is a good one to practice; but pay very close attention to centering the ball throughout, to avoid any possibility of entering an unintentional spin. And since we are on the subject of spins, let me say that there has been an ongoing controversy for many years about whether or not spin training should be required for the private pilot certificate. It is not, as you know; but I believe (and many agree with me) that it is very good training. You learn a new skill, and you add an element of safety to your capabilities. Find an experienced instructor who enjoys doing spins, and have them show you how. Entering a spin intentionally, by applying hard rudder at the moment of a stall, is a real thrill, something like going over the top in a roller coaster.

C. IMMINENT STALLS—POWER ON AND POWER OFF

1. **Objective.** To determine that the applicant:

   a. Exhibits adequate knowledge by explaining the aerodynamic factors associated with imminent stalls (power on and power off), an awareness of speed loss in different configurations, and the procedure for resuming normal flight attitude.

   b. Selects an entry altitude that will allow recoveries to be completed no lower than 1,500 feet AGL.

   c. Establishes either a takeoff, a climb, or an approach configuration with the appropriate power setting.

   d. Establishes a pitch attitude on a constant heading, ± 10°, or in 20°, ± 10°, bank turns that will induce an imminent stall.

   e. Applies proper control to maintain coordinated flight.

   f. Recognizes and recovers from imminent stalls at the first indication of buffeting or decay of control effectiveness by reducing angle of attack and adjusting power as necessary to regain normal flight attitude.

   g. Avoids full stalls, excessive airspeeds, excessive altitude change, spins, or flight below 1,500 feet AGL.

2. **Action.** The examiner will:

   a. Ask the applicant to explain the aerodynamic factors associated with imminent stalls, power on and power off.

> b. Ask the applicant to perform imminent stalls, both power on and power off, in a specified configuration and maneuver, and determine that the applicant's performance meets the objective.
>
> c. Place emphasis on the applicant's ability to promptly recognize and recover from imminent stalls.

The point of this maneuver is to demonstrate that you are aware of all the signs of an impending stall. This means that you increase the angle of attack—in whatever flight configuration you may be in—until the signs of an imminent stall are apparent. As you have learned, a smooth airflow over the wings is required for normal lift to be generated. This airflow makes the aircraft respond sensitively to very slight elevation of the aileron on one side or the other, and the same airflow over the horizontal and vertical stabilizers makes the response to elevator and rudder movement immediate. As the airflow diminishes when the aircraft slows down, controls become sluggish, and at the edge of the stall the airplane is literally wallowing. Associated signs are a quieting of the sound of air rushing past the cabin, and most important, there is a trembling of the aircraft at the edge of the stall. In part this reflects directly the turbulent broken-up airflow at the leading edge of the wings. The nose may begin to oscillate gently up and down. Recovery is immediate when the angle of attack is reduced. Alternatively, one could proceed at this stage to a full stall by applying just a little more back pressure.

D. MANEUVERING AT MINIMUM CONTROLLABLE AIRSPEED

---

1. **Objective.** To determine that the applicant:
   a. Exhibits adequate knowledge by explaining the flight characteristics and controllability associated with maneuvering at minimum controllable airspeeds.
   b. Selects an entry altitude that will allow the maneuver to be performed no lower than 1,500 feet AGL.
   c. Establishes and maintains the airspeed at which any further increase in angle of attack, resulting from an increase in load factor or reduction in power, would result in an immediate stall while
      (1) in coordinated straight and turning flight in various configurations and bank angles, and
      (2) in coordinated departure climbs and landing approach descents in various configurations.
   d. Maintains the desired altitude, $\pm$ 100 feet, when a constant altitude is specified, and levels off from climbs and descents, $\pm$ 100 feet.
   e. Maintains the desired heading during straight flight, $\pm$ 10°.
   f. Maintains the specified bank angle, $\pm$ 10°, in coordinated flight.
   g. Maintains minimum controllable airspeed, + 5, − 0 knots.

2. **Action.** The examiner will:

    a. Ask the applicant to explain the flight characteristics and controllability involved in flight at minimum controllable airspeed.

    b. Ask the applicant to perform flight at minimum controllable airspeed, specifying the configuration and maneuver, and determine that the applicant's performance meets the objective.

    c. Place emphasis on the applicant's ability to recognize minimum controllable airspeed and to maintain correct airplane control.

This is a maximum performance maneuver from the standpoint of piloting skills, and it is also applicable to normal flight situations, typically in a crowded traffic pattern when you wish to slow down in order to provide enough spacing from the aircraft ahead of you.

In its simplest form, slow flight is done with full flaps in straight and level flight. When this has been mastered, it can also be practiced with other flap settings, or no flaps, and in climbs and descents. Always, the point is to fly the airplane at such an airspeed that any increase in angle of attack will cause an immediate stall. Thus, the way the airplane handles in slow flight should be observed and remembered, as indicative of an imminent stall. The point of the maneuver, of course, is to keep the airplane under complete control without stalling.

Start in level cruising flight on a definite heading and maintain this heading throughout. To reduce the airspeed, it is necessary to raise the nose to a higher angle of attack. If this is done at cruise power, the additional lift will result in a climb. However, in this version of the maneuver, the aim is to maintain altitude absolutely unchanged from start to finish. Therefore, the first step is to reduce power. The exact amount of power reduction doesn't matter much; a moderate reduction will do, say from 2600 to 2000 RPM. Power reduction, as you know, will let the nose drop and a descent will begin, unless you prevent it. So bring on increasing back pressure to prevent the descent, watching the altimeter carefully. When the airspeed has fallen into the flap range, add flaps, a little at a time, until you have full flaps. Because of the increasing drag, more power will now be needed to maintain the altitude. In some small trainers, it may require almost full power just to hold the altitude constant with full flaps; that's why in such an airplane a go-around with full flaps is impossible. Ultimately, the airspeed should be just above the stall, with the stall warning indicator operating, and the altitude and heading should be the same as at the start of the maneuver.

The next part of the slow flight exercise is a real test of the pilot's "feel" for the airplane. Maintaining altitude and a minimum controllable airspeed, execute a 30° banked turn. This is difficult because the ailerons won't work very effectively, and excessive bank or excessive back pressure will immediately precipitate a stall. Because the angle of attack is very high, a great deal of right rudder will be needed, even in a left turn, to keep the ball centered. The whole thing is rather like walking a tightrope, but it's a satisfying maneuver when it's done right. When you become proficient, you can do it without the stall warning indicator—just turn off the master switch, having turned off the avionics first, to avoid a voltage surge when you turn the master on again.

The recovery to cruising flight is the reverse—step by step—of the entry into slow flight. The new problem here is that removing flaps tends, at first, to cause an altitude loss because of the loss of lift. Therefore, flaps must be removed bit by bit, with power increases as required to prevent a descent. As the airspeed increases, forward pressure will be required to avoid a climb, and this pressure should gradually be trimmed out. Finally, cruise airspeed is regained, at the same altitude and heading as before.

The usual error in the entry into and recovery from slow flight is inattention to the altimeter and VSI. The VSI is a very sensitive indicator of what the altimeter is about to do. Therefore, immediate action with the throttle—increased power if the VSI shows a descent, decreased power if it shows a climb—will arrest altitude changes before they have a chance to become significant.

When you have mastered the level version of slow flight, try the same thing climbing or descending. The procedure is exactly the same, except that to climb, you will have to add power, while to descend, you will have to reduce power. Since, in general, the airplane stalls at a slightly lower airspeed with power than without, you may have to make appropriate slight airspeed changes to stay at the very edge (within 5 k) of the stall.

A common sequence is to go directly from slow flight into an imminent stall or a full stall, as described above, rather than recovering to cruise.

Examiners and instructors often say (I agree) that slow flight is the single best maneuver for testing piloting skill. You'll have good cause for satisfaction when, in your practice sessions, you really master slow flight.

Score Sheet: 7A. Full Stalls—Power Off—No Flaps

Date											
Clearing turns first, then vigilance for traffic throughout the maneuver											
Ball centered at all times											
Smooth, decisive stall entry											
Prompt recovery											
Imminent stall, **or**											
Full stall											
Altitude loss (ft)											
Climbout to initial altitude at V_X then V_y											
TOTAL SCORE (omit altitude loss)											
Divide by 5 = AVERAGE SCORE											

Score Sheet: 7A. Full Stalls—Power Off—Approach to Landing Stalls

Date									
Clearing turns first, then vigilance for traffic throughout the maneuver									
Ball centered at all times									
Smooth decisive stall entry just as 15° bank is reached									
Prompt recovery									
Imminent stall, **or**									
Full stall									
Altitude loss (ft)									
Prompt flap removal to climb									
Climbout to initial altitude at V_x then V_y									
TOTAL SCORE (omit altitude loss)									
Divide by 6 = AVERAGE SCORE									

Score Sheet: 7B. Full Stalls—Power On—From Level Flight

Date									
Clearing turns first, then vigilance for traffic throughout the maneuver									
Ball centered at all times									
Smooth, decisive stall entry									
Prompt recovery									
Imminent stall, **or**									
Full stall									
Altitude loss (ft)									
Climbout to initial altitude at V_x then V_y									
TOTAL SCORE (omit altitude loss)									
Divide by 5 = AVERAGE SCORE									

Score Sheet: 7B. Full Stalls—Power On—Takeoff and Departure Stalls

Date											
Clearing turns first, then vigilance for traffic throughout the maneuver											
Ball centered at all times											
Maintaining lift-off speed until stall											
Smooth decisive stall entry just as 15° bank is reached											
Prompt recovery											
Imminent stall, **or**											
Full stall											
Altitude loss (ft)											
Climbout to initial altitude at V_x then V_y											
TOTAL SCORE (omit altitude loss)											
Divide by 6 = AVERAGE SCORE											

Score Sheet: 7B. Full Stalls—Power On—Accelerated Stalls

Date												
Clearing turns first, then vigilance for traffic throughout the maneuver												
Ball centered at all times												
Appropriate power reduction												
Smooth decisive stall entry just as 45° bank is reached												
Prompt recovery												
Imminent stall, **or**												
Full stall												
Altitude loss (ft)												
Climbout to initial altitude at V_x then V_y												
TOTAL SCORE (omit altitude loss)												
Divide by 6 = AVERAGE SCORE												

Score Sheet: 7C.   Imminent Stalls—Power On and Power Off

Date									
Understanding and being able to explain the aerodynamics									
Coordinated control, centering the ball at all times.									
Recognizing the sings of an imminent stall.									
Smooth recovery, no loss of altitude.									
TOTAL SCORE									
Divide by 4 = AVERAGE SCORE									

Score Sheet: 7D. Maneuvering at Minimum Controllable Airspeed (Slow Flight)

Date											
Maintaining heading (± 10 degrees)											
Maintaining altitude (± 100 ft) (or stabilized rate of climb or descent)											
Turns to left and right with 30° bank											
Ball centered at all times											
Constant airspeed just above stall											
Clearing turns before starting, and vigilance for traffic during maneuver											
Smooth return to cruise with stepwise flap removal and no loss of altitude											
Inadvertent stall (subtract 50, otherwise no score here)											
TOTAL SCORE											
Divide by 7 = AVERAGE SCORE											

8

TURN MANEUVERS

A. CONSTANT ALTITUDE TURNS

1. **Objective.** To determine that the applicant:

   a. Exhibits adequate knowledge by explaining the performance factors associated with constant altitude turns including increased load factors, power required, and overbanking tendency.

   b. Selects an altitude that will allow the maneuver to be performed no lower than 1,500 feet AGL.

   c. Establishes an airspeed which does not exceed the airplane's design maneuvering airspeed.

   d. Enters a 180° or 360° turn maintaining a bank angle of 40° to 50° in coordinated flight.

   e. Divides attention between airplane control and orientation.

   f. Rolls out at the desired heading, ± 20°.

   g. Maintains the desired altitude, ± 200 feet.

2. **Action.** The examiner will:

   a. Ask the applicant to explain the performance factors associated with constant altitude turns.

   b. Ask the applicant to perform constant altitude turns and specify degree of turn and roll-out heading, and determine that the applicant's performance meets the objective.

   c. Place emphasis on the applicant's ability to control pitch and bank, and maintain coordinated flight.

This maneuver is nearly the same as what has always been called "steep turns," but with an important difference. The classical steep turn was regarded as an advanced maneuver, only required on the Commercial check ride, a bank angle of at least 50° being called for. Here the required bank angle is 40°–50°. So, in introducing the maneuver into the Private Pilot check ride for the first time, FAA has made it a little easier. Even so, it is difficult to carry out perfectly, and therefore a deviation of 200′ above or below the entering altitude is permitted, as compared with only 100′ in the classical Steep Turns maneuver. Nevertheless, this has to be regarded as primarily an exercise in coordination, and a test of the pilot's "feel" for the airplane, rather than a procedure that would be applied in ordinary normal flight.

The steep bank angle places the aircraft in the region of overbanking tendency, due to the more rapid forward movement of the outer (high) wing, causing more lift than on the inner (low) wing. In addition, the steep bank significantly decreases the vertical component of total lift, producing a nose-down diving tendency, which has to be overcome with back yoke pressure, increasing the angle of attack. G forces are increased, and the stall speed is significantly higher than in level flight, as the table in your Owner's Manual shows. As a result of the increased angle of attack, right rudder is needed to keep the ball centered, sometimes even in a steep turn to the left. Obviously, rolling into and out of a steep turn will exercise the pilot's coordination skills to the utmost. To add to the difficulty of the maneuver, many small trainers require addition of full power to avoid altitude loss. Finally, leading the rollout accurately is much more difficult than in shallow or medium turns. The maneuver calls for a 180° or 360° turn, with rollout exactly on the entry heading. Disorientation can occur, unless one keeps careful track by reference to terrain and the heading indicator.

Start at maneuvering speed (V_A), in level flight toward a definite terrain reference, such as a distant landmark or a straight highway, and also note your heading. Roll briskly into a 45° bank, using rudder initially in the direction of the turn, and glancing at the ball to keep it centered. Bring in more power if your airplane requires it. Simultaneously bring in back pressure to keep the nose in a fixed position with relation to the horizon. As the desired bank angle is attained, neutralize aileron and rudder, and maintain back pressure on the yoke. Now you have to find out what aileron position will oppose the overbanking tendency; it probably will require some opposite aileron (toward the outside of the turn) throughout the maneuver. You also have to find out what rudder pressures you will need to keep the ball centered. You might need right rudder only in right turn, or you might need it in the left turn, too.

Your center of attention should be outside the aircraft, especially on the position of the nose or cowling against the horizon. An occasional glance at the altimeter and vertical speed indicator is useful, but if the nose is made to follow a circle around the horizon, without dropping or rising, the altitude will not change. If things do get out of hand, and you start to lose altitude, the best way to recover is to shallow the bank; with a steep bank already, further back pressure will do more to tighten the turn than to initiate a climb.

Now, with everything stable, you should be watching the terrain to note when the degree of turn has been completed. Say it out loud. It is surprisingly easy to forget the rollout heading. Then about 20 degrees before you come to it, roll out, coordinating rudder with aileron. The trickiest part of the maneuver is the smooth relaxation of back pressure as you roll out. Otherwise, you'll balloon upward as you unbank and regain normal lift. If power was increased in the turn, reduce it as you roll out.

Turns to the left and to the right will require different apparent positions of the nose on the horizon, since you are sitting off to the left side of the cabin. In a turn to the left you are below the center of the nose cowling, so it seems higher on the horizon than in a turn to the right, when your own position is above the center of the nose. Practice enough turns in each direction to become thoroughly familiar with this important difference. Use your attitude indicator (artificial horizon), provided it was set correctly in level flight, to help you learn the correct positions of the nose on the horizon.

The ultimate form of this maneuver, which you should practice, requires a smooth entry into the opposite turn after each completion. This means rolling, without hesitation, directly from a 45° bank to the left over to a 45° bank to the right, and vice versa. Obviously, this reversal of direction will keep you busy, coordinating aileron, rudder, back pressure, and power—all perfectly smoothly, and without change of altitude. This exercise puts a maximum demand on the pilot's abilities, which accounts for it being a favorite of instructors and examiners who want to find out what the pilot can really do.

While you are doing these steep turns, you can't easily spot traffic, but you have to try. At least make sure to clear the area thoroughly before you begin.

B. DESCENDING TURNS

1. **Objective.** To determine that the applicant:
   a. Exhibits adequate knowledge by explaining the performance factors associated with descending turns while maintaining the airplane's position in relation to the surface.
   b. Establishes a glide at the recommended airspeed when power loss is simulated.
   c. Selects a suitable area over which a descending turn can be performed.
   d. Enters the descending turn, not to exceed a bank angle of 40° at the steepest point, over the selected area with the desired radius of turn.
   e. Maintains a radius which is approximately constant over the selected area.
   f. Divides attention between airplane control, planning, flightpath, and orientation.

    g. Mainains the desired airspeed, ± 10 knots.

    h. Recovers at a safe altitude and position from which an emergency landing could be accomplished.

2. Action. The examiner will:

    a. Ask the applicant to explain the performance factors associated with descending turns while maintaining the airplane's position in relation to the surface.

    b. Ask the applicant to perform a descending turn combining this task with high altitude simulated emergencies, and determine that the applicant's performance meets the objective.

    c. Place emphasis on the applicant's ability to plan and maintain the desired flightpath in relation to the surface.

Like the preceding maneuver, this is a modified version of one that was formerly only required on the Commercial check ride, where it was called "Steep Spirals." There the steepest bank was specified as 50°–55°; in the present maneuver it is 40°. Unlike the Constant Altitude Turns, Descending Turns has a real usefulness. The aim is to descend in a glide over a fixed spot, maintaining a constant radius about that spot. The turns will always be to the left, since this is the only way the pilot can keep the ground below in constant view. The principal use of the maneuver would be to descend directly over a point of intended landing after an engine failure. Another use would be to descend, VFR, through a relatively small break in the clouds.

The airspeed must be exactly the **best glide speed** (see Chapter 1). The method of keeping a constant radius is the same as will be discussed at length in Chapter 9, C (Turns Around A Point). The key is to make the bank shallower coming upwind and steeper going downwind, with a maximum bank angle of 40°. The logic is easy to understand. Divide the circle mentally into an upwind half and a downwind half. You will spend longer flying the upwind half, and therefore you need a shallower bank angle in order to avoid completing the half-circle before you have covered enough ground. On the downwind half-circle, the opposite applies—you have to hold a steeper bank in order to avoid being carried too far before completing it. Some people find it helpful to imagine a crossroads, with four posts at an equal distance along each road, and the requirement that you cross directly over each post as you go around the circle.

You should clear the engine periodically in any simulated engine failure to avoid turning it into a real one through spark plug fouling or excessive engine cooling. Return the throttle briefly to the cruise setting, but don't let the additional power make you lose coordination. This takes some practice. Both the changing angle of bank in the glide and the periodic application of power alter the pitch attitude you need in order to maintain a constant airspeed. For example, at a steeper bank, the nose will be lower; and when power is applied, the nose has to be raised.

The descending turns should be stopped when you reach an altitude from which a smooth transition to an emergency landing can be accomplished. The technique for doing this is described in Chapter 11, A.

Score Sheet: 8A. Constant Altitude Turns

Date													
Careful clearing turns													
Turns to the left													
Smooth entry, ball centered													
Altitude control													
Maintenance of constant 45° bank													
Rollout on entry heading after turn													
Turns to the right													
Smooth entry, ball centered													
Altitude control													
Maintenance of constant 45° bank													
Rollout on entry heading after turn													
Smooth transition from turns in one direction to turns in opposite direction													
TOTAL SCORE													
Divide by total number of items attempted = AVERAGE SCORE													

Score Sheet: 8B. Descending Turns

Date									
Careful clearing turns with attention to what is below.									
Constant radius about the spot.									
Maximum bank angle 40° downwind.									
Constant best-glide airspeed.									
No disorientation.									
Proper clering of engine without disturbing the maneuver.									
TOTAL SCORE									
Divide by 6 = AVERAGE SCORE									

9
FLIGHT MANEUVERING BY
REFERENCE TO GROUND OBJECTS

Obviously, clearing turns are a must, before performing any maneuvers, whether high or low. Climbing straight ahead at a steep pitch attitude should be avoided wherever possible; if you can't see everything over the nose, perform your climb by a series of alternating shallow turns, and scan for traffic at all times. Be alert and aware of special places where collision conflicts are most likely, such as over a VOR (where many aircraft may be converging), in certain practice areas, and at the specific points in the traffic pattern that were discussed earlier.

There are three maneuvers conducted at low altitude, which are very similar in concept and require the same skills. These are:

A. Rectangular Course,
B. S Turns Across a Road,
C. Turns Around A Point.

Two additional interesting ones are found in Chapter 14.

The point of all these is to control the airplane by outside reference to the ground, maintaining altitude within ± 100 feet, and executing the required ground track with smoothness and precision. The key to all of them is proper wind correction. In each maneuver, turns are made, which require different technique depending upon the wind direction. It is useful to practice at first without significant wind, in order to perfect the techniques under the simplest conditions. But the real test is to carry them out equally well with a brisk wind.

The first principle in all the ground reference maneuvers concerns division of attention—inside and outside the airplane. You have to be trimmed for level flight at whatever power setting you are using (usually a low cruise RPM, for example 2300 RPM in a light trainer). Now, in order to maintain an exact altitude, you will have to keep the pitch constant, by holding the nose in a fixed position on the distant horizon. In order to trace a perfect ground track, you have to look frequently at the road, rectangular field, crossroad, or other reference point on the ground. Finally, in order to ensure that altitude really doesn't vary, you have to glance at the altimeter from time to time. The best way to do all this is systematically, by the procedure known as PPAT—Pitch, Point, Altitude, Traffic. Keep your eyes and neck moving. First check the nose on the horizon, then look over at the ground reference point, then glance at the altimeter, then as you move your scan outside, look around for other airplanes. The last is the most important, because a mid-air collision definitely is disqualifying in all ground reference maneuvers!

Some pilots find altitude control the most difficult part of these ground reference maneuvers. This may simply be a question of not being able to see a distant horizon. If there are hills or mountains nearby, these may block your view of the true horizon. You have to imagine a line, part way up the mountain range, that would coincide with the distant horizon if the mountains were transparent. If you forget this and use the ridge line, you will pitch up and tend to climb. The other common altitude control problem results from failing to use sufficient back pressure in banks. This results in a diving tendency, which is especially alarming since you are already at a low altitude.

The only other matter of importance is wind correction. Here a simple general principle holds for all these maneuvers: **Steepest bank downwind, shallowest bank upwind**. Suppose you want to fly a perfect circle around a tree, as illustrated in Fig. 9-1. At top is shown the effect on your ground track if you maintain a constant bank. As you come downwind, you are carried far down beyond the tree, and as you come upwind, you make much slower progress. Your ground track will look like a series of loops, and you will soon leave the tree far behind on your crosscountry flight. The solution is illustrated at the bottom of the figure. The steeper the bank, the faster the turn, and the smaller the radius of turn. Therefore, steepest bank coming downwind means shorter exposure to the wind, so the crosswind part of the circle can be started at a reasonable distance from the tree. Coming upwind, the shallow bank permits the aircraft to make greater progress against the wind (since it will spend a longer time on the upwind part of the circle), and so it can turn crosswind at the same distance from the tree.

In all the ground reference maneuvers there are changing bank angles to follow a desired ground track and to compensate for wind. Changing bank angles mean changing rudder pressures so that every turn remains coordinated. It is essential, therefore, to include the ball in your instrument scan. Uncoordinated slipping or skidding turns are very common—and disqualifying—errors in all the ground reference maneuvers.

Turns to the left are much easier than turns to the right, because you can keep your ground references in view. In turns to the right, you may have to do a good deal of stretching and neck-craning to see anything useful. Therefore, practice the maneuvers to the left first. Then, after you've become proficient, you'll find the turns to the right much easier to perform.

If you're doing a check ride or biennial flight review, expect a low altitude forced landing to be thrown at you in the middle of one of these maneuvers. Be prepared (see Chapter 11)!

The ground reference maneuvers may be performed at any altitude between 600 and 1000 feet. Some advocate 800 feet because this is the

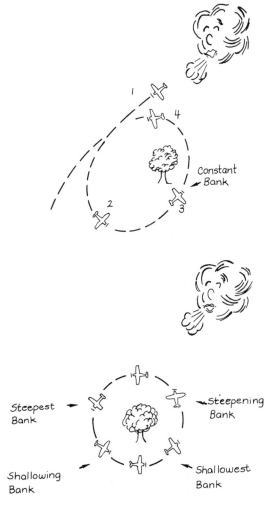

Fig. 9-1 Ground reference maneuvers: The wind correction principle

customary pattern altitude. However, the appropriate altitude will depend very much on the local situation, the height of any towers or buildings in the practice area, and whether or not there are homes below. Even if the area is lightly settled, so that the regulations permit flying to within 500 feet of a house or person, I think that is poor advertising for general aviation. Unless the area is completely unpopulated, I recommend an altitude of 1000 feet above the ground.

Finally, a warning. Whenever you are flying at low altitude, you should keep the airspeed indicator in your scan at all times. Inattention, or distraction by the particular demands of a maneuver, can allow an excessive pitch attitude (excessive angle of attack) to develop. Tension usually results in a pull on the yoke, and this contributes to the same danger. One thing you definitely do **not** want at low altitude is an unexpected stall. It would certainly be disqualifying on a check ride, and it could even disqualify you permanently!

A. RECTANGULAR COURSE

1. **Objective.** To determine that the applicant:
   a. Exhibits adequate knowledge by explaining wind-drift correction in straight and turning flight and the relationship of the rectangular course to airport traffic patterns.
   b. Selects a suitable reference area.
   c. Enters a left or right pattern at a desired distance from the selected reference area and at 600 to 1,000 feet AGL.
   d. Divides attention between airplane control and ground track, and maintains coordinated flight control.
   e. Applies the necessary wind-drift corrections during straight and turning flight to track a uniform distance outside the selected reference area.
   f. Maintains the desired altitude, ± 100 feet.
   g. Maintains the desired airspeed, ± 10 knots.
   h. Avoids bank angles in excess of 45°.
   i. Reverses course as directed by the examiner.

2. **Action.** The examiner will:
   a. Ask the applicant to explain wind-drift correction as it relates to the rectangular course and airport traffic patterns.
   b. Ask the applicant to perform flight around a suitable rectangular area course, and determine that the applicant's performance meets the objective.
   c. Place emphasis on the applicant's correct airplane control and proper wind-drift corrections.

This maneuver, illustrated in Fig. 9-2, is simply a square pattern around the borders of a field or other rectangular area. The principles of wind compensation are applied by using the correct crab angle into the wind on each of the four straight courses. The only difficult part of the maneuver is to adjust the bank angle for turning each corner according to the wind direction and velocity. The principle "shallow bank coming upwind, steep bank coming downwind" applies to these cornering turns just as it did in the maneuvers already discussed.

This maneuver should be entered on a 45 degree angle to one of the long straight legs, just as in the normal entry to a traffic pattern. If it is convenient, the entry should be to the downwind leg; then the whole procedure will simulate a traffic pattern. Don't make the mistake of flying too close to the edge of the field; you should be far enough out (at least several hundred feet) so that you can conveniently see it at all times. Maintaining a correct crab angle along the straight edges will not be difficult. If you see yourself starting to drift to the left, you can crab a little to the right, and vice versa. The trick is to roll out of the turns, at the corners of the pattern, with the correct crab angle already established. In other words, with a diagonal wind (as shown in the figure), some turns require heading changes of greater than 90 degrees, while others may require heading changes of less than 90 degrees.

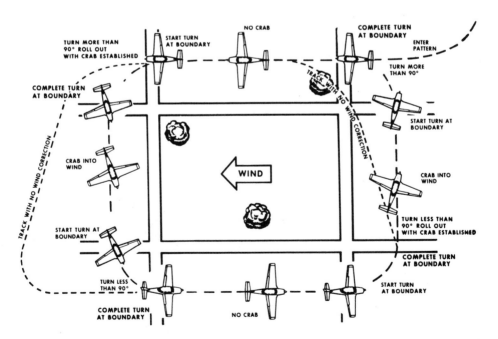

Fig. 9-2 Rectangular Course

After perfecting your technique in the left pattern, reverse direction and fly a right pattern. You should try to maintain the same distance from the edges of the field as you did before. This will be more difficult because you will be unable to see the edge of the field without leaning across to the right side of your cabin, and you can obviously do this only periodically. Therefore, you will have to use more accessory cues, especially those some distance ahead of and to the sides of the airplane.

B. S-TURNS ACROSS A ROAD

---

1. Objective. To determine that the applicant:

   a. Exhibits adequate knowledge by explaining the procedures associated with S-turns, and wind-drift correction throughout the maneuver.

   b. Selects a suitable ground reference line.

   c. Enters perpendicular to the selected reference line at 600 to 1,000 feet AGL.

   d. Divides attention between airplane control and ground track, and maintains coordinated flight control.

   e. Applies the necessary wind-drift correction to track a constant radius turn on each side of the selected reference line.

   f. Reverses the direction of turn directly over the selected reference line.

   g. Maintains the desired altitude, ± 100 feet.

   h. Maintains the desired airspeed, ± 10 knots.

   i. Avoid bank angles in excess of 45°.

2. Action. The examiner will:

   a. Ask the applicant to explain wind-drift correction as it relates to S-turns across a road.

   b. Ask the applicant to perform a series of S-turns across a selected reference line, and determine that the applicant's performance meets the objective.

   c. Place emphasis on the applicant's correct airplane control and wind-drift corrections.

For this maneuver you have to find a road or power line or other long, straight feature of the landscape, running perpendicular to the wind. The idea of the maneuver (Fig. 9-3) is to cross the road with wings level, then to describe a perfect half-circle and return to the road again, once more crossing with wings level, then a half-circle in the other direction, and so on.

The maneuver should be entered downwind. You have to roll into your steepest bank immediately as you cross the road, then progressively shallow the bank as you return to the road again, as Fig. 9-3 illustrates.

Unless the wind is exactly perpendicular to the road, you should carry out the maneuver in a generally upwind direction, for you will move quite a distance up the road anyway; travelling into the wind will keep you from going quite so far.

In this maneuver, as in all ground reference maneuvers, the steepest bank is downwind, the shallowest bank upwind, in order to yield a symmetrical ground track. A common error is to overbank and then correct by shallowing the bank, or to keep too shallow a bank and then suddenly steepen the bank as you approach the road. The key to this maneuver is smoothness. All bank changes are progressive, never jerky, and never with overshoots that require correction. Thus, in the upwind half of the "S," after crossing the road with wings level, you start a very very gentle bank. Look at your ground track and project the semicircle in your mind's eye, so that you are always planning for the airplane to be at a certain point ahead of you. Make a gradual increase in the bank angle, just enough to bring you to the planned point. Steepen the bank very slowly and continuously as you reach the crosswind part of the semicircle, then continue increasing the bank as you come downwind, reaching the steepest bank—but not greater than 45°—just as you approach the road.

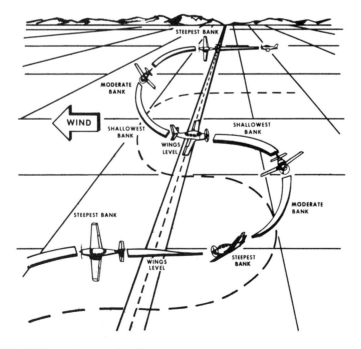

Fig. 9-3 "S"-Turns Across a Road

As shown in the figure, since you will still be travelling downwind, but have to change direction, you will need your steepest bank in the opposite direction as soon as you cross the road. Thus, coming across the road, flying downwind, a rapid roll is needed, from one steep bank to the opposite steep bank. Then, through the semicircle on the downwind side of the road, the bank will be progressively shallowed, so that you cross the road again with wings level.

Remember that the constantly changing bank will require constantly changing rudder pressures throughout this maneuver, so keep a close eye on the ball as part of your scan of the instruments.

C. TURNS AROUND A POINT

---

1. **Objective.** To determine that the applicant:
   a. Exhibits adequate knowledge by explaining the procedures associated with turns around a point and wind-drift correction throughout the maneuver.
   b. Selects a suitable ground reference point.
   c. Enters a left or right turn at a desired distance from the selected reference point at 600 to 1,000 feet AGL.
   d. Divides attention between airplane control and ground track, and maintains coordinated flight control.
   e. Applies the necessary wind-drift corrections to track a constant radius turn around the selected reference point.
   f. Maintains the desired altitude, ± 100 feet.
   g. Maintains the desired airspeed, ± 10 knots.

2. **Action.** The examiner will:
   a. Ask the applicant to explain the procedures associated with turns around a point and necessary wind-drift corrections.
   b. Ask the applicant to perform turns around a point, and determine that the applicant's performance meets the objective.
   c. Place emphasis on the applicant's correct airplane control and wind-drift corrections.

Turns about a point (Fig. 9-4) require the airplane to describe a perfect circle on the ground, with the chosen point in the center of the circle, and the maximum angle of bank 45°. This maneuver is most easily carried out if the chosen point is a crossroad intersection, so that the crossing point on each arm of the crossroads can be projected mentally ahead of the airplane. This process aids in maintaining a constant distance from the point—the principal requirement in this maneuver. Entry is accomplished by flying downwind, abreast of the point, and at the correct distance from it. Immediate roll into the steepest bank (45°) is then called for, followed by gradual shallowing of the bank as you turn crosswind.

The difficult part of this maneuver is judging at the outset how far from the point you should be so that your steepest bank will be 45°. The common error is to start the maneuver too far from the point. Once you have perfected your technique for left turns, reverse direction. If you are at the proper distance, you will be able to see the point quite easily through the window on the right side of the airplane when you are at your steepest bank, turning to the right.

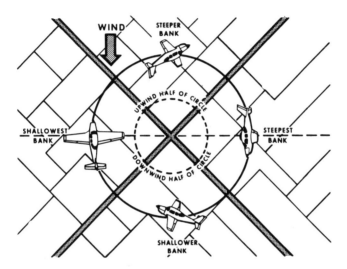

Fig. 9-4 Turns Around a Point

Score Sheet: 9A. Rectangular Course

Date										
Smooth entry										
Altitude control										
Smoothness of bank changes										
Ball centered at all times										
Ground path at constant distance from borders of field										
Rolling out of turns on correct heading with appropriate crab correction										
Vigilant lookout for traffic										
TOTAL SCORE										
Divide by 7 = AVERAGE SCORE										

Score Sheet: 9B. "S" Turns Across A Road

Date										
Smooth entry										
Altitude control										
Smoothness of bank changes										
Ball centered at all times										
Symmetrical ground path										
Vigilant lookout for traffic										
TOTAL SCORE										
Divide by 6 = AVERAGE SCORE										

Score Sheet: 9C. Turns Around A Point

Date											
Smooth entry rolling into 45° bank											
Altitude control											
Smoothness of bank changes											
Ball centered at all times											
Ground path at constant distance from point											
Vigilant lookout for traffic											
TOTAL SCORE											
Divide by 6 = AVERAGE SCORE											

10
NIGHT FLIGHT OPERATIONS

A. PREPARATION AND EQUIPMENT

1. **Objective.** To determine that the applicant exhibits adequate knowledge by explaining:
   a. Preparation and equipment essential for night flying.
   b. Factors related to night vision including those which will change night vision.
   c. Airplane, airport, and navigation lighting.
   d. Weather conditions, terrain features, and unlighted areas that may affect night flight operations.

2. **Action.** The examiner will:
   a. Ask the applicant to explain preparation essential for night flying, characteristics of night vision, lighting, weather conditions, terrain features, and effect of unlighted areas on night flight operations, and determine that the applicant's performance meets the objective.
   b. Place emphasis on the applicant's knowledge of the hazards of night flight into areas of deteriorating weather and areas devoid of lights.

Flying after dark is a beautiful and thrilling experience, but it is potentially hazardous. It is important to become proficient at night flying because delays on a crosscountry trip could result in your reaching your destination after dark.

The first technique to practice and master is the decision-making as to whether or not a safe night flight, VFR, can be attempted. The essential point is to be able to see clouds. This is easy on a moonlit night, and in populous areas there may be enough diffuse light from the ground to show you the difference between a cloud formation and the black sky. But on a dark moonless night, especially if there is a high overcast, this may be impossible. If there is a choice, don't fly on nights like that unless you are IFR rated.

The next essential is to study the sectional chart very thoroughly, marking prominently any obstructions that could be a problem if they were invisible. Especially helpful is the safe terrain clearance number shown in the center of each grid rectangle on the chart. You know that you can relax when your altitude is well above that shown, and conversely, that you need to be on the alert when you are lower. As long as terrain is a factor, you must keep very careful track of your position at all times, using landmarks, lights, and VOR radials to help you. It is all too easy, in night sightseeing expeditions, to fly around this way and that, without any particular plan or headings, become distracted by beautiful light patterns on the ground, and fly directly into a hillside. Hills and mountains are invisible on a dark night, and the lights of houses on the hillsides can be mistaken for stars. So, as you plan your flight, work out in advance how you will avoid such problems. Choose a certain VOR radial that you won't cross, set it up with your omni bearing selector, then, while you are flying, glance at the needle from time to time, to make sure it stays on the same side of center.

Airport lighting requires some consideration. At a completely unlighted airport, night flight is very hazardous. You may manage the takeoff, but how will you find the airport again for landing? And even if you are familiar with the locale, and aware of the obstructions in the approach path, how will you orient your airplane for a final approach to an unlighted runway? Finally, even after touchdown, unless there is a prominent white center-line, how will you prevent a high-speed roll off to the side before you can brake to a stop?

If there is lighting, you should be familiar with it. There will be a row of white lights marking the edges of the runway, the threshold will be marked by a line of green lights, and the taxiway lights will be blue. The windsock, tetrahedron, or wind tee will also usually be lighted.

There are two kinds of obstruction lights—red ones (steady or flashing) and white strobes. If there is a rotating beacon (shown on the sectional chart), be sure you know whether it is on the airport or whether it is some distance away. There are many locations where the beacon is a mile or two to one side, and often on a hill overlooking the airport. In such a case, flying to the beacon could be disastrous. The alternating green and white flashes of the beacon are primarily to help you locate the vicinity of the airport from a distance. The fact that beacons at military airports have a double white flash alternating with a single green can be very useful orientation when military and civilian airports are in the same general area.

Before you fly at night, you will need to be thoroughly familiar with the lighting system of your own aircraft. You should be able, by feel alone, to operate the switches for the navigation lights, the rotating beacon and strobes, and the landing light, as well as the controls for the panel lighting. Since electrical failure is always a possibility, it is unthinkable to fly at night without a flashlight that has recently been checked. Without panel lights and without a flashlight you cannot see your instruments, you become entirely dependent on outside references, yet it is quite common at night not to be able to see the horizon. Your situation could quickly become desperate, much as if you tried to fly in the clouds without any instruments. You should have learned already, through practice under the hood, that you absolutely cannot control the airplane without a means of leveling the wings, and you cannot do that without some instruments or an outside horizon reference. As I remarked in an earlier chapter, what this means to me is that **two** working flashlights are cheap life insurance for night flights.

A particularly insidious situation that often develops at night is the sudden formation of fog. When the temperature and dewpoint meet, the water vapor may precipitate as fog, over a wide area in a short time. Be alert to the temperature-dewpoint spread before you make a night flight, and cancel if fog seems imminent. While you are flying, you (or your passengers) may observe the very beautiful formation of fog patches below you that irregularly blot out surface lights. Admire it while you make a beeline for the nearest runway.

B. NIGHT FLIGHT

1. **Objective.** To determine that the applicant:
   a. Exhibits adequate knowledge by explaining night flying procedures including safety precautions and emergency actions.
   b. Inspects the airplane by following the checklist which includes items essential for night flight operations.
   c. Starts, taxies, and performs pre-takeoff check adhering to good operating practices.
   d. Performs takeoffs and climbs with emphasis on visual references.
   e. Navigates and maintains orientation under VFR conditions.
   f. Approaches and lands adhering to good operating practices for night flight operations.

2. **Action.** The examiner will:
   a. Ask the applicant to explain or demonstrate (as required by the examiner) essential elements relating to night flight operations, and determine that the applicant's performance meets the objective.
   b. Place emphasis on the applicant's knowledge of the factors affecting safety during night flight operations including emergency procedures.

A night takeoff is no different from a daytime takeoff, as far as flying technique is concerned. After all, the airplane doesn't know the time of day. But at the moment of lift-off, something new happens. As you raise the nose for the climbout, you suddenly may lose visual contact and become disoriented. No horizon, no distinctive terrain, no distant landmarks. On a dark, moonless, starless night, everything is a pool of ink. Worse, on a starry night, the stars and the lights on the ground may look identical, giving you a sudden case of up-down vertigo. The key to avoiding problems during the climbout is to concentrate on your instrument panel, especially on the attitude indicator. You know that the little airplane has to be a certain distance above the horizon bar for your climb, and you know your best-rate airspeed, and you know you need to keep wings level. After a few minutes, when you have reached a safe altitude, there is time enough to begin taking in the view outside.

Before takeoff you have to know—either by familiarity with the terrain or by studying the sectional chart—whether or not there are significant obstructions in the climbout path. This, of course, will determine if you climb at the usually V_y, or if you make a short-field takeoff and climb at V_x. In the landing approach, too, you have to be aware of obstacles, which will be invisible unless lighted. Night landing approaches, in general, are made fairly steeply, unless there is a VASI system in operation. Certainly, you don't want to drag it in low when trees, power lines, towers, buildings, and fences will all be invisible. Another good reason for flying a steep approach path at night is that you can't see very clearly what glide slope was flown by a jet aircraft landing ahead of you, yet to avoid wake turbulence, you want to fly above its approach path at all times.

Night landings are difficult until they are mastered. At first, they should be practiced with the landing light, but later, as proficiency develops, it is important to be able to land without a landing light (after all, it could burn out, or you could have electrical failure). At night you seem to be landing in a pitch black chasm between the two rows of runway lights. It is a good idea to use power, in order to have fine control of your rate of descent. You will probably flare too high, for fear of flying into the ground, and skillful use of the throttle will then let you descend in a level attitude until you touch down. With a landing light, you will suddenly see the runway when you are about 20 feet high, and the rest of the landing can be routine. Without a landing light, you have to pay especial attention to the runway lights, by glancing sideways, all the while you hold the airplane in a level attitude and carry just enough power to cushion your landing. After you turn off the runway, if there is a parallel taxiway, so that you will be facing the approach threshold, it is courteous to turn off your landing light to avoid blinding the pilot who is about to land. Taxiing at night should be slower than in the daytime, because your limit of visibility may be no farther than the reach of your landing light.

Not everything about night flying is dangerous. The risk of mid-air collision is very much less than in the daytime, because the characteristic lights of other aircraft can be seen many miles away. Strobes are flashing, red beacons are blinking, red and green navigation lights are moving against the background of dark sky or dark terrain. You can tell the direction of flight of other aircraft relative to you by noting the relationship of their green and red navigation lights. Since the green is on the tip of the right wing and the red on the tip of the left, if you see green on your left and red on your right, you are looking at the other airplane head-on (do something!). If you only see green, you are looking at the right side of the other aircraft, so it must be moving toward your right.

This sounds very easy. The problem is that the distance of lights is very difficult to judge at night. After all, the planet Venus, which is millions of miles away, is brighter than many an aircraft light only a few miles away. At night, therefore, even more than in the daytime, it is important to apply the collision course rule. If you hold a constant heading, a light that remains in the same position on your windscreen is on a collision course, or is moving along with you on a parallel course. You have to assume it is on a collision course, until you find out otherwise, even if it turns out to be the planet Venus. A light that moves on your windscreen is no problem. But at night, it is very difficult to avoid being confused by movement of the other aircraft's light against a background of lights on the ground or sky. The collision rule has nothing to do with movement of the target against the background—which is irrelevant—but only its movement on your windscreen. Put your finger on it. If it moves, you're safe.

If you can see the horizon, you can also apply the rule that an aircraft light seen against the sky must be above you, and one seen against the ground must be below you; but this is hard to do on a dark night over unpopulated terrain. The biggest problem in seeing another aircraft at night is picking out its lights against the varied illumination pattern of a town or city. But in that case, the other aircraft is below you, and unless one of you is climbing or descending, there is no hazard.

In crowded airspace, particularly in busy terminal areas, it is wise policy to keep on your landing light at all times. This makes a very big difference in the ability of other aircraft to see you. Obviously, if your airplane is equipped with strobe lights, they should always be operating in night VFR flying.

The general rule in night flying is to depend much more on the instruments than you normally would in VFR conditions. You are looking at lights on the ground, lights on hillsides, lights on mountain tops, and lights in the sky (stars). Sometimes, you feel suddenly certain that you are diving, or climbing, because you confuse these different light sources. That won't happen (or if it does, it will be short-lived) if you are constantly glancing at the attitude indicator, the turn indicator, the heading indicator, and the airspeed indicator. If you have any trouble with this, ask your instructor to take you up for more hood practice, including recoveries from unusual attitudes.

If you do have a starry sky, understand that any area in which stars are blotted out means a cloud formation or a mountainside. If it's ahead of you, do a 180 fast. But suppose you do fly into a cloud by accident, what will it be like. Very suddenly, you will be surrounded by the flashing glow of your rotating beacon and strobes. React at once, in a disciplined way. First note your heading, and focus your attention completely on the instruments, just as though you were under the hood. This is no time for fancy mental arithmetic, just make a quick 180. When you note the heading, just use two digits, exactly as it is shown on the heading indicator—thus, 15, not 153, for example. Now add or subtract 18—15 plus 18 equals 33. Then 33 (really 333, but never mind) is the heading for rollout. Once on the new heading, keep flying until you emerge from the cloud, which you will know by glancing outside. The reflections of the beacon and strobes inside the cloud are said to produce vertigo, and well they may, if you stare out at them. However, in the emergency situation described here, it is better not to turn them off, since they will be your best guide to when you are clear of cloud again.

Assuming you don't do anything really foolish while enroute, the trickiest part of a night flight will be your approach and landing. An amazing number of **very** experienced pilots—I mean air carrier pilots with thousands of hours—have come to grief on night approaches, especially at airports not served by an instrument landing system (with glideslope guidance) or a VASI. Psychological research has revealed numerous optical illusions that can persuade you that you are too high. Here is a simple example. You have been accustomed to flying at night out of an airport with a 150-foot wide runway that is 2 miles long. The appearance of the runway lights is built into your memory bank—the way it looks when you are on a 1-mile final at 600′ AGL. Now you make a night flight to an airport with a 50-foot wide runway that is 3000 feet long. At 600′ AGL on a 1-mile final you will seem to be very high, because the spacing of the runway lights from side to side, as well as the lengthwise perspective, are the same as they would be from 1800′ AGL at your home base. You can see the danger. You might think "Well, as long as I look at the altimeter, I'm safe." Wrong! You have no way of knowing how far out you are, so you can't tell what your altitude should be. There will be a great temptation to descend well below the safe glide path into that black void that conceals hills, trees, power lines, water towers, and what-not.

There is only one good reliable rule that will keep you out of trouble: Unless there is glide slope guidance (ILS or VASI), **never make a straight-in approach at night**! Enter the downwind leg of the traffic pattern by the usual 45° method or from a position directly over the runway at about 1500' AGL. You know for sure that the pattern is safe, or it wouldn't be there. You know the safe procedures for the transition from downwind to base to final, with appropriate altitude step-downs at each phase. For example, if you are downwind at 800' AGL opposite the threshold, 600' turning base, 400' turning final, and if you turn base at the appropriate position when you can sight back to the threshold at about a 45° angle, you can have complete confidence of being safely above obstructions all the way to touchdown.

One further warning concerning the ILS. IFR pilots are trained not to entrust their lives to a glideslope needle without being absolutely certain it is working properly. If you should be on a final approach at night with only the ILS for glide path guidance, make doubly sure that no red flag is showing, and also that you can hear the identifier on the ILS frequency. It has happened that a pilot flew an inoperative glide slope needle right into the ground!

Score Sheet: 10A. Preparation and Equipment

Date											
Decision making about safety of night weather conditions for VFR flight											
Familiarity with airport lighting											
Eyes-closed operation of all aircraft lighting											
Possession of operating flashlight, easily accessible											
TOTAL SCORE											
Divide by 4 = AVERAGE SCORE											

Score Sheet: 10B. Night Flight

Date										
Safe climb path on takeoff withV_x or V_y as appropriate										
Safe landing path, steep approach or glide path guidance, knowledge of terrain										
Use of power to touchdown										
Smooth landings with and without landing light										
Slow taxi speed										
Vigilance for traffic, recognition of collision hazards from aircraft lights										
Use of landing light in flight in crowded airspace										
Awareness of problems of spatial disorientation										
Performance of 180-degree turns unexpectedly										
TOTAL SCORE										
Divide by 9 = AVERAGE SCORE										

11

EMERGENCY OPERATIONS

A. EMERGENCY APPROACH AND LANDING (SIMULATED)

1. **Objective.** To determine that the applicant:

   a. Exhibits adequate knowledge by explaining approach and landing procedures to be used in various emergencies.

   b. Establishes and maintains the recommended best-glide airspeed and configuration during simulated emergencies.

   c. Selects a suitable landing area within gliding distance.

   d. Plans and follows a flight pattern to the selected landing area, considering altitude, wind, terrain, obstructions, and other factors.

   e. Follows an appropriate emergency checklist.

   f. Attempts to determine the reason for the simulated malfunction.

   g. Maintains correct control of the airplane.

2. **Action.** The examiner will:

   a. Ask the applicant to explain emergency approach and landing procedures.

   b. Simulate emergencies at various altitudes and in various situations, and determine that the applicant's performance meets the objective. (Examiner should terminate the emergency approach at or above minimum safe altitude.)

   c. Place emphasis on the applicant's judgment, planning, and control during the simulated emergencies.

Power malfunctions in a single engine aircraft call for two actions, in the following order: (1) Find a suitable place for a forced landing, if it should become necessary, and set up the proper glide to make the field, and then (2) analyze the problem and see if power can be restored.

Partial loss of power may be due to an over-lean mixture, as when you have descended from a higher altitude but failed to enrich with the descent. The most common cause of a partial power failure is carburetor icing, and therefore, the **immediate** first reaction to a drop in RPM or MP should be to apply carburetor heat. In a fuel-injected engine, there may be induction system icing; again, heat should be applied, and/or an alternate source of induction air should be actuated, if that does not occur automatically. When carburetor heat is applied, it should be applied fully, and kept on until the proper RPM is restored.

A rough engine is usually due to magneto problems, so the immediate action should be to try each magneto system separately. If the problem is solved by switching to one of the two magnetos, the flight can be continued and a landing should be made at an appropriate airport as soon as practicable.

Fire in the engine compartment presents a very serious problem, the only solution to which is to shut off the main fuel valve, and thus to starve the fire. At the same time it may be possible to slip the aircraft, so that fire and smoke are discharged to the side away from the slip instead of through the firewall into the cabin. Smoke in the cabin should be vented by opening a window, reducing airspeed as necessary if there is a restriction on window-opening at a high airspeed.

A complete power failure, occurring without warning—means either that a fuel tank has been allowed to run dry, or that the engine has suffered a serious mechanical malfunction. The immediate response to a complete power failure is to switch fuel tanks (if your aircraft doesn't operate on cross-feed normally) and to use the booster fuel pump to move fresh fuel past the empty lines. Indeed, failure of the engine-driven fuel pump could be the cause of the problem, and the accessory fuel pump will then solve it.

If you do experience a partial or complete power failure, you will need a systematic, planned and rehearsed sequence of procedures to cover all the possibilities, once you have picked out a field for possible landing. Since an actual emergency engenders panic, it is wise to carry a clear emergency checklist in a specific place that is easily reached. This checklist should contain the following items: MIXTURE, FUEL PUMP, CARB HEAT, SWITCH TANKS, MAGS. If none of these restores full power, you have two choices: either make a forced landing (with complete power failure this is your only choice), or make a decision, depending upon terrain and other factors, as to whether you may be able to make a nearby airport. When time allows, call MAYDAY on 121.5, and get whatever assistance may be available.

A forced landing from a high altitude is in some ways simpler than one from low altitude, because there is ample time to choose a field and to maneuver into the right position to enter base leg and make a normal landing. On the other hand, there are more choices to make and more opportunity to commit errors of judgment. When you have a simulated (or real) engine failure, the first thing to do is to set up a normal glide at the appropriate best-glide speed, which is usually about the same as the best rate of climb speed. Trimming is essential; then you can give your full attention to choosing a field without worrying about flying the airplane. The important thing to understand is how far you can comfortably glide, since nothing is more futile than trying to land on a beautiful and inviting field (even a concrete runway) that you can't possibly reach.

How can you tell instantly, at a glance, what is within your gliding distance? The method is very simple. What you have to know in advance is your glide ratio. This is given in your Owner's Manual for the no-wind condition. An average small trainer will glide at approximately a 10:1 ratio, meaning that from 5000 feet you can glide nearly 10 miles. Now, the farthest point you can reach in a glide will be the same **angular distance** below the horizon as your glide angle. A 10:1 glide ratio means a glide angle of 4.5 degrees. So if you could measure 4.5 degrees **down** from the horizon in any direction, you would be able to just reach that point on the ground, but no farther. You are probably chuckling at the idea of doing trigonometry when your engine has just failed, but the nice trick is that all the measurements are done in advance.

You only have to know that if you hold your thumb at a certain distance (e.g., at arm's length), with its tip on the horizon, the line of sight through its base gives the limit of your glide. Of course, everyone's arm is a different length, and so is everyone's thumb, but you can work out your own system in advance. For a 10:1 glide angle, you only have to establish a 10:1 sighting arrangement, as illustrated in Fig. 11-1. The principle is shown in the diagram, at the left, and its application is illustrated at the right. My own outstretched arm is 24 inches long from the position of my eye to my upraised thumb, and my thumb is about 2.4 inches from tip to base. So that's the 10:1 ratio. In the diagram, the airplane is assumed to be 1 mile high, so that the limit of the glide will be 10 miles. The geometry is obvious. The small triangle composed of the 24-inch outstretched arm and the 2.4-inch thumb has the same 10:1 ratio of its sides as the large triangle with 1-mile and 10-mile sides. Thus, if you set the tip of your thumb on

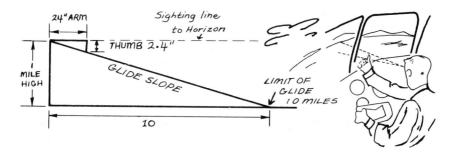

Fig. 11-1 Estimating glide range in a forced landing

the horizon, as the pilot is doing at the right, the line of sight through the base of your thumb shows you how far you can glide in the no-wind condition. The elegant part of this system is that it has nothing to do with your altitude, since glide angles, and ratios of the arms of triangles, are independent of altitude. Moreover, the measuring apparatus I've described is always with you, you can't forget to bring it along!

Once you have established, by rule of outstretched thumb, how far you can glide, you may add or subtract a bit if you are pretty confident of the wind direction and velocity, but play it safe. The field you pick should be well within gliding range. Keep it in sight at all times, circling to the left as required to place yourself in position to enter a normal base leg at the usual height (about 800 feet) above the field. From there on, it is a normal landing approach, except that flaps should be held off until you are sure the field is made. Slips are fine for losing altitude if you're too high. Finally, when everything looks right, bring in full flaps and reduce to your normal approach speed. The field will be rougher than a concrete runway, so you'll want to touch down in a full stall, at minimum airspeed, and once you touch down, hold the yoke all the way back, to roll out with the nose wheel well off the ground.

In a simulated forced landing, as soon as you are ready to touch down, execute a clean go-around procedure (see Chapter 12, C). In a real forced landing, turn off mags and master switch, shut off the fuel valve, and have your passengers protect their faces and heads, before touchdown. It is also wise to open a door to expedite evacuation of the aircraft.

Forced landings from a low altitude are more difficult, because there is so little time, but they are also easier, in a way, just because there are so few decisions to make. You have to pick a field very quickly, head for it, and land. Here it is especially important to gauge accurately how far you can glide. Use the same rule of thumb, and don't make the mistake of aiming for a field you can't make. From the standpoint of perspective, from a low altitude, the fields you can make will seem to lie pretty much directly under the airplane. If you can manage, make a normal entry onto a base leg; but often this will be quite out of the question, and you just have to get there one way or the other, as soon as you can.

If your engine failure occurs as low as a few hundred feet off the ground, there is nothing to do but put the nose down and land, as best you can, maneuvering gently to avoid major obstructions. This unpleasant situation is like what you face if you have an engine failure on takeoff. Below about 500 feet, there is no way you can safely manage a 180 degree turn to land downwind on the runway; just land straight ahead. Between 500 and 800 feet, you might be able to make it back, but be certain to keep the nose down, since distraction and panic could easily lead you into a stall-spin situation. Above 800 feet, you can easily make it back for a downwind landing. If you are already well along a downwind leg, you should be able to manage a normal landing. These guidelines should be firmly in your head whenever you start your takeoff roll, and as you pass through each critical altitude, you should review in your mind what you would do if you had an engine failure just then.

A final word of caution. Power lines are death. In all forced landings, but especially in forced landings from low altitude, never never land toward a power line. If you are **surely** high enough to clear it with plenty of room to spare, that's fine. Otherwise, land parallel to the power line, even if you have to land crosswind or downwind. This rule must be followed even more rigorously in simulated forced landings than in real ones, because you'll have to climb out again, and you certainly don't want to be climbing toward a power line.

If you have an airport to yourself, with little traffic in the pattern, practice precision landings. Although this is not required on the private pilot flight test, it is excellent practice for developing judgment in forced landing situations. On downwind leg, opposite the numbers, throttle back to idle, and work your way around to a perfect power-off landing. This maneuver starts—as in all forced landing practice—at best-glide airspeed. At every moment, you have to judge how high you are and how far from the field. The trick is to be high on base leg, and then to slip as you come down final, applying flaps only after you are sure the field is made. Don't worry about square turns to base and to final; if you seem to be low, cut in toward the runway as required. An hour of precision landing practice will pay off richly in sharpening your skills for forced landings.

B. SYSTEMS AND EQUIPMENT MALFUNCTIONS

---

1. **Objective.** To determine that the applicant:
   a. Exhibits adequate knowledge by explaining causes, indications, and pilot actions for various systems and equipment malfunctions.
   b. Analyzes the situation and takes appropriate action for simulated emergencies such as -
      (1) partial power loss.
      (2) rough running engine or overheat.
      (3) carburetor or induction icing.
      (4) loss of oil pressure.
      (5) fuel starvation.
      (6) engine compartment fire.

  (7) electrical system malfunction.

  (8) gear or flap malfunction.

  (9) door opening in flight.

  (10) trim inoperative.

  (11) loss of pressurization.

  (12) other malfunctions.

2. Action. The examiner will:

 a. Ask the applicant to explain causes, indications, and remedial action for various systems and equipment malfunctions.

 b. Simulate various equipment malfunctions, and determine that the applicant's performance meets the objective.

 c. Place emphasis on the applicant's ability to analyze the situation and take action appropriate to the simulated emergency.

This is a grab-bag of possible malfunctions that you have to know how to handle. You need to know, and to rehearse, what to do if one electrical component fails (where are the fuses and circuit breakers? do you have spare fuses?), and for complete electrical failure. What will you do if the flaps won't extend or won't retract? What about failure of the gear extension system in a retractable gear aircraft? What about trim tab failure? How will you handle an electrical fire, usually accompanied by acrid smoke? (Certainly, you'll turn off the master switch, but what then?) Emergency procedures for all these and other possible malfunctions are covered in your Owner's Manual, and they differ for each model of aircraft, so you have to study them as they apply to your own airplane.

Among the 12 items listed above on the FAA list, a few deserve comment. A **partial power loss** has to be regarded as the harbinger of a complete power loss in a single-engine aircraft. Something is wrong, but you don't know what. If it doesn't respond immediately to switching mags, turning on a fuel pump, or switching fuel tanks, forget about it and direct all your attention to the possibility of a landing. Here some balancing of risks and benefits will be called for. Can you try to make the airport that is 25 miles away, or are you better off landing right here and now on the rural road just under you? It all depends. How good is the terrain between you and the airport? How bad does the engine sound? On these judgment calls, no one who is not actually there with you at the time can possibly suggest what is your best course of action.

Electrical system malfunction is not rare. It usually means you have lost your generator/alternator, perhaps through a mechanical failure, perhaps through an electrical short circuit. If you become aware of the failure immediately, while the battery is still fully charged, you can carry on safely for a while, but only if you conserve electricity. This means shutting down all lights and all or most avionics. You should understand that the biggest current drains are from transmitters—this means your COM transmitter, the transponder, and the DME. Since you are VFR, you don't actually need any of those anyway—just save your radio for arrival at the destination. If you fail to notice anything amiss until the battery is dead, you will first discover the problem when your radio fails. Another way it can happen suddenly is through an electrical fire, with acrid fumes of burning insulation—then you will immediately turn off the master switch.

You should have a mental list at all times of which instruments are operated electrically and would therefore fail if the electricity failed. In most airplanes the turn indicator would fail, but this is not of much importance since you have both a working attitude indicator and a working heading indicator. Naturally, all the lights will fail, and all the COM and NAV equipment. Pilots have been unnecessarily alarmed by the indications of zero fuel and possibly zero oil pressure (depending on the type of system). A good idea is to turn off the master switch the next time you are flying, and carefully scan the entire panel to see just how things would look. In some retractables an electric hydraulic pump is required, otherwise manual or gas-operated gear extension is required. The point is simply to know, for your airplane, what the situation would be in a complete electrical failure.

Even if you were in a situation where you required radionavigation, you could substitute radar assistance—if only you could talk to the controllers. This potential problem is solved by a back-up radio transceiver. Several excellent ones are on the market now. For IFR flight I consider one of these an absolutely essential piece of equipment, but even in VFR flight it can be very useful. Fig. 11-2 shows one of the more popular units. It operates on rechargeable batteries, receives and transmits on all the authorized frequencies, and three frequencies can be programmed into memory and recalled at a finger-touch. Although the unit has a self-contained microphone, an extension microphone (available as an accessory) is a worthwhile addition because then the little antenna can be held conveniently close to a window for optimum transmission and reception. Such a unit also has a non-emergency use—one can call Clearance Delivery or Ground Control before firing up the engine at a busy airport where delays can be expected.

A VFR situation in which such a backup transceiver can be a lifesaver is night flight or flight over the top of an overcast, when you have to depend much more on radios than in ordinary daytime ground-contact VFR. It doesn't even take a complete electrical failure to endanger the safety of a flight. Most radio speakers in small aircraft are tinny affairs of poor quality. What if the speaker fails and you don't carry earphones (you should!).

Fig. 11-2 A portable aircraft-band transceiver. The unit shown is a popular and efficient one, which operates on all authorized frequencies (including the VOR frequencies). View of the whole unit, with its short flexible antenna, is shown at left. Inset is magnified view looking down on top of the unit. Frequencies are selected by the little knurled wheels on top. Up to three frequencies (for example, 121.5, and your home tower frequencies) can be stored in memory for instant recall by a little slide switch on top. The model shown here is the TR-720, manufactured by Communications Specialists, Inc., 426 W. Taft Ave., Orange, CA 92665-4296.

Suppose you have only one COM radio and it blows a transistor. Suppose you have two COM radios and a malfunction in the audio panel kills them both. Suppose your NAV and COM antennas ice up in freezing rain and break off. After you add your own scenarios to this list, you'll probably go out and buy a portable transceiver!

Finally, a few words about **door opening in flight.** This is a much over-rated hazard. It makes alot of noise and it frightens the passengers, but the truth is it doesn't make much difference to the performance or handling of the airplane. The only proper response is to stay cool. If it happens just after takeoff (that's the usual time), go around the pattern and land, reas-suring the passengers, and handling the airplane exactly as you always do. However, if the door comes unlatched during cruising flight, it is probably worthwhile trying to close it. This requires slow flight (remember the flaps), so you can reduce the pressure of the airstream enough to let you force it open wider and then slam it shut. But don't become so preoccupied with this non-problem that you stall the airplane. The best way is for you to concentrate on flying the airplane while someone competent in the right seat works on the door.

Score Sheet: 11A. Emergency Approach And Landing (Simulated)

Date									
Picking a field immediately, and setting up the glide									
Checklist for possible remedial actions									
Power-off glide to base leg at 800 ft.									
Making the field, with slips and flaps as required									
Smooth go-around from the approach when field is made									
TOTAL SCORE									
Divide by 5 = AVERAGE SCORE									

Score Sheet: 11B. Systems And Equipment Malfunctions

Date										
Knowing location of all fuses and circuit breakers										
Knowing what to do for generator or alternator failure										
Knowing what to do for electrical fire and smoke in cockpit										
Knowing what to do for flap and gear malfunctions										
Knowing what to do for trim tab malfunctions										
Actual handling of door opening in flight										
TOTAL SCORE										
Divide by 6 = AVERAGE SCORE										

12
APPROACHES AND LANDINGS

A. NORMAL APPROACH AND LANDING

1. **Objective.** To determine that the applicant:
   a. Exhibits adequate knowledge by explaining the elements of a normal approach and landing including airspeeds, configurations, and related safety factors.
   b. Maintains the proper ground track on final approach.
   c. Establishes the approach and landing configuration and power required.
   d. Maintains the recommended approach airspeed, ± 5 knots.
   e. Makes smooth, timely, and correct control application during the final approach and transition from approach to landing roundout (flare).
   f. Touches down smoothly at approximate stalling speed, beyond and within 500 feet of a specified point, with no appreciable drift, and the airplane's longitudinal axis aligned with the runway centerline.
   g. Maintains directional control during the after-landing roll.

2. **Action.** The examiner will:
   a. Ask the applicant to explain the elements of a normal approach and landing including airspeeds, configurations, and related safety factors.
   b. Ask the applicant to perform a normal approach and landing, and determine that the applicant's performance meets the objective.
   c. Place emphasis on the applicant's demonstration of correct airplane control particularly during the after-landing roll.

The normal landing requires coordination of the left hand (on the yoke) and the right hand (on the throttle)—and little else. When the airspeed is slow enough, the airplane will stop flying. The aim, of course, is to have it stop flying on the runway surface, with the main gear touching down.

With full flaps, in a normal landing, your approach on final is with a nose-low attitude. At the right moment, about 10 feet off the runway, you flare, i.e., you raise the nose to a higher attitude, usually with the cowl just on the horizon. If you don't change the power (or if you are making a power-off landing), raising the nose automatically makes the airspeed fall off. As the airspeed decreases, the nose "wants" to drop. Back pressure on the yoke will keep it from dropping. Excessive back pressure, however, will make the airplane balloon upward. So the back pressure on the yoke has to be just enough to keep the nose on the horizon. This additional back pressure causes further decrease of airspeed, with further nose-dropping tendency, which you continue to oppose by bringing the yoke farther and farther back. The whole process is called "holding it off." In a perfect landing, as the airplane settles—always in a slightly nose-high condition—and the yoke continues to come back, the stall is reached exactly as the main gear touch down. At this point the yoke should be full back against the stop, and the stall warning should be operating.

The only problem in executing this perfect landing is to have it all end on the runway surface. If the stall is reached too soon, the airplane stops flying several feet off the runway, and it drops in. But this is easily prevented with power. If you are dropping too fast for comfort, an immediate burst of power will pull you forward as you settle, so that the touchdown occurs at a reasonable angle rather than perpendicular to the runway. The usual mistake made by the inexperienced pilot is not to use enough throttle, or, if enough is used, to allow the nose to pitch up as it always does when more power is applied. There is no reason to be satisfied with less than a perfect landing, and once everything falls into place, all landings should be nearly perfect.

Clumsy and jerky use of throttle is the principal error. You should hold the throttle control in such a way that tiny changes (a few millimeters) can be made smoothly. This means using several fingers to act as a stop, in contact with the panel (or quadrant). If you hold the throttle control entirely by its knob (or lever handle), it is impossible to achieve the fine control that is necessary. Ask your instructor to demonstrate this, if you don't understand it. Then you can make frequent small power adjustments smoothly, all the way to touchdown.

The commonest error made by inexperienced pilots on the landing approach is not to respond sufficiently with throttle when the approach is quite obviously too high or too low. If your pitch attitude (i.e., your air-speed) is correct, with the nose just where it should be, you can easily judge whether you'll land short of the numbers, or whether you'll land at some other airport. The trick of watching the numbers in the windscreen works well, but **only** if the pitch attitude is constant. If the numbers stay in the same place on the windscreen, as they come closer, you'll touch down fine. If the numbers move up, you are clearly going to touch down short, unless you do something. And if the numbers move down, you'll overshoot, unless you do something. Either way, that "something" is to adjust the power—more power to arrest the descent, less power to descend faster. For some strange reason, student pilots who **know** they are high, and will even remark to the instructor that they're high, nevertheless continue to carry power all the way past the numbers to the point where a landing is impossible. If you're really high, kill the power completely, let the ship settle, then bring power in again, when needed. If you're really low, bring in a lot of power, even full power (remember the tremendous drag of those flaps) to get back onto a reasonable glide slope, then reduce power again when things look better.

When the approach on final is high, the novice may unconsciously try to dive at the runway, despite all the instructor's explanations about the uselessness of this maneuver. Diving means increasing the airspeed, so when you flare, you are bound to float—farther, it turns out (because of ground effect) than if you hadn't made the diving "correction" in the first place. At all phases of the final approach, concentrate on keeping the **airspeed constant** with a **constant pitch attitude**, and **control your descent with power**. Reducing to idle power, with full flaps, results in a very efficient descent (it drops like a rock), and if necessary the descent can be increased further by slipping (if your ship allows slips with full flaps) without change in airspeed.

After the touchdown, hold the yoke back to keep the weight on the main gear for good braking action, and apply the brakes. Flaps can be raised to further reduce lift and place weight on the main gear. But in retractable gear aircraft, the risk of reaching for the gear handle during the rollout outweighs the convenience of sparing the brakes, so wait until you are on the taxiway, and then very deliberately raise the flaps.

You should practice normal landings with all flap settings, and without flaps. The principal difference will be a faster approach speed with less flaps (to stay safely above the stall speed), and a flatter pitch attitude during the approach. Gusty winds, even right down the runway, require less flaps and a higher approach speed. This is because the momentum of the airplane prevents its rapid response to changing wind. If you are approaching at 60 k into a 40 k headwind, your airspeed is 60 k (although your groundspeed is only 20 k) as long as the wind is steady. However, a sudden drop in wind velocity to 25 k would subject the airplane to an instantaneous drop of 15 k in the relative wind. Since 60 k minus 15 k equals 45 k, the airplane will stall if its stalling speed is 45 k or higher in the particular landing configuration.

The preceding argument might suggest that full flaps should be used in gusty winds, in order to make the stalling speed as low as possible. However, this would create problems immediately after landing. A very low stalling speed also means a very low flying speed, so a gust could more easily lift you off again than if you had less flaps. The procedure for gusty-wind landings, therefore, is to use **little or no flaps** and a considerably **higher approach speed** than usual.

B. FORWARD SLIPS TO LANDING

---

1. **Objective.** To determine that the applicant:
   a. Exhibits adequate knowledge by explaining the elements of a forward slip to a landing including the purpose, technique, limitation, and the effect on airspeed indications.
   b. Establishes a forward slip at a point from which a landing can be made in a desired area using the recommended airspeed and configuration.
   c. Maintains a ground track aligned with the runway centerline.
   d. Maintains an airspeed which results in little or no floating during the landing roundout.
   e. Recovers smoothly from the slip.
   f. Touches down smoothly at approximate stalling speed, beyond and within 500 feet of a specified point, with no appreciable drift and the airplane's longitudinal axis aligned with the runway centerline.
   g. Maintains directional control during the after-landing roll.

2. **Action.** The examiner will:
   a. Ask the applicant to explain the elements of forward slips to a landing including the purpose, technique, limitation, and the effect on airspeed indications.
   b. Ask the applicant to perform a forward slip to a landing, and determine that the applicant's performance meets the objective.
   c. Place emphasis on the applicant's demonstration of airspeed control and correct airplane control.

Slips have two important uses in the landing approach, so this is a good time to consider them. As you know from watching the ball, in a slip the airplane slides obliquely in the direction of the low wing. Since the airflow changes from its normal direction from front to rear across the wings, and since the relative wind now meets the unstreamlined side face of the airplane fuselage, there is both loss of lift and increase of drag. In a power-off glide, the slip provides a means of rapid descent without diving and therefore without increase of airspeed. This use of the slip can be helpful in correcting too-high landing approaches. Some aircraft are prohibited from slipping with full flaps, so make sure about yours before you try.

The other important use of the slip is to permit the aircraft to fly a straight track with wing low, and thus, by slipping into a crosswind, to remain aligned with the runway throughout the landing approach.

In order to lose altitude by slipping, you have to drop a wing. Ordinarily, this will initiate a turn. To prevent the turn, you bring in opposite rudder. How much rudder? Just enough to keep the nose fixed on a distant landmark, i.e., just enough to maintain your heading constant. The more the wing is dropped, the more opposite rudder will be required. If the pitch attitude is maintained constant, the airspeed will not change, but you will observe a considerable increase in rate of descent on the VSI. Naturally, since the aim is to descend rapidly, the power will be at idle throughout the maneuver. Usually you will slip to the left so that you can readily see where you are going, but when slipping as part of a crosswind landing you will always slip into the wind.

All slips are side slips. You should not be confused by the distinction made in some manuals (and even by FAA) between side slips and so-called "forward slips." This is merely a question of where you point the nose of the airplane. Suppose there is no wind, and you are making a straight ground track toward a distant mountain. If you continue to hold the nose straight ahead, while you slip to either side, your ground track will change. Your new course will be the resultant of the sideways slipping motion and the continued forward motion. Therefore, if you wish to maintain your original ground track while slipping, you have to turn the nose somewhat away from the low wing. In this type of slip, you usually lower the left wing and turn the airplane slightly to the right, so that you can observe the airspace in the direction you are moving. You may think of this as a "forward slip" because the slipping movement is more or less in the direction of your ground track.

On the other hand, if a wind is blowing from the left, you can continue on your original heading, and maintain the same ground track, by merely flying in a slip with the left wing low. You will be holding left aileron and keeping the nose lined up with right rudder. The extent of bank will be determined by the crosswind velocity; the stronger the wind, the steeper the bank in order to counteract the wind drift. This, of course, is exactly the procedure for a crosswind landing, as described below.

Slips should be practiced at altitude, with and without power. Without power, you should observe how the rate of descent, on the VSI, depends upon how steeply you bank, always keeping the nose on the same distant point. The commonest error in slipping to lose altitude is allowing the nose to drop, so that airspeed increases. Be sure you trim for the appropriate approach airspeed. Then, in the slip, some back pressure may be required.

With power, you should simulate a reasonable rate of descent (say 400 fpm) for a landing approach, while you slip. Try it to the right and the left, and at different rates of descent, as well as in level flight.

In a perfect slip, aileron and opposite rudder are nicely coordinated, with constant aileron to hold a constant angle of bank, and just enough rudder to hold the nose on track. The heading is not allowed to vary, and the airspeed remains absolutely fixed. This is the one maneuver, in single-engine aircraft, in which the ball will be far out toward the low wing. The prescribed manner of flying a twin with a dead engine is to bank 5° into the working engine, thus flying in a slip with the ball off center toward the low wing (see Chapter 13).

C. GO-AROUND FROM A REJECTED LANDING

1. **Objective.** To determine that the applicant:
   a. Exhibits adequate knowledge by explaining the elements of the go-around procedure including timely decision, recommended airspeeds, drag effect of wing flaps and landing gear, and coping with undesirable pitch and yaw tendencies.
   b. Makes a timely decision to go around from a rejected landing.
   c. Applies takeoff power and establishes the proper pitch attitude to attain the recommended airspeed.
   d. Retracts the wing flaps as recommended or at a safe altitude.
   e. Retracts the landing gear, if retractable and recommended, after a positive rate of climb has been established.
   f. Trims the airplane and climbs at V_Y, ± 5 knots, and tracks the appropriate traffic pattern.

2. **Action.** The examiner will:
   a. Ask the applicant to explain the elements of a go-around from a rejected landing including timely decisions, recommended airspeeds, drag effect of wing flaps and landing gear, and coping with undesirable pitch and yaw tendencies.
   b. Present a situation in which a go-around from a rejected landing would be required, and determine that the applicant's performance meets the objective.
   c. Place emphasis on the applicant's judgment, prompt action, and ability to maintain correct airplane control during the go-around.

In every landing approach you should anticipate the possibility of a go-around, either because of traffic on the runway, or because you are not completely satisfied with the approach. A go-around is mandatory if you have not touched down soon enough for sufficient runway to remain for easy stopping, even if your brakes were to prove defective.

The go-around procedure (Fig. 12-1) is essentially the same as the recovery from an approach-to-landing stall, already discussed in Chapter 7, A. The sequence is (1) full power, (2) gear up, (3) remove half flaps, (4) establish V_y or (if there are obstacles) V_x, (5)remove the remaining flaps in a stepwise fashion, (6) climb out and enter the traffic pattern for another landing approach. If you were properly trimmed for approach airspeed, very little re-trimming will be needed for an obstacle climb, since the usual approach speed and V_x are both about 1.3 times the stall speed in landing configuration. If you wish to go around at V_y—the more usual situation—you should be aware that forward yoke pressure will be needed until you trim for a more nose-down climbout. In a go-around, immediate removal of half the flaps is absolutely essential, since most small trainers cannot climb at all with full flaps because of the great drag.

Practicing go-arounds is rarely done enough. Try them occasionally when you're almost ready to flare. The tower doesn't really need warning, but it's courteous to tell the controller what to expect.

D. CROSSWIND APPROACH AND LANDING

1. **Objective.** To determine that the applicant:
   a. Exhibits adequate knowledge by explaining the elements of a cross-wind approach and landing including crosswind limitations, and related safety factors.
   b. Maintains the proper ground track on final approach.
   c. Establishes the approach and landing configuration and power required.

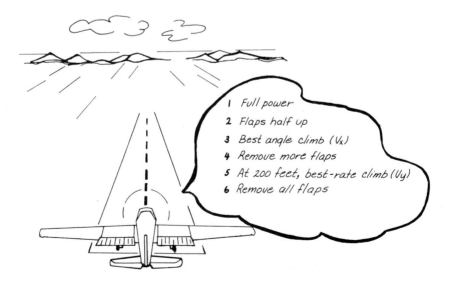

Fig. 12-1 The go-around

    d. Maintains the recommended approach airspeed, ± 5 knots.

    e. Makes smooth, timely, and correct control application during the final approach and transition from approach to landing roundout (flare).

    f. Touches down smoothly at approximate stalling speed, beyond and within 500 feet of a specified point, with no appreciable drift and the airplane's longitudinal axis aligned with the runway centerline.

    g. Maintains directional control, increasing aileron deflection into the wind, as necessary, during the after-landing roll.

2. Action. The examiner will:

    a. Ask the applicant to explain the elements of a crosswind approach and landing including crosswind limitations and related safety factors.

    b. Ask the applicant to perform a crosswind approach and landing, and determine that the applicant's performance meets the objective. (NOTE: If a crosswind condition does not exist, the applicant's knowledge of the TASK will be evaluated through oral questioning.)

    c. Place emphasis on the applicant's control of wind drift during the approach and landing.

Crosswind landings require a special technique and a great deal of practice. Before you try, make sure your airplane and you can manage the crosswind component, as discussed in Chapter 4, B.

The whole point of a crosswind landing is to touch down without sideways drift (which could impose excessive forces on the gear), and with the upwind wing held firmly down to prevent the wind from lifting it and upsetting the airplane. The best way to accomplish this is to slip into the wind, just enough to overcome the wind drift, so that the airplane will track true down the runway as it touches down (Fig. 12-2).

You could, of course, crab into the wind until the very moment of touchdown, but this requires a very high degree of proficiency, since at the last moment you have to kick the nose straight with downwind rudder. It is a demanding maneuver. The preferred way is to carry the slip all the way down final until the touchdown. This means that the upwind gear actually lands first. Many pilots are reluctant to land in a wing-low attitude, but this is an exaggerated fear. As soon as the upwind gear settles onto the runway, the other gear settles down, since the airplane has stopped flying, and there is really nothing else it can do. Some pilots are also reluctant to use whatever downwind rudder is necessary to keep the nose straight in the slip. The best way to deal with this is to imagine the nose linked to the rudder pedal, and simply do whatever has to be done to keep the nose lined up with the runway. Excellent practice for the crosswind landing is provided by slips at safe altitude, and by Dutch rolls (see Chapter 14).

Just as with a crosswind takeoff (Chapter 4, B), it is very important not to permit any floating, during which a sideways movement could occur. For this reason it is wise to land with less flaps than usual, especially if the crosswind is gusty. Adequate forward speed must be maintained, and the airplane is virtually "flown on." A full stall landing is out of the question, because while you hold it off at an airspeed just above the stall, you have very little aileron effectiveness, the wind is bound to blow you sideways, and you will touch down in lateral motion.

E. SHORT-FIELD APPROACH AND LANDING

1. **Objective.** To determine that the applicant:
   a. Exhibits adequate knowledge by explaining the elements of a short-field approach and landing including airspeeds, configurations, and related safety factors.
   b. Considers obstructions, landing surface, and wind conditions.
   c. Selects a suitable touchdown point.
   d. Establishes the short-field approach and landing configuration, airspeed, and descent angle.
   e. Maintains control of the descent rate and the recommended airspeed, ± 5 knots, along the extended runway centerline.

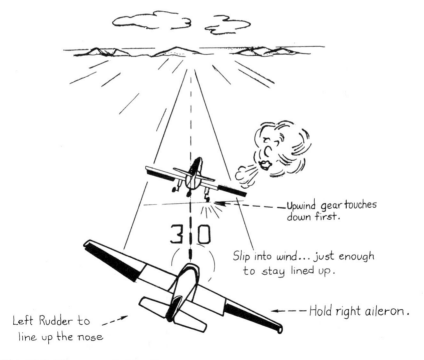

Fig. 12-2 The crosswind landing

    f. Touches down beyond and within 200 feet of a specified point, with minimum float and no appreciable drift and the airplane's longitudinal axis aligned with the runway centerline.

    g. Maintains directional control during the after-landing roll.

    h. Applies braking and controls, as necessary, to stop in the shortest distance consistent with safety.

2. Action. The examiner will:

    a. Ask the applicant to explain the elements of a short-field approach and landing including airspeeds, configurations, and related safety factors.

    b. Ask the applicant to perform a short-field approach and landing, and determine that the applicant's performance meets the objective.

    c. Place emphasis on the applicant's control of descent rate, airspeed, and use of flight controls.

In a short field landing, as in a short field takeoff (Chapter 4, C), an obstacle is assumed. It is more difficult that way, and if you can do it well with an assumed obstacle, you'll have no trouble at all without one. The problem, then, is to come into a short field with a 50-foot tree near the runway threshold. The aim is to approach more steeply than usual, clearing the tree by at least 50 feet, and touch down **at the stall**. You want the airplane to stop flying the moment you flare and set it on the runway. Then quick and decisive braking will bring you to a very fast stop, within a few hundred feet.

The key to the technique is to level off at about 200 feet on your final approach, carrying power and full flaps until the point where you can start the steep descent that will carry you safely past the obstacle. Do not change your glide slope once this final descent has begun. The important thing, as usual, is the airspeed. It should be just enough above the stall to leave you room to flare, i.e., to allow you to shake off the difference between your approach speed and the stall speed, during those few seconds after you flare. A good rule of thumb is to use 1.3 times the power-off full flaps stall speed. In general, this will be nearly the same as V_x, the airspeed you used for best angle of climb in a short-field takeoff. A gusty wind will require a higher speed for safety, but a strong headwind will shorten the float and landing roll to compensate for this. A good short-field landing is a pleasure, because the flare is followed immediately by a smooth touchdown at minimum airspeed, and you will have the satisfaction of taxiing off the active at the very first turnoff. It is a maneuver that requires a lot of practice, since flaring a little high will call for a quick burst of power, without delay, to avoid a hard landing. On the other hand, since the airspeed is so low during the final approach, the nose will be higher than usual already, and therefore the flare itself will require less effort.

Without an obstacle, a short-field landing is easier because a steep glide slope is not required. It is poor technique, however, to drag the ship in along the ground, very slow and with lots of power, for the obvious reason that you should not place yourself in a situation where a power failure would make you land short of the runway, or a wind-shift would make you stall. Simply make a normal approach at low airspeed, and set it down on the numbers.

F. SOFT-FIELD APPROACH AND LANDING

1. **Objective.** To determine that the applicant:

    a. Exhibits adequate knowledge by explaining the elements of a soft-field approach and landing procedure including airspeeds, configurations, operations on various surfaces, and related safety factors.

    b. Evaluates obstructions, landing surface, and wind conditions.

    c. Establishes the recommended soft-field approach and landing configuration and airspeed.

    d. Maintains recommended airspeed, ± 5 knots, along the extended runway centerline.

    e. Touches down smoothly at minimum descent rate and groundspeed with no appreciable drift and the airplane's longitudinal axis aligned with runway centerline.

    f. Maintains directional control during the after-landing roll.

    g. Maintains proper position of flight controls and sufficient speed to taxi on soft surface.

2. **Action.** The examiner will:

    a. Ask the applicant to explain the elements of a soft-field approach and landing procedure including airspeeds, configuration, operations on various surfaces, and related safety factors.

    b. Ask the applicant to perform a soft-field approach and landing, and determine that the applicant's performance meets the objective.

    c. Place emphasis on the applicant's demonstration of touchdown at minimum descent rate, proper airspeed, and use of flight controls on a soft surface.

This is probably the most difficult of the landings to execute properly. The idea, as in the soft-field takeoff (Chapter 4, D), is to hold the nose wheel out of the mud, soft grass, snow, or slush. In the takeoff, this became easier and easier as the airspeed increased; here it becomes harder and harder as the airspeed decreases after touchdown. The technique, fundamentally, is to land the airplane in slow flight, just above the stall, and carrying a great deal of power. This means, of course, a very nose-high pitch. After touchdown, power is reduced and the yoke is held increasingly farther back to hold the nose off, as the declining lift tends to make the nose fall. Very little braking action is needed on a soft field, but brakes will be required when the maneuver is simulated on a hard runway. Even after the nose wheel contacts the runway, full back yoke should be held, to keep as much weight as possible off the nosewheel. In a low-wing airplane it is a good idea to retract the flaps after touchdown, to prevent damage by mud or slush thrown up by the wheels; but in a retractable, follow the rule of not reaching for anything until you can do it carefully, after you have turned off the runway.

Score Sheet: 12A. Normal Approach And Landing

Date									
Airspeed control in landing approach (± 5 k)									
Glideslope control									
Smooth flare and hold-off for touchdown									
Power control to cushion landing if necessary (10 points if not necessary)									
Touchdown in first portion of runway									
Directional control during rollout									
TOTAL SCORE									
Divide by 6 = AVERAGE SCORE									

Score Sheet: 12B. Forward Slips To Landing

Date								
Maintaining constant bank angle								
Holding nose on point with opposite rudder								
Airspeed control								
Vertical speed control (including level flight) with power (Score 10 if power off)								
Smooth recovery from slip								
TOTAL SCORE								
Divide by 5 = AVERAGE SCORE								

Score Sheet: 12C.   Go-Around From A Rejected Landing

Date									
Prompt application of full power									
Prompt removal of half flaps									
Smooth establishment of V_y or V_x as appropriate									
Stepwise removal of remaining flaps									
Directional control during climbout									
Smooth re-entry into traffic pattern									
TOTAL SCORE									
Divide by 6 = AVERAGE SCORE									

Score Sheet: 12D. Crosswind Approach And Landing

Date										
Establishing correct degree of slip into wind on long final										
Alignment with runway to point of touchdown using opposite rudder										
Controlled rate of descent with power										
Wing held low into wind until upwind gear touches down										
Proper flare and smooth touchdown										
Immediate transition to ground steering with rudder pedals										
Aileron and elevator into wind during rollout, turn-off, and taxi										
TOTAL SCORE										
Divide by 7 = AVERAGE SCORE										

Score Sheet: 12E. Short-Field Approach And Landing

Fill in the correct approach airspeed for your aircraft, or 1.3 times the power-off, full-flaps stall speed (1.3 times V_{SO}) = _____

Date													
Reducing to the correct speed at 200 feet, before reaching the assumed obstacle													
Establishing & maintaining a constant glide path over the assumed obstacle and all the way to the flare													
Airspeed control ± 5 knots													
Controlling rate of descent with throttle, if necessary, while maintaining constant airspeed													
Flare, power-off, at the right height above touchdown													
Correcting high flare and rapid descent with burst of power, if needed													
Touchdown at the stall, with stall warning operating													
Immediate braking to a short stop with simultaneous retraction of flaps													
Full stop within distance shown in Owner's Manual													
TOTAL SCORE													
Divide by 9 = AVERAGE SCORE													

Score Sheet: 12F. Soft-Field Approach And Landing

Date									
Normal approach with full flaps and power, airpeed 1.3 times V_{SO}(± 5 k)									
Slow flight at edge of stall as you touch down									
Yoke back smoothly (up elevator) during rollout, with power maintained as needed									
Avoid becoming airborne again while holding nosewheel off ground									
Retract flaps during rollout, maintaining positive control									
TOTAL SCORE									
Divide by 5 = AVERAGE SCORE									

13

SPECIAL CONSIDERATIONS IN TWIN-ENGINE FLIGHT

This chapter is devoted to the special requirements in flying twin-engine aircraft. I reproduce here the entire Table of Contents of the FAA's Practical Test Standard for Airplane Multiengine Land (AMEL). Then follows extracts of all material that is substantially different from the single-engine test standard on which the previous chapters were based. In these extracts I include only the **Objectives**, which are the heart of the matter. Of course, the twin is heavier, and its systems are more complex. But the major difference has to do with engine-out procedures. In a single with one engine out, the pilot only has a single skill to exercise—the ability to make an emergency landing with the least possible injury to people and damage to the aircraft. In a twin with one engine out, on the other hand, there are sometimes (not always) options other than an emergency landing, but only if the pilot is proficient. After presenting all the extracts from the Practical Test Standard, I shall discuss the many issues concerning twin-engine safety. My aim will be to teach you how to assess the risks, and how to develop your own personal standards for twin-engine safety.

AIRPLANE MULTIENGINE LAND
(AMEL)
Practical Test Standard

CONTENTS

1. **PREFLIGHT PREPARATION**
   A. Certificates And Documents
   B. Obtaining Weather Information
   C. Cross-Country Flight Planning

2. **MULTIENGINE OPERATION**
   A. Airplane Systems
   B. Emergency Procedures
   C. Normal Procedures
   D. Determining Performance And Flight Planning
   E. Weight And Balance/Equipment List
   F. Flight Principles—Engine Inoperative

3. GROUND OPERATIONS
   A. Visual Inspection
   B. Cockpit Management
   C. Starting Engines
   D. Taxiing
   E. Pre-Takeoff Check

4. AIRPORT AND TRAFFIC PATTERN OPERATION
   A. Radio Communications And ATC Light Signals
   B. Traffic Pattern Operations
   C. Airport And Runway Marking And Lighting

5. TAKEOFFS AND CLIMBS
   A. Normal Takeoff And Climb
   B. Cross-Wind Takeoff And Climb
   C. Short-Field Takeoff And Climb

6. CROSS-COUNTRY FLYING
   A. Pilotage And Dead Reckoning
   B. Radio Navigation
   C. Diversion To Alternate
   D. Lost Procedures

7. FLIGHT BY REFERENCE TO INSTRUMENTS
   A. Straight-And-Level Flight
   B. Straight, Constant-Airspeed Climbs
   C. Straight, Constant-Airspeed Descents
   D. Turns To Headings
   E. Critical Flight Attitudes
   F. Radio And Radar Navigation

8. INSTRUMENT FLIGHT
   A. Engine Failure During Straight-And-Level Flight And Turns
   B. Instrument Approach—All Engines Operating
   C. Instrument Approach—One Engine Inoperative

9. FLIGHT AT CRITICALLY SLOW AIRSPEEDS
   A. Stalls, Gear-Up And Flaps-Up
   B. Stalls, Gear Down And Approach Flaps
   C. Stalls, Gear Down And Full Flaps
   D. Maneuvering At Minimum Controllable Airspeed

10. TURN MANEUVERS
   A. Constant-Altitude Turns
   B. Descending Turns

11. FLIGHT MANEUVERING BY REFERENCE TO GROUND OBJECTS
   A. Rectangular Course
   B. S-Turns Across A Road
   C. Turns Around A Point

12. NIGHT FLIGHT OPERATIONS

A. Preparation And Equipment

B. Night Flight

13. EMERGENCY OPERATIONS

A. Systems And Equipment Malfunctions

B. Maneuvering With One Engine Inoperative

C. Engine Inoperative Loss Of Directional Control Demonstration

D. Demonstrating The Effects Of Various Airspeeds And Configurations During Engine Inoperative Performance

E. Engine Failure En Route

F. Engine Failure On Takeoff Before V_{MC}

G. Engine Failure After Lift-Off

H. Approach And Landing With An Inoperative Engine

14. APPROACHES AND LANDINGS

A. Normal Approach And Landing

B. Go-Around From A Rejected Landing

C. Crosswind Approach And Landing

D. Short-Field Approach And Landing

---

2. MULTIENGINE OPERATION

A. AIRPLANE SYSTEMS

1. **Objective.** To determine that the applicant exhibits adequate knowledge by explaining the airplane systems and their operation including:

a. Primary flight controls and trim.

b. Wing flaps, leading edge devices, and spoilers.

c. Flight instruments.

d. Landing gear -

   (1) retraction system.

   (2) indication system.

   (3) brakes and tires.

   (4) nosewheel steering

e. Engines -

   (1) controls and indicators.

   (2) induction, carburetion, and injection.

   (3) exhaust and turbocharging.

   (4) fire detection.

f. Propellers -

   (1) constant-speed control.

   (2) feather, unfeather, autofeather, and negative torque sensing.

   (3) synchronizing, synchrophasing.

    g. Fuel system -

        (1) tanks, pumps, controls, and indicators.

        (2) crossfeed and transfer.

        (3) fueling procedures.

        (4) normal operation.

    h. Hydraulic system -

        (1) controls and indicators.

        (2) pumps and regulators.

        (3) normal operation.

    i. Electrical system -

        (1) controls and indicators.

        (2) alternators or generators.

        (3) battery, ground power.

        (4) normal operation.

    j. Environmental system -

        (1) heating.

        (2) cooling and ventilation.

        (3) controls and indicators.

        (4) pressurization.

    k. Ice prevention and elimination.

    l. Navigation and communication.

    m. Vacuum system.

B. EMERGENCY PROCEDURES

NOTE: Demonstration of intentional spins and recovery are not required on the practical test and are prohibited in most multiengine airplanes. However, the examiner will ask the applicant to explain the recommended spin recovery procedure for the particular airplane used. This knowledge is essential for recovery if an unintentional spin occurs. This is a knowledge requirement **ONLY**. It is not intended that spins be practiced in multiengine airplanes.

1. **Objective.** To determine that the applicant exhibits adequate knowledge by explaining the airplane's emergency procedures including:

    a. Emergency checklist.

    b. Partial power loss.

    c. Engine failure -

        (1) engine failure before lift-off.

        (2) engine failure after lift-off.

        (3) engine failure during climb and cruise.

        (4) engine securing.

    d. Single-engine operation -

        (1) approach and landing.

        (2) restart.

    e. Emergency landing -

       (1) precautionary.

       (2) without power.

       (3) ditching.

    f. Engine roughness or overheat.

    g. Loss of oil pressure.

    h. Smoke and fire -

       (1) engine.

       (2) cabin.

       (3) electrical.

       (4) environmental.

    i. Icing.

    j. Crossfeed.

    k. Pressurization.

    l. Emergency descent.

    m. Pitot static system and instruments.

    n. Electrical.

    o. Landing gear.

    p. Wing flaps (asymmetrical position).

    q. Inadvertent door openings.

    r. Emergency exits.

D. DETERMINING PERFORMANCE AND FLIGHT PLANNING

1. **Objective.** To determine that the applicant exhibits adequate knowledge by explaining and using the airplane's performance data for flight planning including:

    a. Accelerate-stop distance.

    b. Accelerate-go distance.

    c. Takeoff performance, all engines, single engine.

    d. Climb performance, all engines, single engine.

    e. Service ceiling, all engines, single engine.

    f. Cruise performance.

    g. Fuel consumption, range, endurance.

    h. Descent performance.

    i. Go-around from rejected landings.

    j. Landing distance.

F. FLIGHT PRINCIPLES—ENGINE INOPERATIVE

1. **Objective.** To determine that the applicant exhibits adequate knowledge by explaining the flight principles related to operation with an engine inoperative including:

    a. Factors affecting single-engine flight -

       (1) density altitude.

     (2) drag reduction (propeller, gear, and flaps).

     (3) airspeed (V_{SSE}, V_{XSE}, V_{YSE}).

     (4) attitude (pitch, bank, coordination).

     (5) weight and center of gravity.

     (6) critical engine.

  b. Directional control -

     (1) reasons for loss of directional control.

     (2) reasons for variations in V_{MC}.

     (3) indications of approaching loss of directional control.

     (4) safe recovery procedure if directional control is lost.

     (5) determines V_{MC} in relation to stall speed.

     (6) a decision made as to whether engine inoperative loss of directional control demonstration can be safely accomplished in flight.

  c. Takeoff emergencies -

     (1) takeoff planning.

     (2) decisions after engine failure.

     (3) single-engine operation.

3. GROUND OPERATIONS

E. PRE-TAKEOFF CHECK

  1. Objective. To determine that the applicant:

    a. Exhibits adequate knowledge of the pre-takeoff check by explaining the reasons for checking the items.

    b. Positions airplane to avoid creating hazards.

    c. Divides attention inside and outside of the cockpit.

    d. Ensures that the engine temperatures and pressures are suitable for run-up and takeoff.

    e. Follows the checklist.

    f. Touches the control or switch, or adjusts it to the prescribed position after identifying a checklist item.

    g. States the instrument reading, when appropriate, after identifying the checklist item.

    h. Ensures that the airplane is in safe operating condition emphasizing -

      (1) flight controls and instruments.

      (2) engine and propeller operation.

      (3) seat adjustment and lock.

      (4) safety belts and shoulder harnesses fastened and adjusted.

      (5) doors and windows secured.

    i. Recognizes any discrepancy and decides if the airplane is safe for flight or requires maintenance.

    j. Reviews the critical takeoff performance airspeeds and takeoff distances for existing operating conditions considering engine malfunction.

k. Describes takeoff emergency procedures with emphasis on -

    (1) engine inoperative cockpit procedures.

    (2) engine inoperative airspeeds.

    (3) engine inoperative route to follow considering obstructions and wind conditions.

l. Obtains and interprets takeoff and departure clearance.

m. Notes takeoff time.

5. TAKEOFFS AND CLIMBS

A. NORMAL TAKEOFF AND CLIMB

1. Objective. To determine that the applicant:

a. Exhibits adequate knowledge by explaining the elements of a normal takeoff and climb profile including airspeeds, configurations, and emergency procedures.

b. Aligns the airplane on the runway centerline.

c. Advances the throttles smoothly to maximum allowable power.

d. Checks the engine's instruments.

e. Maintains directional control on the runway centerline.

f. Rotates at the airspeed to attain lift-off at V_{MC} + 5, V_{SSE}, or the recommended[1] lift-off airspeed.

g. Establishes the single-engine, best rate-of-climb pitch attitude and accelerates to V_Y.

h. Establishes the all-engine best rate-of-climb pitch attitude when reaching V_Y and maintains V_Y, ± 5 knots, or V_Y, + 10 knots, to avoid high pitch angles.

i. Retracts the wing flaps as recommended or at a safe altitude.

j. Retracts the landing gear after a positive rate of climb has been established and a safe landing cannot be made on the remaining runway, or as recommended.

k. Climbs at V_Y to 400 feet AGL or to a safe maneuvering altitude.

l. Maintains takeoff power to a safe maneuvering altitude.

m. Uses noise abatement procedures as required.

n. Establishes and maintains a cruise climb airspeed, ± 5 knots.

o. Maintains a straight track over the extended runway centerline until a turn is required.

p. Completes after-takeoff checklist.

---

[1]The term "recommended" as used in this standard refers to the manufacturer's recommendation. If the manufacturer's recommendation is not available, the description contained in AC 61–21 will be used.

C. SHORT-FIELD TAKEOFF AND CLIMB

1. Objective. To determine that the applicant:

a. Exhibits adequate knowledge by explaining the elements of a short-field takeoff and climb profile including the significance of appropriate airspeeds, configurations, emergency procedures, and expected performance for existing operating conditions.

b. Positions the airplane at the beginning of the takeoff runway aligned on the runway centerline.

c. Advances the throttles smoothly to maximum allowable power.

d. Checks the engines' instruments.

e. Adjusts the pitch attitude to attain maximum rate of acceleration.

f. Maintains directional control on the runway centerline.

g. Rotates at the airspeed to attain lift-off at V_{MC} + 5 knots, V_X, or at the recommended airspeed, whichever is greater.

h. Climbs at V_X or the recommended airspeed, whichever is greater (no lower than V_{MC}) until obstacle is cleared, or at least 50 feet above the surface, then accelerates to V_Y, and maintains V_Y, ± 5 knots, or V_Y, + 10 knots to avoid high pitch angles.

i. Retracts the wing flaps as recommended or at a safe altitude.

j. Retracts the landing gear after a positive rate of climb has been established or a safe landing cannot be made on the remaining runway or as recommended.

k. Climbs at V_Y to 400 feet AGL or to a safe maneuvering altitude.

l. Maintains takeoff power to the safe maneuvering altitude.

m. Uses noise abatement procedures as required.

n. Establishes and maintains a cruise climb airspeed, ± 5 knots.

o. Maintains a straight track over the extended runway centerline until a turn is required.

p. Completes after-takeoff checklist.

8. INSTRUMENT FLIGHT

A. ENGINE FAILURE DURING STRAIGHT-AND-LEVEL FLIGHT AND TURNS

1. Objective. To determine that the applicant:

a. Exhibits adequate knowledge by explaining the reasons for the procedures used if engine failure occurs during straight-and-level flight and turns while on instruments.

b. Recognizes engine failure promptly during straight-and-level flight and during standard-rate turns.

c. Sets the engine controls, reduces drag, and identifies and verifies the inoperative engine.

d. Establishes the best engine-out airspeed and trims the airplane.

e. Verifies the prescribed checklist procedures for securing the inoperative engine.

f. Establishes and maintains a bank toward the operating engine as required for best performance in straight-and-level flight.

g. Maintains a bank angle as required for best performance in a turn of approximately standard rate.

h. Attempts to determine the reason for the engine malfunction.

i. Maintains an altitude or a minimum sink rate sufficient to continue flight considering -

   (1) density altitude.

   (2) service ceiling.

   (3) gross weight.

   (4) elevation of terrain and obstructions.

j. Monitors the operating engine and makes necessary adjustments.

k. Maintains the desired altitude ± 100 feet, if within the airplane's capability, the desired airspeed ± 10 knots, and the desired heading ± 10° if in straight flight.

l. Recognizes the airplane's performance capability and decides an appropriate action to ensure a safe landing.

m. Avoids imminent loss of control or attempted flight contrary to the single-engine operating limitations of the airplane.

9. FLIGHT AT CRITICALLY SLOW AIRSPEEDS

NOTE: No stall will be performed with one engine throttled or cut off and the other engine(s) developing effective power.

Full stalls using high-power settings have been deleted from the multiengine practical test because of excessive high pitch angles necessary to induce these stalls which may result in uncontrollable flight.

Examiners and instructors should be alert to the possible development of high sink rates when performing stalls in multiengine airplanes with high wing loadings; therefore, the tolerance of − 50 feet loss of altitude during stall entries has been incorporated in these TASKS.

A. STALLS, GEAR-UP AND FLAPS-UP

1. **Objective.** To determine that the applicant:

   a. Exhibits adequate knowledge by explaining the aerodynamic factors associated with stalls, gear up and flaps up, and an awareness of stall speed in the configuration, power, pitch, and bank required, and the procedure for resuming normal flight.

   b. Selects an entry altitude that will allow recoveries to be completed no lower than 3,000 feet AGL.

   c. Stabilize the airplane at approach airspeed in level flight with a gear-up, flaps-up configuration and appropriate power setting.

d. Establishes a pitch attitude, straight ahead and in 20° (±10°) bank turns, that will induce a stall with a power setting to maintain altitude + 50 feet, − 50 feet.

e. Applies proper control to maintain coordinated flight.

f. Recognizes and recovers from stalls at the first indication of buffeting or decay of control effectiveness by immediately reducing angle of attack and increasing power.

g. Returns to entry airspeed and configuration.

h. Avoids full stalls, excessive pitch change, excessive altitude loss, spirals, spins, or flight below 3,000 feet AGL.

B. STALLS, GEAR DOWN AND APPROACH FLAPS

1. Objective. To determine that the applicant:

a. Exhibits adequate knowledge by explaining the aerodynamic factors associated with stalls, gear down and approach flaps, and an awareness of stall speed in the configuration, power, pitch, and bank required, and the procedure for resuming normal flight.

b. Selects an entry altitude that will allow recoveries to be completed no lower than 3,000 feet AGL.

c. Stabilizes the airplane at approach airspeed in level flight with a gear down and approach flap configuration and appropriate power setting.

d. Establishes a pitch attitude straight ahead, and in 20°, ± 10°, bank turns, that will induce a stall with a power setting to maintain altitude + 150 feet, − 50 feet.

e. Applies proper control to maintain coordinated flight.

f. Recognizes and recovers from stalls at the first indication of buffeting or decay of control effectiveness by immediately reducing angle of attack and increasing power.

g. Returns to entry airspeed and configuration.

h. Avoids full stalls, excessive pitch change, excessive altitude loss, spirals, spins, or flight below 3,000 feet AGL.

C. STALLS, GEAR DOWN AND FULL FLAPS

1. Objective. To determine that the applicant:

a. Exhibits adequate knowledge by explaining the aerodynamic factors associated with stalls, gear down and full flaps, and an awareness of stall speed in the configuration, power, pitch, and bank required, and the procedure for resuming normal flight.

b. Selects an entry altitude that will allow recoveries to be completed no lower than 3,000 feet AGL.

c. Stabilizes the airplane at approach airspeed in level flight with a gear down and full flaps configuration and appropriate power setting.

d. Establishes a pitch attitude straight ahead, and in 20°, ± 10°, bank turns, that will induce a stall with a power setting to maintain altitude + 150 feet, − 50 feet.

e. Applies proper control to maintain coordinated flight.

f. Recognizes and recovers from stalls at the first indication of buffeting or decay of control effectiveness by immediately reducing angle of attack and increasing power.

g. Returns to entry airspeed and configuration.

h. Avoids full stalls, excessive pitch change, excessive altitude loss, spirals, spins, or flight below 3,000 feet AGL.

D. MANEUVERING AT MINIMUM CONTROLLABLE AIRSPEED

NOTE: Examiners, instructors, and applicants should be cautioned that maneuvering at minimum controllable airspeed may be at a speed below V_{MC}, and should be alert to recovery procedures if an engine fails at this speed.

1. **Objective.** To determine that the applicant:

   a. Exhibits adequate knowledge by explaining the flight characteristics and controllability associated with maneuvering at minimum controllable airspeeds.

   b. Selects an entry altitude that will allow the maneuver to be performed no lower than 3,000 feet AGL.

   c. Establishes and maintains the airspeed at which any further increase in angle of attack, resulting from an increase in load factor or reduction in power, would result in an immediate stall or the activation of a stall warning device while -

      (1) in coordinated straight and turning flight in various configurations and bank angles, and

      (2) in coordinated departure climbs and landing approach descents in various configurations.

   d. Maintains the desired altitude, ± 100 feet, when a constant altitude is specified, and level off from climbs and descents, ± 100 feet.

   e. Maintains the desired heading during straight flight ± 10°.

   f. Maintains the specified bank angle ± 10° in coordinated flight.

   g. Maintains minimum controllable airspeed + 5, − 0 knots.

   h. Recognizes buffet if it occurs and recovers immediately.

13. EMERGENCY OPERATIONS

B. MANEUVERING WITH ONE ENGINE INOPERATIVE

NOTE: The feathering of one propeller should be demonstrated in any multiengine airplane equipped with propellers which can be safely feathered and unfeathered in flight. Feathering for pilot flight test purposes should be performed only under such conditions and at such altitudes (no lower than 3,000 feet above the surface) and positions where safe landings on established airports can be readily accomplished in the event difficulty is encountered in unfeathering. At altitudes lower than 3,000 feet above the surface simulated engine failure will be performed by throttling the engine to zero thrust.

In the event a propeller cannot be unfeathered during the practical test, it should be treated as an emergency.

1. **Objective.** To determine that the applicant:

   a. Exhibits adequate knowledge by explaining the flight characteristics and controllability associated with maneuvering with one engine inoperative.

   b. Sets the engine controls, reduces drag, identifies and verifies the inoperative engine after simulated engine failure.

   c. Attains the best engine-out airspeed and trims the airplane.

   d. Maintains control of the airplane.

   e. Attempts to determine the reason for the engine malfunction.

   f. Follows the prescribed checklist to verify procedures for securing the inoperative engine.

   g. Establishes a bank toward the operating engine as required for best performance.

   h. Turns toward the nearest suitable airport.

   i. Monitors the operating engine and makes necessary adjustments.

   j. Demonstrates coordinated flight with one engine inoperative (propeller feathered, if possible) including -

   (1) straight-and-level flight.

   (2) turns in both directions.

   (3) descents to assigned altitudes.

   (4) climb to assigned altitudes, if airplane is capable of climbs under existing conditions.

   k. Maintains the desired altitude, ± 100 feet, when a constant altitude is specified, and levels off from climbs and descents, ± 100 feet.

   l. Maintains the desired heading during straight flight, ± 15°.

   m. Maintains the specified bank angle, ± 10°, during turns.

   n. Divides attention between coordinated control, flightpath, and orientation.

   o. Demonstrates engine restart in accordance with prescribed procedures.

C. ENGINE INOPERATIVE LOSS OF DIRECTIONAL CONTROL DEMONSTRATION

NOTE: There is a density altitude above which the stalling speed is higher than the engine inoperative minimum control speed. When this density altitude exists close to the ground because of high elevations and/or high temperatures, an effective flight demonstration of loss of directional control may be hazardous and should not be attempted. If it is determined prior to flight that the stall speed is higher than V_{MC} and this flight demonstration is impracticable, the significance of the engine inoperative minimum control speed should be emphasized through oral questioning, including the results of attempting engine inoperative flight below this speed, the recognition of loss of directional control, and proper recovery techniques.

To conserve altitude during the engine inoperative loss of directional control demonstration, recovery should be made by reducing angle of attack and resuming controlled flight. If a situation exists where reduction of power on the operating engine is necessary to maintain airplane control, the decision to reduce power must be made by the pilot to avoid uncontrolled flight. Emphasis should be placed on conservation of altitude but not at the expense of uncontrolled flight.

Recoveries should never be made by increasing power on the simulated failed engine.

The practice of entering this maneuver by increasing pitch attitude to a high point with both engines operating and then reducing power on the critical engine should be avoided because the airplane may become uncontrollable when the power on the critical engine is reduced.

1. **Objective.** To determine that the applicant:
   a. Exhibits adequate knowledge by explaining the causes of loss of directional control at airspeeds less than V_{MC} (minimum engine inoperative control speed), the factors affecting V_{MC}, and the safe recovery procedures.
   b. Selects an entry altitude that will allow recoveries to be completed no lower than 3,000 feet AGL.
   c. Establishes the airplane's configuration with -
      (1) propeller set to high RPM.
      (2) landing gear retracted.
      (3) flaps set in takeoff position.
      (4) cowl flaps set in takeoff position.
      (5) engines set to rated takeoff power or as recommended.
      (6) trim set for takeoff.
      (7) power on the critical engine reduced to idle (avoid abrupt power reduction).
   d. Establishes a single engine climb attitude (inoperative engine propeller windmilling) with the airspeed representative of that following a normal takeoff.
   e. Establishes a bank toward the operating engine as required for best performance.
   f. Reduces the airspeed slowly with the elevators while applying rudder pressure to maintain directional control until full rudder is applied.
   g. Recognizes the indications of loss of directional control.
   h. Recovers promptly by reducing the angle of attack to regain control and, if necessary, adjusts power on operating engine sufficiently to maintain control with minimum loss of altitude.
   i. Recovers within 15° of the entry heading.

D. DEMONSTRATING THE EFFECTS OF VARIOUS AIRSPEEDS AND CONFIGURATIONS DURING ENGINE INOPERATIVE PERFORMANCE

1. **Objective.** To determine that the applicant:
   a. Exhibits adequate knowledge by explaining the effects of various airspeeds and configurations on performance during engine-inoperative operation.

b. Selects an entry altitude that will allow recoveries to be completed no lower than 3,000 feet AGL.

c. Establishes V_{YSE} with critical engine at zero thrust.

d. Varies the airspeed from V_{YSE} and demonstrates the effect of the airspeed changes on performance.

e. Maintains V_{YSE} and demonstrates the effect of each of the following on performance -

  (1) extension of landing gear.

  (2) extension of wing flaps.

  (3) extension of both landing gear and wing flaps.

  (4) windmilling of propeller on the critical engine.

E. ENGINE FAILURE EN ROUTE

1. Objective. To determine that the applicant:

a. Exhibits adequate knowledge by explaining the techniques and procedures used if engine failure occurs while en route.

b. Sets the engine controls, reduces drag, and identifies and verifies the inoperative engine after simulated engine failure.

c. Attains the best engine inoperative airspeed and trims the airplane.

d. Maintains control of the airplane.

e. Attempts to determine the reason for the engine malfunction.

f. Follows the prescribed checklist to verify procedures for securing the inoperative engine.

g. Establishes a bank toward the operating engine as required for best performance.

h. Turns toward nearest suitable airport.

i. Maintains an altitude or a minimum sink rate sufficient to continue flight considering -

  (1) density altitude.

  (2) service ceiling.

  (3) gross weight.

  (4) elevation of terrain and obstructions.

j. Monitors the operating engine and makes necessary adjustments.

k. Maintains the desired altitude, $\pm$ 100 feet, if within the airplane's capability, the desired heading, $\pm$ 15°, and the desired airspeed, $\pm$ 5 knots.

l. Divides attention between coordinated airplane control, flightpath, and orientation.

m. Contacts appropriate facility for assistance, if necessary.

F. ENGINE FAILURE ON TAKEOFF BEFORE V_{MC}

1. Objective. To determine that the applicant:

a. Exhibits adequate knowledge by explaining the reasons for the procedures used for engine failure on takeoff before V_{MC} including related safety factors.

    b. Aligns the airplane on the runway centerline.

    c. Advances the throttles smoothly to maximum allowable power.

    d. Checks the engines' instruments.

    e. Maintains directional control on the runway centerline.

    f. Closes throttles smoothly and promptly when engine failure occurs.

    g. Maintains directional control and applies braking as necessary.

G. ENGINE FAILURE AFTER LIFT-OFF

    1. Objective. To determine that the applicant:

      a. Exhibits adequate knowledge by explaining the reasons for the procedures used if engine failure occurs after lift-off including related safety factors.

      b. Recognizes engine failure promptly.

      c. Sets the engine controls, reduces drag, and identifies and verifies the inoperative engine after simulated engine failure.

      d. Establishes V_{YSE} if there are no obstructions; if obstructions are present, establishes V_{XSE} or $V_{MC} + 5$, whichever is greater, until obstructions are cleared, then V_{YSE} and trims the airplane.

      e. Maintains control of the airplane.

      f. Follows the prescribed checklist to verify procedures for securing the inoperative engine.

      g. Establishes a bank toward the operating engine as required for best performance.

      h. Recognizes the airplane's performance capability; if a climb is impossible, maintains V_{YSE} and initiates an approach to the most suitable landing area.

      i. Attempts to determine the reason for the engine malfunction.

      j. Monitors the operating engine and makes necessary adjustments.

      k. Maintains the desired heading, $\pm 20°$, and the desired airspeed, ± 5 knots.

      l. Divides attention between coordinated airplane control, flightpath, and orientation.

      m. Contacts the appropriate facility for assistance, if necessary.

H. APPROACH AND LANDING WITH AN INOPERATIVE ENGINE

    1. Objective. To determine that the applicant:

      a. Exhibits adequate knowledge by explaining the procedure used during an approach and landing with an inoperative engine.

      b. Sets the engine controls, reduces drag, and identifies and verifies inoperative engine after simulated engine failure.

      c. Establishes the recommended airspeed and trims the airplane.

      d. Follows the prescribed checklist to verify procedures for securing the inoperative engine and completes pre-landing checklist.

      e. Establishes a bank toward the operating engine as required for best performance.

    f. Maintains proper track on final approach.

    g. Establishes the approach and landing configuration and power.

    h. Maintains a stabilized descent angle and the recommended final approach airspeed (not less than V_{YSE}) until landing is assured.

    i. Touches down smoothly beyond and within 500 feet of a specified point, with no appreciable drift and the longitudinal axis aligned with the runway centerline.

    j. Maintains correct control during after-landing roll.

There are two aspects of flying light twins that require discussion here, because they are the two things that get pilots into trouble most frequently. These are engine failure during takeoff and climb, and single-engine landings. But first let me clarify something about the statistics of light-twin safety. You will hear all kinds of arguments about the safety of twins compared with singles, and every argument will be buttressed with statistics. You will understand the old saying "There are lies, damn lies, and statistics!" What is the truth? One truth is indisputable—a twin has twice the probability of engine failure compared with a single, because there are two engines to fail instead of one. But the companion truth is the more important one. In case an engine does fail, the outlook is very much better in a twin, **provided that** it is handled correctly. Another way of putting this is that when an engine fails in a single, there is going to be a landing within the next few seconds or minutes (depending on altitude), and usually it will be an off-airport landing. In off-airport landings, major damage to the aircraft is typical, and personal injuries (even fatal injuries) are likely on hostile terrain. In contrast, when an engine fails in a twin— except for a critical few seconds at takeoff—there is no reason for an accident to happen at all. The worst outcome should be the same as with a single, namely, an emergency landing.

These obvious truths notwithstanding, the accident record shows that there are a great many light twin accidents that result from engine failure. Why? A clue is found in the fact that these accidents are much more frequent (per engine failure) in general aviation light twins flown by low-time pilots than in corporate aircraft flown by professionals. For every engine failure in a twin, the probability that an accident will result is greatest in light twins, less in heavier corporate twins, least of all in air carrier twins. This suggests that pilot proficiency is the key to the correct handling of engine failure in a twin. I am going to explain why. A fuller discussion is found, with illustrations from NTSB accident reports, in my book FLYING OUT OF DANGER (Airguide Publications Inc., Long Beach, CA 90801). My approach to this subject is based on analysis of actual accidents. I am also much indebted to Richard N. Aarons for his common-sense writings in Business & Commercial Aviation; his approach agrees closely with mine. I have concluded that much of what is written about engine-out procedures—even by FAA—is nonsense, in that theory dominates over reality. They tell you what you have to do (as in the extracts from FAA's Practical Test Standards reproduced above), and they test you in simulated conditions to see if you can do it, but the truth is **you can't possibly do it** in an engine failure at a critical moment during takeoff.

Let's see why. A typical general aviation light twin is not required to meet any standards whatsoever for single-engine performance. At gross weight, typical sea-level single-engine best rate of climb is 200'–400' per minute. Let me give a few actual examples. In 1985 these numbers (in feet per minute) were as follows, according to the Business & Commercial Aviation Handbook: Piper Seneca II, 240; Beech Baron B55, 397; Beech Baron 58P, 223. Ten years earlier, the numbers were: Piper Aztec E, 240; Cessna 310Q, 327; Beech Queen Air B80, 210. Nothing has changed. Notice also that turbocharging has no big effect on sea-level performance; its chief value is in giving sea-level performance at high density altitude, where the power obtainable from a normally aspirated engine would go down substantially.

This is a good place to repeat a familiar point concerning performance in twins that lose an engine. Losing half the horsepower reduces performance by 80% or more, **not** by 50%, because nearly half the rated horsepower is needed just to sustain the weight of the aircraft against the force of gravity. Performance (speed or climb capability) is due to the **excess** over this basic minimum. That is why even at sea level, climb rates of as high as 1500' per minute with both engines working can be reduced to the measly 200' per minute already noted when an engine fails. You might be thinking that a couple of hundred feet per minute climb is not really all that bad, and feel reassured. I have to destroy your complacency! The bad news is that you will **never** actually see those advertised figures in the period immediately after an engine failure. They are based on absolutely perfect conditions—full power on the working engine, gear retracted, flaps retracted, dead propeller feathered, and 5° bank into the working engine. Until all these conditions are achieved, you will not climb at all, and you might not even be able to maintain altitude.

Let's look at the worst-case scenario. You start your takeoff roll, reach V_{MC} + 5k (just as FAA recommends), rotate, and lift off. Unless the runway is exceptionally long, it will only be a few seconds before you are beyond the point where you could still land safely. Suddenly there is a jolt, and the aircraft pulls sharply to the right. You are startled, but you recover your wits quickly and realize you've lost an engine. Several seconds have passed. FAA describes the situation: "...experience has shown that an unexpected engine failure so surprises the unseasoned pilot that proper reactions are extremely lagging ... as though he is 'swimming in glue.' By the time the initial shock wears off and the pilot is ready to take control of the situation, the excess speed has dissipated and the airplane is still barely off the ground." You look at the airspeed indicator and it is practically at the V_{MC} redline. "Have to get this cleaned up fast," you think, and reach for the gear handle. In some aircraft the moving gear and the opening and closing of the gear doors creates more drag than the extended gear alone. The airspeed sags below V_{MC}. A few more seconds have passed. You haven't even begun to feather the inoperative prop; indeed, you haven't even confirmed for sure which one it is. Remember the drill you were taught? Both throttles forward (well, you were at takeoff, so they are already forward), then **carefully** pull back what you think is the dead throttle, confirm that there is no change in power, and then—only then—feather the corresponding prop. Which prop control is the "corresponding" one? Do you think it possible, under the intense stress of such an episode, that you could reach for the wrong one? It doesn't really matter any more, because by now—only 10 seconds into this engine failure—the airspeed has fallen to the critically dangerous level below V_{MC}. The aircraft is only 30' above the runway, and descending. It is also in an increasingly steep bank to the right. Unless you kill the power on the working engine **immediately**, you will be another statistic. Directional control has been lost, the stall speed is being approached, and the next sure event is a fiery crash in a near-inverted attitude.

Now it is true that **if** you practiced engine-out emergency procedures in a simulator, with the element of surprise present, and **if** you did this regularly under the supervision and monitoring of a check pilot—in other words, **if** you maintained your proficiency to the same level as air carrier pilots and the best corporate pilots, you might be able to handle those first 10 seconds exactly right. But we are talking about **you**, not about them. There is simply no way you are going to handle an engine failure on takeoff safely—not without some very specific guidelines for action, which will be personally tailored to your own capabilities.

If you think about the scenario just described, you will realize at once that you need three things to manage an engine failure in the takeoff-and-climb phase of flight—**airspeed**, **altitude**, and **time**. To be able to climb to a safe altitude, you need the best-rate single-engine airspeed (V_{YSE}) or V_{XSE} in case of obstacles ahead. If you haven't got it yet, there's no way you will get it until the airplane is completely cleaned up. In the time it takes to do that, you have absolutely no choice but to put the nose down, thus trading altitude for the airspeed you need in order to survive. This is where you are really in a bind! And the situation is not much better if you already have those airspeeds, because trying to maintain altitude before the airplane is clean will bleed off speed quickly. So the question comes down to—how long will it take you to clean everything up from the moment of engine failure? In that time you are either going to lose airspeed or lose altitude. If airspeed falls below V_{MC} while you continue to carry full power on the good engine, you are dead. If you avoid this by reducing power on the good engine, you go down faster. In summary, you are going to lose some altitude one way or the other before you can climb out. The only question is: How much?

The answer to the question just posed is your personal guideline for how high you have to be, AGL, in order to continue safely. I suggest that for most moderately proficient pilots this number is not less than 500′. You can find out for yourself by going up to a safe altitude, simulating the takeoff, and having an instructor cut an engine without warning. Then find out how much altitude you lose before you are established again in a solid climb. Let's assume 500′ turns out to be a safe conservative number for you. Then you have a firm rule: **Below 500′ I am flying a single.** Nothing to think about—engine failure means immediately bringing both throttles back and landing straight ahead or nearly straight ahead as well as you can. Above 500′ the rule is: **Lower the nose, to maintain at least V_{XSE}, get the gear and flaps up, bank 5° into the good engine, feather the dead prop ("dead foot, dead engine"), and establish a climb.**

The biggest safety hazard in this procedure is psychological. To put it crudely, if a single quits, the eerie silence leaves no doubt about what you have to do. But when the only working engine in a twin makes so much noise and sounds so powerful, it is hard to believe it won't get you out of the mess you're in. It won't! You need the disciplined professional attitude that will let you damage your airplane to save your life and the lives of your passengers. And the only way to make the right decision is to have it made **in advance** before you start your takeoff roll. Some people tell themselves out loud as they advance the throttles, "Abort the takeoff." Then as they rotate, they tell themselves, "Both throttles back and land straight ahead." Then when they reach their predetermined safe altitude, they say, "Now clean up and fly." In this way they establish a certain psychological "set"—a readiness to act instantly without wasting precious seconds in decision-making. If all multiengine pilots who do not maintain proficiency to a professional level adopted this approach and followed through on it, there would be some damaged airplanes, but lives would be saved.

These recommendations apply to airplanes at gross weight. Obviously, they can be relaxed slightly at less than gross, since performance is better, the lighter the aircraft is loaded. Experience will also teach you to modify the guidelines according to when the failure occurs. The correct procedure, as you know, is to build up speed in ground effect, from $V_{MC} + 5$ k at rotation, to V_Y. Then an immediate climb at V_Y is initiated, in order to gain precious altitude as quickly as possible. So common sense has to be applied. If you are at 400' AGL and climbing at V_Y in a clean configuration when an engine fails, you will obviously have enough time and airspeed and altitude to identify and feather and continue climbing at V_{YSE}, even if your "guideline" altitude at takeoff was 500'.

The recommendations also have to be modified for normally aspirated engines at high density altitude. Look at the manufacturer's claim about your single-engine service ceiling. Typical would be 5,000' for an Aztec, 7,000' for a Beech Baron or Cessna 310. Turbocharged, these same numbers become 15,000'–18,000'. Of course, this very much influences what happens enroute if you lose an engine—that needs no elaborating upon. My point here is that if you are taking off from a field with a density altitude of 5,000'–7,000'—not at all an unusual state of affairs, especially in the summer—you really **are** flying a single, because there is **no way** you can climb, dirty or clean.

Now we come to the other major problem—single-engine landings. It seems very strange that engine failures enroute cause no problem until the landing, and then result in an extraordinary number of serious accidents. This needs some careful analysis. Here the whole difficulty is psychological, since there is no question of performance—the aircraft only has to go down, from cruising altitude, steadily and systematically, until it touches down on the runway of intended landing. Why should this be a problem?

Let's begin again with a look at performance. **Rule 1** about single-engine landings is that a go-around is impossible. You will hear some arguments that it could be done under some circumstances (for example, if you are well under gross), but let's keep this simple. For the same reason you were not able to climb out on a single engine until you **first** reached a critical altitude AGL, and cleaned up the airplane, you will not be able to reject a landing and climb out safely. There are two conclusions. One is that you will not, under any circumstances, attempt a single-engine go-around. The other is that you make this perfectly clear to the tower controller. Every engine failure in a twin is an emergency, and you should have declared the emergency while enroute, so there ought to be no question about exercising your emergency authority to ensure that no circumstance will arise in which you might have to go around. It is worth making sure that the tower controller understands the situation. I was once approaching to land with an engine out, and I **thought** it was clear to the controller what kind of priority I needed. To my horror, he cleared someone for takeoff just as I turned final. Suppose that aircraft had to abort? Where would that have left me? What happened was my own fault for not clarifying fully what I needed.

I think the trouble in single-engine landings starts with the knowledge that a go-around will not be possible. This makes the pilot very anxious, and the fatigue level is already high. It is not only the end of a long flight, but a flight in which the engine failure had to be dealt with—certainly not the most relaxed state of affairs. Now here comes the landing, and we **must** get it right, we have only one shot at it. What happens then is that instead of just flying a normal pattern and a normal approach to a normal touchdown, the pilot tries to keep it high, just to be **sure** of making the runway. Or maybe instead of carrying normal landing flaps, a no-flaps landing is tried. Or something else is done differently. The net result is a touchdown point way down the runway, threatening an overshoot. Then, despite all the knowledge about the danger of attempting a go-around, it is tried anyway—full power on the good engine, airspeed dangerously low, even below V_{MC}—and another statistic is born! Let me be brutally frank. If you have never seen a light twin that crashed inverted into the runway on a go-around attempt, carrying the pilot and passenger to instant death—as I did at our own airport—you can't imagine how horrible it is. Our runway is only 2,300' long. This twin almost touched down at the halfway point, then started a go-around. Had they stuck to the rule, they probably would have run off the end, and the airplane would have suffered some damage, but the people would very likely have walked away uninjured.

The rule for single-engine landings is to keep the airplane in a clean configuration until it is clear that there will be no further need to climb. Only then is it permissible to lower the gear and to begin adding flaps. Once that process begins, no climbs whatsoever will be permissible. This raises a big question about IFR approaches under conditions where a missed approach may be forced by the weather. Fortunately, this is a VFR book, so I don't have to deal with that one now.

In summary, most of what FAA requires of you in the lengthy materials reproduced at the beginning of this chapter is technique. It is technique you have to learn, because you are going to use it primarily for an enroute engine failure. I hope that by setting safe and conservative limits for yourself, you will not come to grief because of an engine failure during takeoff and the early part of the climbout. And I hope that by recognizing the virtual impossibility of a go-around in single-engine operation, you will keep yourself from becoming a statistic at that phase of flight. The key to all this is the attitude of professionalism and discipline that is needed to overcome foolhardy risk-taking born of overconfidence and a "macho" attitude. Flying is adventuresome, so there's a little bit of that in all of us. Recognizing it's there can help keep it from killing us.

Score Sheet: 13. Multiengine Operation

Date									
Familiarity with airplane systems and their operation									
Understanding the rationale for all emergency procedures									
Knowing the numbers for takeoff, especially the accelereate-stop and accelerate-go distances									
Understanding dangers and procedures with engine inoperative									
Pre-takeoff checks, including advance decision-making about speeds, distances, and altitudes for rejecting takeoff or climbout									
Takeoff, rotation, acceleration in ground effect, and climb at appropriate airspeeds									
Short-field takeoff procedures									

Score Sheet: 13. Multiengine Operation (continued)

Date											
Management of engine failure during level flight, recognition and feathering of dead engine, maintaining 5° bank into working engine with ball off center toward working engine											
Engine-inoperative approach procedure											
Stalls, gear-up and flaps-up											
Stalls, gear-down, approach flaps											
Stalls, gear-down, full flaps											
Maneuvering at minimum controllable airspeed (slow flight)											
Maneuvering with one engine inoperative											
Demonstration of incipient loss of directional control with one engine inoperative and other engine at takeoff power											
Management of engine failure enroute											

Score Sheet: 13. Multiengine Operation (continued)

Date										
Management of engine failure on takeoff before V_{mc} (rejected takeoff)										
Management of engine failure after lift-off, with airspeed and altitude determining decision to climb out or to land										
Approach and landing with one engine inoperative										
TOTAL SCORE										
Divide by 19 = AVERAGE SCORE										

14
ADVANCED THEORY AND PRACTICE

This chapter presents two interesting maneuvers that are not required on the private pilot check ride, followed by explanations of some fundamental principles of aerodynamics that many pilots find confusing.

A. DUTCH ROLLS

This is a marvelously satisfying training maneuver, which is often neglected because it is not required for the private ticket. I recommend it strongly for every pilot, at whatever stage of flying experience, because it teaches coordination so beautifully. It is also excellent practice for crosswind landings, because it teaches how to use just the right amount of rudder pressure to keep the nose in a constant position.

The first thing to practice is flying in a slip. Lower one wing to a 10° bank angle, and use exactly enough opposite rudder to hold the heading absolutely constant by reference to a point on the horizon and to the heading indicator. When you are in stable slipping flight, return to the wings level condition, and simultaneously (or with a slight lag) release the rudder pressure. The point is never to let the nose wander from its fixed position on the horizon, and thus never to let the heading vary. You will find that the only way to exert fine control over the rudder pressures is to use **both** feet at all times. You get the best control by working one foot against the other.

When you can manage this for slips to the left and slips to the right, increase the bank angle to 20°, and find out how much extra rudder pressure you need to hold the heading. Eventually increase to 30° bank angle, or to a point where you run out of opposite rudder. Practice these stepwise, moving from one bank angle to another, both in left banks and in right banks. Since you maintain cruise airspeed throughout these slipping maneuvers, the warnings you have heard and read about crossed controls have no relevance here. Slips are perfectly safe maneuvers. You should practice them at altitude, but eventually, in crosswind landings, you will be doing them close to the ground.

Dutch rolls consist of alternate slips to the left and to the right, performed smoothly and rhythmically, and without the slightest deviation from a constant heading (Fig. 14-1). Set up normal cruise with good attention to proper trim, and head for a distant landmark. Now bank gently (about 10°) to the left, and before the ship can begin to turn, bring in just enough right rudder to keep the nose on the landmark. Now roll into a 10° bank to the right, perfectly smoothly, and without hesitating at the wings-level position. Hold the same right rudder pressure **until the nose begins to move** to the right, and then switch smoothly from right rudder to left rudder, now using just enough left rudder to hold the nose on the distant point.

The key to Dutch rolls is using aileron and rudder one after the other, **not simultaneously**. The beauty of the maneuver is in the rhythm, like a ballet in the sky—roll left, **then** right rudder, roll right, **then** left rudder, and so on. You will find this a rather difficult maneuver to master, but the satisfaction of doing it perfectly is worth the practice. As you get better at it, you should increase the bank angle, to 20°, then 30°. Greater bank angle means greater opposite rudder pressure, and more difficult coordination in switching pressure smoothly from one foot to the other. Incidentally, this is not a good maneuver to do with a passenger; it can produce air-sickness in someone who is passive, but it rarely disturbs the pilot.

B. EIGHTS—ALONG A ROAD, ACROSS A ROAD, AROUND PYLONS

For eights along a road (Fig. 14-2), find a road or other straight-line feature of the landscape that is aligned with the wind. Fly along the road and directly over it, heading downwind. The object is to make a 360 to the

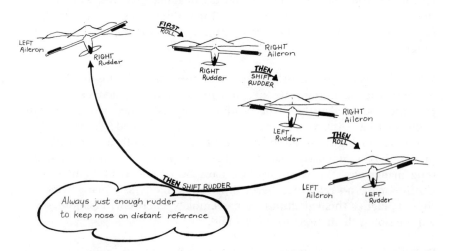

Fig. 14-1 Dutch rolls.

left, returning to the road at the same place you left it, then a 360 to the right, and so on. The loops of the "8" should be equal and symmetrical, and the changing bank angles should be smooth and gradual, as in "S" turns across a road (Chapter 9, B).

Since you start flying downwind, you have to roll into your steepest bank immediately. This bank is then gradually shallowed as your turn brings you upwind. The shallowest bank is in the upwind part of the circle, at the moment when you are again parallel to the road. Then you have to start steepening the bank again, so that when you return to the road you will have your steepest bank. Here, as was the case with "S" turns, you have to roll from one steep bank to another as soon as you are at the road and facing downwind. The exercise is more interesting (and more difficult) if the wind is from a quartering angle rather than right down the road, because the changes in bank angle then require some more thoughtful advance planning.

In eights across a road (Fig. 14-3) the main requirement is that the extended arms of the "8" must always cross the road at the same place. It is convenient if this place is a crossroad or other prominent feature along the road. In this maneuver the road should be perpendicular to the wind or, as in the figure, almost perpendicular to the wind. At each loop of the "8," you fly upwind and, therefore, at your shallowest bank. To aid in keeping the loops equal and symmetrical, you should choose a terrain

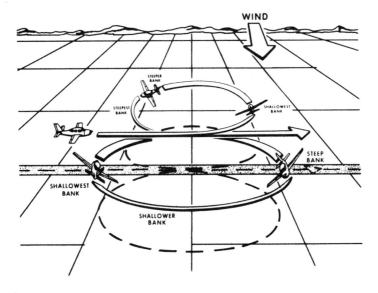

Fig. 14-2 Eights Along a Road

feature along the road at each end of the "8," equally distant from the crossroad or other feature chosen already as your crossing point.

Eights around pylons (Fig. 14-4) is a modification of turns around a point (Chapter 9, C). Two points are chosen, about 10 seconds flying time apart. The airplane is maneuvered around one point, describing a perfect circle at first, but then decreasing the bank angle in order to cross the road midway between the two points, with wings level. When a position abeam the second point is reached, roll into a bank and describe a circle about it, then roll out and fly level, crossing the midway point again with wings level.

The maneuver should be entered downwind, at 45 degrees to the line connecting the two pylons. As this line is crossed, roll into a 45° bank,

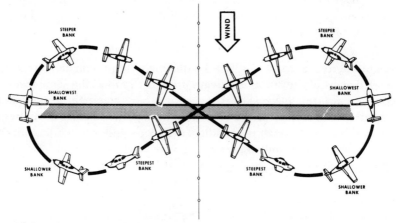

Fig. 14-3 Eights Across a Road

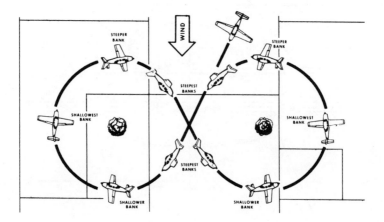

Fig. 14-4 Eights Around Pylons

which will be the steepest bank in the entire maneuver. As you go around the pylon, keeping a constant distance from it, the maneuver is identical to turns about a point. The shallowest bank will be at the moment you are coming directly upwind, on the outside of the "8." As you complete the turn, you will need to steepen the bank again. At the same time, you will have to establish a crab angle in order to arrive at a correct position opposite the other pylon. This means learning, by trial and error, how to sight a line (and aim the airplane) to the pylon itself or even upwind of the pylon to compensate for the downwind drift.

C. THEORY OF THE TURN

To understand turns, and to grasp some important practical consequences, you have to understand the relationships between **airspeed, angle of bank, radius of turn,** and **rate of turn.**

Consider, first, what happens when you have been flying straight and level, and you enter a turn by establishing a bank angle. Fig. 14-5 represents an airplane (the heavy diagonal bar) in a left turn. When the airplane was flying straight and level, all the lift was directed vertically upward, and it exactly balanced the weight of the airplane (represented by **W** in the figure). Now, in the banked turn, the lift is directed at some angle from the vertical, equal to the bank angle. Clearly, all of the lift is no longer directed vertically upward, although it is still all directed perpendicular to the wing surfaces. If the airplane is to remain in level flight while it turns,

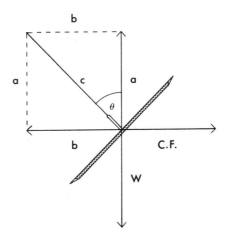

Fig. 14-5 Theory of the turn.

the vertical lift must be kept the same, just equal to **W**. The way this is accomplished, of course, is to increase the angle of attack, just as discussed earlier in connection with steep turns.

The steeper the bank, the more you have to increase the angle of attack in order to keep the vertical lift (**a**, in the figure) constant. Now the total lift, **c**, can be resolved into a vector acting vertically upward (**a**) and another acting horizontally, toward the center of the circle (**b**). Indeed, the horizontal component of lift can be thought of as the force that "lifts" the airplane around the circle. In a steady flight condition, all the forces acting on the airplane are balanced. The airplane neither climbs nor descends because you have increased the angle of attack just enough to make **a** equal to **W**, as it was in straight flight. The inward (centripetal) component, **b**, exactly balances the centrifugal force (**C.F.**) that is generated by the circular motion (i.e., by the speed of the airplane as it moves around the circumference of the circle).

The simplest relationship to understand is that between the angle of bank on the one hand, and the radius and rate of turn on the other. Suppose that, as in Fig. 14-5, you are making 360-degree turns to the left at a constant airspeed and a constant angle of bank. If you now bank more steeply, you will have to increase the angle of attack in order to avoid a descent. You will keep **a** constant, but you will obviously increase **b**. Thus, you will have created an imbalance of the centripetal over the centrifugal force. Consequently, the airplane will tend to move inward, to fly in a smaller circle. At some point the balance will be restored, because an object moving at the same velocity in a smaller circle produces more centrifugal force. At the radius (and circumference) at which the new value of **b** is exactly matched by **C.F.**, a steady condition will again exist.

In summary, then, at constant airspeed, greater bank angle means smaller radius of turn. Since the circumference is always about six times the radius ($C = 2 \pi r$), it will decrease in exactly the same way as the radius. Since the airspeed is unchanged, and the total distance to be flown (the circumference) is decreased, you will complete the turn faster, i.e., the rate of turn will increase.

Now what will happen if you increase the airspeed and maintain the **same angle of bank**? The same arguments apply. Since lift depends upon airspeed, if you don't reduce the angle of attack, you are bound to start climbing. So, to maintain altitude, you will trim nose-down while holding the same bank angle. This bank angle determines the partition of lift into its vertical and horizontal components. Fig. 14-5 shows the case for a 45° bank, in which the two components are equal. It follows that whatever the bank angle, as long as it is held constant, when you change airspeed and then alter your angle of attack to keep **a** constant, you will also be holding **b** constant. Here too, then, you have produced an imbalance of forces. If you increased the airspeed, the centrifugal force also increased (it actually increased as the **square** of the velocity), while the opposing, centripetal force remained the same. Consequently, the airplane moves outward to describe a larger circle. When a certain larger radius is attained, at which the centrifugal force is decreased until it again matches the centripetal force, you will again be in a steady flight condition. It turns out that the radius (and circumference) of the new circle will have increased as the square of the airspeed; doubling the airspeed, for example, will result in a circle of four times the radius (and circumference).

In summary, at a fixed angle of bank, the greater the airspeed, the greater the radius of turn. It is interesting to examine a practical consequence of this relationship at different airspeeds and a 45° angle of bank. These numbers give an indication of the minimum amount of room you would need to make a 180-degree course reversal, since a 45° bank angle is generally the maximum you would want to use except in a dire emergency.

Airspeed, at 45° bank (k)	Radius of turn (ft)	Diameter of turn (statute miles)
80	567	1/5
100	886	1/3
160	2268	4/5

If you are interested in the computations used to arrive at the results in the table, here they are. If you are not, just skip them.

Referring again to Fig. 14-5:

$\tan \theta = $ **b/a**

where θ is the bank angle. If $\theta = 45°$, then $\tan \theta = 1.0$

b is the centripetal force, which is equal to the centrifugal force;

a is the vertical component of lift, which is equal to **W**, the weight of the airplane.

Now centrifugal force $=$ **b** $=$ **W** $\times$ **V²/(g** $\times$ **r)**

where **V** is the airspeed, **g** is the gravitational constant, and **r** is the radius of turn.

Then $\tan \theta = 1.0 = \dfrac{\mathbf{W} \times \mathbf{V^2}}{\mathbf{g} \times \mathbf{r}} \times \dfrac{1}{\mathbf{W}} = \dfrac{\mathbf{V^2}}{\mathbf{g} \times \mathbf{r}}$

and r $=$ V²/g

It remains only to convert to the same units of feet and seconds:

1 knot $=$ 6080 ft/hr $=$ 1.689 ft/sec

g $=$ 32.2 ft/sec²

Then $\mathbf{r} = \dfrac{(1.689)^2}{32.2} \times \mathbf{V}^2 = 0.0886 \times \mathbf{V}^2$

There are several important lessons to be learned from the table of turn diameters for different airspeeds at a 45° angle of bank. First, think about that 1/5 mile minimum required for a course reversal the next time you are tempted to fly into a narrow canyon. Second, note the tremendous advantage of slowing down, if you are ever in a tight spot and need to reverse course. Third, note the importance of flying near one side of a steep valley, so the whole valley width (not just half of it) will be available for a course reversal. And finally, note that these figures are for a no-wind condition. This brings out clearly how important it is to fly the **downwind** side of the valley, so that any course reversal will turn you into the wind initially, thus reducing the radius of turn of your ground track.

The final question to be considered is the bank angle required for a **standard rate turn** at different airspeeds. The answer follows from the previous discussion. As the airspeed increases, the radius (and circumference) of the turn also increases, but to an even greater extent, as the square of the airspeed. This disproportionate increase in the radius (and circumference) can be seen in the above table by comparing turn radius for 160 k with that for 80 k. Therefore, it would take longer to complete a full circle at a faster airspeed. In order to do it in the same 120 seconds, you must therefore bank more steeply.

In summary, for a standard rate turn, the slower the airspeed, the shallower must be the bank angle, and the faster the airspeed, the steeper must be the bank angle. The exact relationship is given by the formula $\tan \theta = 0.00274 \times V$, where V is the airspeed in knots. In the speed range where small aircraft fly, a rough rule for finding the bank angle for a standard rate turn is simply to divide the airspeed in knots by seven. At 100 k, your required bank angle is 15°. A jet at 400 k (the rough rule won't work) would be in a 48° bank and pulling a very high G load. To avoid this, fast aircraft make turns at half standard rate.

D. LIFT, STALLS, PERFORMANCE, AND LOAD FACTORS

The subject of **lift** causes a remarkable amount of confusion for many pilots. The simple and fundamental question is—what makes an airplane fly?

Newton's Third Law states that to every action there is an equal and opposite reaction. This means that if an airplane is to be kept **up** against the force of gravity, a continuous stream of air has to be forced **down**. The power required to do this is provided by the engine as it turns the propeller, producing forward thrust that draws the wings through the air. An airplane flies because there is enough downwash to hold it up, and the downwash results from the movement of the wings, **at a positive angle of attack**, against the relative wind.

The airfoil shape causes a smooth and efficient downwash of air, but it has nothing fundamental to do with flying. If you had a lot of power to spare, you could fly a barn door by setting it at a positive angle of attack and pulling it through the air. As the relative wind struck the under surface, which would be tilted slightly upward, a stream of air would be deflected downward. Anyone who has pulled a kite through still air has seen this simple principle in operation. Most kites don't have airfoil shapes.

Some textbooks attribute lift primarily to Bernouilli's Principle and to the shape of the airfoil. This principle states that in a region of faster fluid flow, there is a reduction of fluid pressure. Because of the airfoil shape, it is argued, the air flowing over the top of the wing is moving faster (since it has farther to go) than that flowing under the wing, and therefore the pressure is lower above the wing than below it. Lift is attributed to this difference in pressure.

It is certainly true that the pressure against the underside of the wing is higher than that against the upper surface. But this is obviously because of the impact pressure from the forward movement of the wing, set at a positive angle of attack, into the relative wind. It is primarily **this** pressure (or the downwash, which amounts to the same thing) that creates lift. What the airfoil shape does is to provide a smooth path for air to be deflected downward—air that is flowing over the top of the wing as well as that striking the under surface.

If you still believe that the shape of the airfoil is responsible for lift, rather than the angle of attack, and that the longer path over the top than under the wing is critically important for Bernouilli's Principle to lift the airplane, try to explain inverted flight. Any airplane—as far as its wings are concerned—can be flown inverted, provided you establish a positive angle of attack. Of course, in inverted flight the flat side of the wing will be uppermost and the curved side will be underneath, but the lift will still be directed upward.

Another source of confusion is the way "angle of attack" is defined, as the angle between the chord line of the wing and the relative wind. This is a convenient definition, but when the chord line is exactly parallel to the relative wind ("zero angle of attack," by definition), the under surface of the wing still presents a slight positive angle to the relative wind. At a **truly** zero angle of attack (which would be defined, technically, as negative), there would be no downwash, and no lift would be generated.

When we speak of a downwash of air, we mean that a certain number of molecules of air are driven downward, with a certain velocity, per second. It is this **rate** of downward air flow that determines the amount of lift. At a given angle of attack, if the airspeed is increased, the wings collide with and drive downward more molecules of air per second, and thus, more lift results. At a given airspeed, increasing the angle of attack imparts a greater downward component of velocity to the downwash, thereby creating more lift.

A **stall** results when the angle of attack becomes too high (generally greater than about 18°), so that the airstream impacts at too perpendicular an angle to the wing surface and can no longer be deflected smoothly downward. Turbulence results, the smooth flow over the wing breaks up into eddies, a major part of the lift is suddenly lost, and the airplane stops flying.

The wings will always stall at the same critical angle of attack. This angle of attack, however, will correspond to different airspeeds in different flight situations. Thus, an airplane can be stalled at any airspeed. The use of flaps will lower the stall speed because the airspeed is slower at a given angle of attack with flaps than without flaps. Stalls with power generally occur at a lower airspeed than stalls in a glide. Most important, the stall speed will rise dramatically with increasing angle of bank, or in abrupt pull-ups, as discussed below in connection with load factors.

In the light of the discussion so far, the effects of altitude and of temperature upon airplane **performance** are easy to understand. With increasing altitude, the air becomes less dense. This is because the entire atmosphere is a rather thin shell, with fewer air molecules in a given volume, the higher you go. Increasing temperature affects air density in the same way, because air expands as it is warmed, and thus a given volume contains fewer molecules. The effect of both factors is embraced in the term **density altitude**. At a high density altitude (low air density), at any given true airspeed and angle of attack, less lift is generated, because fewer molecules of air per second are driven downward.

The airspeed indicator registers the impact of air molecules in the pitot tube. It is really a pressure instrument, but for convenience it is marked with airspeeds. These markings refer only to standard temperature at sea level. If you fly at a true airspeed of 100 k on a standard temperature day at sea level, the indicated airspeed (ignoring any instrument error) will be 100 k. Now if you climb to 5,000 ft and then cruise at the same **true** airspeed, fewer air molecules will enter the pitot tube per second, and the indicated airspeed will be less than 100 k. If you want to know your true airspeed, you will make a correction, using the altitude and the outside air temperature and your computer, and thus you will learn that your true airspeed is 100 k.

That kind of correction is useful in figuring out when you will get to your destination, but from the standpoint of the airplane's performance it is not very useful. Since the number of molecules of air impacting on the pitot tube is a direct reflection of the number impacting on the wings, the **indicated** airspeed tells you how the airplane will fly at all altitudes and temperatures. The wings will stall at the same indicated airspeed, and, as discussed more fully on p. 1–21, your speeds in the pattern, on final, in the flare, and at touchdown should all be the same **indicated** airspeeds at high density altitude as at sea level.

The speeds for best angle of climb (V_x) and best rate of climb (V_y) do change as you climb to higher altitudes or experience higher temperatures. This is obvious from the following argument. At sea level, V_x is always considerably lower than V_y. As you go to higher altitudes, the actual rates of climb decrease. Eventually, at the absolute ceiling, all the engine's available horsepower is needed just to maintain altitude. The absolute ceiling must be reached at one particular airspeed, at which no further climb is possible. If any increase or decrease of airspeed gave you climb capability, you would not yet be at the absolute ceiling. Thus, this particular airspeed at the absolute ceiling must be **both** V_x and V_y. In other words, V_x and V_y converge at the absolute ceiling. What this means for intermediate altitudes is that as you climb higher, V_x increases and V_y decreases. The actual best-angle and best-rate airspeeds for different altitudes can be found in the performance tables or graphs for your airplane.

Climb performance depends on the excess of available thrust horsepower over that needed to maintain altitude. At all altitudes, performance is better, the lighter the airplane is loaded below gross weight. The excess horsepower diminishes with increasing altitude because the normally aspirated engine cannot get enough oxygen (because of the low air density) to produce full power, yet the power required to fly level remains nearly the same. Thus, climb performance deteriorates seriously with increasing density altitude.

At high density altitude, takeoff performance is impaired because in order to attain flying speed (i.e., the **indicated** airspeed for rotation), a much higher ground speed is needed than at sea level. With less power available, an exceptionally long ground run will be needed to accelerate to this airspeed, compared with that required at sea level.

Landing performance is affected because the groundspeed at touchdown is much faster than usual (since you stop flying at the same **indicated** airspeed as usual). A very long rollout is needed, therefore, in order to come to a stop with reasonable braking. On a slick runway this problem could become critical for safety. Fortunately, most high altitude runways are much longer than those at sea level.

Load factors are important for the safety of flight. In straight and level flight a force of 1 G is exerted on the airplane. Any deflection from straight and level flight imposes a load on the airplane structure, because centrifugal force is generated. In a balanced turn, for example, forces in excess of 1 G act on all parts of the airplane structure and on the pilot, too. You can feel these G forces, which push you down into your seat. The same effect occurs in a pullout from a dive, which is simply a turn in the vertical plane. If you enter a dive abruptly, you can feel the negative G forces as you are lifted out of your seat, momentarily weightless. Most light aircraft are designed to withstand positive load factors of approximately 4 G. An airplane turning with a 60° bank angle at constant altitude experiences a load factor of 2 G, and this increases very sharply at steeper bank angles. If you exceed 75° of bank, in level flight, you will also exceed the 4 G limit, and you might well tear off the wings.

The stalling speed increases with load factor, just as it does with aircraft weight. The stalling speeds shown in your Owner's Manual are for gross weight of your airplane; the speeds are lower at lighter weights. Load factor is really the same thing as weight; at 2 G, the airplane (and the pilot) "weigh" twice what they ordinarily do. A load factor of 4 G **doubles** the stalling speed, and in general, the stalling speed increases as the square root of the load factor. Suppose an airplane stalls normally at 45 k. Then with a 2 G load factor it will stall at 64 k, with a 3 G load factor at 78 k, and with a 4 G load factor at 90 k. Accelerated stalls (Chapter 7, B) illustrate this effect.

E. PITCH, POWER, TRIM, AND AIRSPEED

Airspeed determines the performance of an aircraft, for the basic aerodynamic reason that the airflow past the wings and elevator determines what the aircraft will do—indeed, whether it will fly at all. That is why, for every aircraft, there are specific critical airspeeds ("the numbers") to learn—the airspeed at which it stalls, power-off; and the airspeeds for best angle of climb, optimal cruise climb, normal cruise, best power-off glide, approach to landing, and so on. For every desired flight condition there is a "speed to fly."

What is the best way to establish a desired airspeed and to achieve a given aircraft performance? You know, from theory and your own experience, that the performance of an airplane is determined by both power and pitch, not by either one alone.

You can not say what performance or what airspeed will result from a given power setting, unless you also have information about the pitch. Consider, for example, a fixed throttle setting at full power. The aircraft could be at a very low airspeed in an extreme nose-up attitude and about to stall. With the same full power, on the other hand, it could be in a maximum performance climb at 1.3 times the power-off stall speed. Finally, with the same full power it could be in a dive and exceeding the red-line airspeed.

Neither does pitch alone determine the airspeed. At a certain nose-high pitch, you can be climbing at 70 k with full power, or you can be stalling at 48 k with idle power. At a certain nose-low pitch, you can be gliding, power off, at 70 k, or you can be in a full-power descent at 130 k.

There is, however, a single factor that directly determines the airspeed in each particular configuration of the aircraft. By "configuration" is meant the position of the gear and flaps. To keep matters simple, let's confine the discussion to the clean configuration, with gear and flaps up. For each angle of attack, in this configuration, there is a corresponding indicated airspeed, from the stall speed up to red-line and above.

There is a control surface that effectively sets the angle of attack, namely, the elevator. The position of the elevator, in turn, is set by the position of the yoke. And unless you are pulling or pushing on the yoke, its position is determined by the setting of the trim wheel. In short, the trim wheel, through the trim tab, determines the elevator position, effectively setting the angle of attack, and thus it comes close to being the single control that determines the airspeed.

The above description, even for a given configuration of the aircraft, is only approximate. It is not to be taken literally. It would, indeed, apply to an ideal perfect aerodynamic machine, but no actual airplane comes close to that ideal. Nevertheless, as we will demonstrate, it is a very useful approximation to the truth.

The most elegant explanation of this subject was written by Wolfgang Langewiesche in his classic book STICK AND RUDDER (McGraw-Hill, 1944, and reprinted often since then), which every pilot should read. Langewiesche pointed out that you could place a ruler alongside the stick (or a set of lines on the column of the yoke), and mark off the different airspeeds, and regardless of power setting, you would not be very many knots off the mark.

Note that angle of attack, which is determined by the position of the yoke, is very different from pitch, which is a complex result of the interplay between power and angle of attack. Fig. 14-6 illustrates the point. It shows three flight conditions at the same moderate airspeed—a climb at a high pitch angle, level flight at a moderate pitch angle, and descent at a nose-low pitch angle. In each case the pitch is different; and, of course, the power is different, too. But the angle of attack—the angle between the longitudinal axis of the airplane (more exactly, the chord line of the wing) and its flight path (relative wind)—is the same in all three cases. Same angle of attack, same airspeed. Well, not exactly the same in real airplanes, but nearly so. The day a student first grasps the difference between pitch

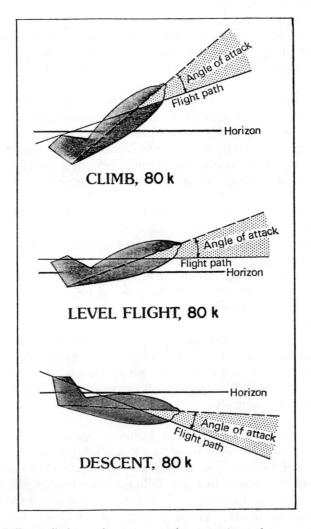

Fig. 14-6 Different flight configurations at the same airspeed.

and angle of attack, he feels that a bright light has suddenly illuminated his whole understanding of flying.

You can easily prove to yourself how nearly the yoke position, as set by the trim wheel, determines the airspeed in your own airplane. Set up level flight at a moderate airspeed—say 80 k in a typical light trainer—and take the time to trim perfectly. Use whatever power setting you need to maintain level flight, hands off. By trimming, you have fixed the angle of attack that you established by yoke position. Trimming, through spring loading or by other means, takes over from you the job of holding the yoke position where you set it. You are "trimmed for 80 k." Now, with hands off the yoke (except only to keep the wings level), bring in more power. The nose will go up, and the airplane will climb, at nearly the same airspeed. Reduce the power, and the nose will drop, the airplane will descend, but the airspeed will not change much. Bring the throttle back all the way to idle. The nose will drop further, and the rate of descent will increase, but the airspeed will still not change a great deal. By making an appropriate mark on the yoke column, you can convince yourself that the yoke position does not change during this experiment; the trim holds it where it was because the forces on the elevator do not change. The airplane changes pitch as required to maintain whatever airspeed it is trimmed for, whenever power changes are made. Throughout this experiment the angle of attack remains the same, whether the airplane is flying level, climbing, or descending.

If you try the same experiment at different trim settings, you will find that each trim setting will correspond to a different airspeed. You have read in the primary instruction manuals that you should not fly the airplane with the trim wheel. I think the main value of that is to teach a student the feel of the controls. In my opinion, however, there is nothing wrong with an experienced pilot making airspeed changes by means of the trim wheel.

I did the experiment described above in a Cessna 150 at 3000 feet, to see how the Lnagewiesche principle would work out in actual practice. First, I held the pitch absolutely constant by means of the attitude indicator, while I changed power settings and recorded the indicated airspeeds and the rates of climb or descent. The result, for three different pitch settings, is seen in Fig. 14-7. The result can be summarized very simply by saying that for any given pitch setting, the airspeeds varied through virtually the entire possible range, as the power was changed. In other words, pitch alone was useless as a means of setting up a given airspeed.

Next I held the trim constant by setting the trim wheel and then flying hands-off. The result was completely different, as Fig. 14-8 shows. For any given trim setting the most extreme airspeed change was less than 7 k above or below the average airspeed for which the airplane was trimmed.

For an ideal airplane these curves would be horizontal lines; for each trim setting the airspeed would remain absolutely constant, regardless of the power. The departure from ideal behavior in this particular airplane was such that the nose pointed higher with increased power, resulting in a slightly increased angle of attack and a slightly decreased airspeed. But the principle worked well enough to be useful in flying the airplane. To a good enough approximation, the trim alone determined the airspeed, regardless of the power setting.

At constant airspeed, the effect of power is to determine if the airplane flies level, climbs, or descends. In this convenient method of flying, the yoke controls the airspeed, and the throttle controls altitude (i.e., climb, descent, or level flight).

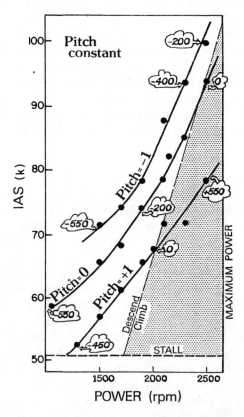

Fig. 14-7 Airspeed as a function of power with pitch constant. Cessna 150, 2000 feet MSL. Pitch settings represent bar widths on the altitude indicator. Numbers in cloud symbols are rates of climb (+) or descent (−) in feet per minute. Shaded area contains all combinations of power and pitch for climb, clear area contains all combinations for descent.

Now let's apply the principle to everyday flying. From takeoff to touch-down, in every phase of flight, you first choose a correct airspeed—the "the speed to fly" for that particular phase of flight. You do that with the yoke, pulling or pushing with just the right force, then trimming out the force so the airplane will fly itself. Let's begin with a short-field, obstacle-clearance takeoff. You apply full power, and bring the yoke back to the position that gives the specified airspeed for maximum angle of climb, say 60 k. But note that if the trim wheel had appropriate markings, you could have set the trim for 60 k before your takeoff roll; then, after lift-off, the obstacle clearance climb at 60 k would have been automatic.

Once over the obstacle, how do you change to best rate of climb airspeed, say 70 k? You move the yoke forward a bit, lowering the nose a little, and find the new yoke position that will give the right airspeed. And you trim

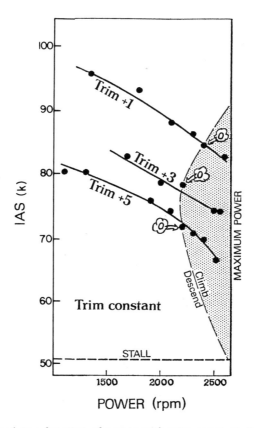

Fig. 14-8 Airspeed as a function of power with trim constant. Cessna 150, 2000 feet MSL. Trim settings are arbitrary, as measured by notches on the trim wheel. Symbols as in Fig. 14-7. Descent is at a greater rate, the lower the power setting. Climb is at a greater rate, the higher the power setting.

again, to continue the climb. Once more, if you had a mark on the trim wheel, you could simply have "dialed in" the 70 k. The same principle applies to the next airspeed change, to cruise climb, and finally to the transition to level flight.

Descent at cruise airspeed—the simplest kind of descent—requires only a power reduction. The airplane is already trimmed for the right cruising airspeed, and the throttle controls the descent—the less power, the greater the rate of descent at approximately the same airspeed.

Of course, you could start the descent by pushing forward on the yoke without any power adjustment. But let's see what happens. The angle of attack will decrease, and the airspeed will increase. Since you want to descend at the original cruising airspeed, you will then have to reduce the power. This, in turn, will compel another adjustment of the yoke. Eventually, after much trial and error, you will be right back to the same trim setting you were using in cruising level flight, and the same reduced power setting described in the previous paragraph.

It is actually dangerous to think that the yoke controls climb or descent, because such thinking could lead you to do the wrong thing in a crisis. At very low airspeeds, raising the nose actually increases the rate of descent, and in the extreme case could stall the airplane. Don't try this, but just imagine executing a go-around from a very slow airspeed just before touchdown. If you have become accustomed to the false idea that pulling on the yoke makes the airplane go up, you will be in very big trouble! On the contrary, the only possible procedure is to apply full throttle first, and then to adjust the yoke for best-rate-of-climb airspeed. To do that, you will have to move the yoke forward rather than pulling it back!

The same principles apply when you want to slow the airplane in level flight. Just as in every other situation, to get a slower airspeed you have to increase the angle of attack. But here, if you pull on the yoke, you are bound to climb, because at an increased angle of attack there is more power than is needed to sustain level flight. Therefore, to avoid climbing, you have to reduce the power first—it doesn't matter how much. This maneuver allows you to bring the yoke back gradually, letting the airspeed fall off to the desired value while maintaining altitude. Then, at the right airspeed, you bring in power again, just enough to prevent a descent, but not enough to climb. Returning to cruise airspeed is the reverse process. You bring in cruise power, but at the same time you have to start pushing the yoke forward to get an increase in airspeed. Otherwise, the airplane would simply climb at the airspeed it was already trimmed for. Finally, in power-off glides (and always, in gliders) it is completely obvious that yoke controls airspeed.

The emphasis I place on airspeed and on control of airspeed by yoke position is related to safety. Stall-spin accidents take an astonishing toll every year. In general aviation, virtually all inadvertent stalls and spins happen through inattention to airspeed. You could fly quite well without an RPM or MP indicator, using the throttle in whatever way it was needed. But the inexperienced pilot would be in serious potential trouble without an airspeed indicator. Good teaching focuses attention where it belongs. If the airspeed is too low, you have to push on the yoke and get the nose down, to reduce the angle of attack and pick up airspeed. That is the prime safety principle that instructors keep hammering home until it becomes instinctive. That is why we practice stalls and stall recoveries.

In summary, while it is certainly true that airspeed and performance are determined by both pitch and power, interacting with each other, it is also true that yoke position alone (and therefore trim) uniquely determines airspeed. This practical fact can be applied consistently, to fly the airplane smoothly, efficiently, and safely, in all phases of flight.

F. PRESSURE-PATTERN NAVIGATION

For the sophisticated pilot, this is an interesting and elegant technique, which permits an entire cross-country flight to be made in minimal time and at a single unchanging heading, regardless of when, where, or how much the wind changes enroute.

This unusual procedure was invented by Dr. John C. Bellamy, and was described in a lucid article in the AOPA Pilot magazine in May 1968 (page 43) by Barry Schiff.

The theory is explained in the article and will not be discussed here, but using the method is extremely simple. It is based on the fact that above a few thousand feet AGL, where there is negligible effect of terrain upon the winds, the wind flow and wind velocities depend upon pressure differences.

We start with the difference in atmospheric pressure between the destination and departure airports at the altitude to be flown. To a close enough approximation, the altimeter settings can be used after multiplying them by 100 (i.e., dropping the decimal point). A constant K is needed which depends on the latitude; at 28°–31° K is 440, at 31°–34° 400, at 34°–38° 360, at 38°–43° 330, and at 43°–50° 300.

The formula for the amount of drift to be expected if no wind correction were made is:

$$Drift = (P_2 - P_1) \times K / TAS$$

where TAS is the true airspeed in knots.

Let us suppose we are going to make a 400-NM trip at latitude 37° and TAS 120 k, and the altimeter setting is 29.95 at departure, 30.15 at destination. Then we have

$$Drift = (3015 - 2995) \times 360 / 120 = 60 \text{ NM}.$$

A positive result means the drift is to the left, a negative result would mean a drift to the right. From the 60-NM drift on a 400-NM flight, we can obtain the wind correction directly from our flight computer in the usual way—in this case a crab angle of 9° to the right. If this course is held perfectly from start to finish, we will end up over the destination airport in the minimum possible time, even though we may have drifted to right and left of course several times during the flight, as we experienced changing winds along the route.

G. ADVANCED RADIONAVIGATION TECHNOLOGY.

Area navigation (abbreviated **RNAV**) uses the VOR system but greatly extends its use. Microcomputer technology makes it possible to "move" a VOR to any desired location. Thus, you can set up a series of **waypoints,** consisting of phantom VORs that have been shifted from the left or the right onto your course. The course itself can be a straight line for flights of moderate length, or a great circle for longer flights. By moving a nearby VOR to the approach end of a runway, you can give yourself helpful VFR approach guidance from a long distance out, even when there is no navaid of any kind at that airport.

The equipment is extremely simple to operate. In addition to the usual NAV receiver and display, and the DME (which is required), there is a little panel device with two windows and two knobs. One knob sets the radial along which the VOR is to be moved, the other sets the distance it is to be moved. Once this has been done, and the mode selector has been set to "RNAV enroute", the system behaves exactly as though the VOR were actually in the new position. You can center the needle and fly directly to the phantom VOR, just as you would to an actual VOR. The DME gives the distance to the phantom VOR, and you will get a normal TO-FROM reversal when you get there.

An interesting feature of RNAV is that needle deviation is constant for a given distance off course, regardless of how far you are from the VOR. As you know, in ordinary VOR navigation the needle deviation depends on the **angular** displacement from the chosen course; a one-dot deviation, for example, may represent only a few yards when you are very close to the station, but a mile or more at some distance away. Constant deviation offers a very useful option to the VFR pilot—the possiblity of flying a displaced parallel course between VORs, rather than staying on the airway centerline. Even passing one VOR and heading for the next, you can keep your constant distance (say half a mile) to one side, and thus avoid the dangerous zone over a VOR, where aircraft converge from several directions.

An obvious advantage of RNAV is that it utilizes equipment already in the aircraft, and that it requires virtually no pilot training—the microprocessor does the whole job. Any VFR pilot can learn the RNAV techniques in a few minutes, and be using them effectively right away. However, the system suffers from the same important defect as VOR navigation itself, namely, that the high radiofrequencies used can only be received within line-of-sight of range. At low altitudes or in remote parts of the country where the VOR stations are few and far between, being out of range is not a rare experience. If you can't receive the actual VOR, you can't move it to a phantom location. For example, if the VOR is behind a mountain and you are flying in the valley, your RNAV will be useless. So in planning a flight by RNAV, you must pay attention to terrain in relation to your proposed altitude and the locations of the VORs, as you plot your waypoints on the sectional chart.

In my judgment, the enroute use of RNAV is more fun than necessity. I mean that for the average VFR pilot there is usually little value in being able to fly a straight course rather than from VOR to VOR. And in VFR weather you could fly the straight course anyway, by pilotage. Besides, the time and fuel saved by avoiding a few dog legs amount to very little on typical flights of a few hours. Furthermore, if you love to fly, shortening a flight is not always a virtue. I believe that the most valuable application of RNAV is for finding small airports with certainty in unfamiliar surroundings. A typical example was a flight I made to a desert air strip at the Hopi reservation in Northern Arizona. If you've ever flown in that country you know how everything looks alike until you become very familiar with the landmarks. By "moving" a VOR 46 miles along its 101° radial, I was able to fly my VOR needle direct. When I got the TO-FROM reversal, I looked down, and the asphalt strip was directly under me.

The really exciting new system of radionavigation is **Loran C.** Prices are reasonable, and the system is becoming more popular. Very likely Loran will some day replace VOR navigation entirely. At the moment, it makes an extremely useful addition to the VOR system, especially if one were equipping an aircraft from the start. Even in considering additions to an existing basic radionavigation panel, one should think very seriously about Loran as an alternative to a second VOR or a DME.

Loran works on a novel principle. Coded pulses are sent out by chains of Loran stations on low radiofrequencies that are not subject to the line-of-sight limitation and can be received over many hundreds of miles. The microprocessor aboard the aircraft scans automatically for Loran signals, and only accepts those of adequate strength. Each chain consists of a master station and several secondary stations. The pulse coding identifies the station to the receiver. Thus, the aircraft Loran microprocessor can note the time of arrival of the master signal and of each secondary signal. The time delay between reception of a certain pulse in the transmitted signal from the "master" station and reception of the corresponding pulse from another station in the chain locates the aircraft on an "arc of position".

The principle is based on simple geometry and the known velocity of radio waves (1 NM in 6.17 microseconds), as illustrated in Fig. 14.9. Here the delay between reception of the master M and the secondary W is

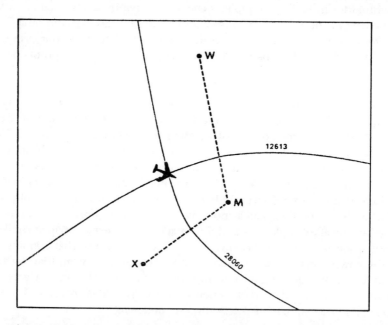

Fig. 14.9 Loran position fix sequence. Time delay between reception of master signal M and secondary signal W is 12,613 microseconds, defining one line of position. Secondary signal X defines another line of position. Aircraft must be at the intersection of the two lines. (From Operating Manual, R-21 Loran System, ARNAV SYSTEMS, Inc., P.O. Box 23939, Portland, OR 97224.)

12,613 microseconds. A large part of this actual delay represents the "emission delay", i.e., the fixed delay between transmission of the same pulse from M and from W. Fixed emission delays—different for each station in a chain—are necessary to permit each secondary signal to be received withoout interference from another. To grasp the concept better, suppose the aircraft were at exactly the same distance from M and W, i.e., anywhere on a line perpendicular to a line connecting M and W. Obviously, the only delay would be the emission delay. Now note what happens if the aircraft—as in the figure—is closer to M. The M signal will reach it sooner, the W signal will take longer, so the delay will increase by an amount determined by the distance from M and from W.

The figure shows the line of position for the W-M delay. Everywhere along this line the delay will be exactly 12,613 microseconds, representing the emission delay plus the difference between the arrival time of the M signal and that of the W signal. Secondary signal X is received with a delay of 28,060 microseconds, giving a second line of position. The intersection of the two lines of position must be the exact position of the aircraft. Note that these seemingly big numbers for the delays actually represent only a few **hundredths** of a second.

In the days of World War II, when Loran was first implemented, the lines of position had to be plotted manually on a chart. The remarkable advances of microprocessor technology make all that automatic now, so the Loran receiver displays latitude and longitude directly. Fig. 14.10 shows the panel display of a popular-priced high-quality general aviation Loran C, produced by a leading manufacturer. This unit computes and displays an updated positon fix every 1.5 seconds.

The mere ability to display precise latitude and longitude coordinates would be useful enough in itself, but the computer memory can do much more than that. For example, any course can be described as a series of waypoints, and the display can give course direction (much as with a VOR needle) to the next waypoint, at the same time displaying distance to go, current groundspeed, ETE, ETA, and so on. An additional available feature is a read-only memory unit that contains pre-stored latitude and longitude coordinates for every public-use airport in North America; then any airport can be called up directly by code name. Consider this interesting safety feature: By punching in "911", you can instantly call up the **nearest** airport, even if you've never heard of it, with course direction for flying to it. Or another amazing capability: Terrain patterns are stored in memory, so that minimum safe altitudes can be displayed as you proceed: the device actually "looks ahead" along your course and gives ample warning to permit a timely climb.

It is not my purpose here to give a complete description of Loran C. But when a new technology is so superior, it obviously should not be omitted, even though relatively few small general aviation aircraft are as yet equipped with it. What remains to be seen is whether, in the very long run, some kind of wholly new satellite-based navigation system will prove superior even to Loran; but such a development is too far in the future to worry about now.

Fig. 14.10. Typical Loran C panel. This popular-priced unit stores up to 200 waypoints and presents information as a LCD display. The unit is remarkably compact, taking only 3.25 × 6.25 inches of panel space, and it weighs only 4.6 pounds. The display includes a full CDI (like a VOR needle) for course guidance. Multiple additional data are also displayed, such as distance, groundspeed, ETE, and minimum safe altitude. The unit shown is the R-21, manufactured by ARNAV SYSTEMS, Inc., P.O. Box 23939, Portland, OR 97224.

Score Sheet: 14A. Slips and Dutch Rolls

Date											
Flying in a slip with 10° bank angle, heading control											
Flying in a slip with 10° bank angle, altitude control											
Flying in a slip with 20° bank angle, heading control											
Flying in a slip with 20° bank angle, altitude control											
Flying in a slip with 30° bank angle, heading control											
Flying in a slip with 30° bank angle, altitude control											
Dutch Rolls, 10° bank											
Dutch Rolls, 20° bank											
Dutch Rolls, 30° bank											
TOTAL SCORE											
Divide by Number of Items Attempted = AVERAGE SCORE											

Score Sheet: 14B. Eights Along a Road

Date											
Smooth entry											
Altitude control											
Smoothness of bank changes											
Ball centered at all times											
Symmetrical ground path											
Vigilant lookout for traffic											
TOTAL SCORE											
Divide by 6 = AVERAGE SCORE											

Score Sheet: 14B. Eights Across a Road

Date										
Smooth entry										
Altitude control										
Smoothness of bank changes										
Ball centered at all times										
Symmetrical ground path										
Crossing at same point on both arms of the eight										
Vigilant lookout for traffic										
TOTAL SCORE										
Divide by 7 = AVERAGE SCORE										

Score Sheet: 14B. Eights Around Pylons

Date									
Smooth entry rolling into 45° bank									
Altitude control									
Smoothness of bank changes									
Ball centered at all times									
Ground path at constant distance from pylons									
Crossing point midway between pylons on both legs									
Vigilant lookout for traffic									
TOTAL SCORE									
Divide by 7 = AVERAGE SCORE									

AvvA, Inc.
735 Dolores St., Dept. B
Stanford, CA 94305

SHIP TO:

_____

Name

_____

Street Address   Apt.

_____

City   State   Zip

Book Title	Qty	Amount	TOTAL
VFR Flight Review		$8.95	
The Right Seat		8.95	
IFR Principles and Practice		8.95	
Flying Out of Danger		8.95	
ALL FOUR BOOKS (15% Discount)		30.00	
		Item Total	
CFI Certificate No. * _____		Less 25%*	
California Residents add Sales Tax:		6.5%	
Shipping: Add 75¢ per book			
		TOTAL	

*Active CFI's: Give CFI Certificate No. for 25% Discount

Method of Payment (Sorry, no COD's):

Amount enclosed: ☐ Check   ☐ Money Order $ _____

Please charge to my account:

☐ MasterCard   ☐ Visa

Account#

Expiration Date: _____

Signature _____

FULL REFUND IF NOT SATISFIED

The widely acclaimed aviation classic by Avram Goldstein —

IFR PRINCIPLES AND PRACTICE:
A Guide to Safe Instrument Flying

"…absolutely first-rate"
(E.K. Gann)

An invaluable book, whether you are just going for your IFR rating or whether you're a 10,000-hour ATP. A clear, logical, step-by-step explanation of flight by instruments and of the ATC procedures.

AvvA, Inc.

735 Dolores St., Dept. B
Stanford, CA 94305

SHIP TO:

_____

Name

_____

Street Address   Apt.

_____

City   State   Zip

Book Title	Qty	Amount	TOTAL
VFR Flight Review		$8.95	
The Right Seat		8.95	
IFR Principles and Practice		8.95	
Flying Out of Danger		8.95	
ALL FOUR BOOKS (15% Discount)		30.00	
		Item Total	
CFI Certificate No. * _____		Less 25%*	
California Residents add Sales Tax:		6.5%	
Shipping: Add 75¢ per book			
		TOTAL	

*Active CFI's: Give CFI Certificate No. for 25% Discount

Method of Payment (Sorry, no COD's):

Amount enclosed: ☐ Check   ☐ Money Order $ _____

Please charge to my account:

☐ MasterCard   ☐ Visa

Account#

Expiration Date: _____

Signature _____

FULL REFUND IF NOT SATISFIED

Also by Avram Goldstein —

FLYING OUT OF DANGER:

A Pilot's Guide to Safety

Lessons from the NTSB Accident Reports

"…an excellent book…"
(Wayne A. Sanderson, President, Jeppesen-Sanderson)

"…well-written and very well-researched …would be of benefit to any pilot."
(Private Pilot *magazine*)

"…very impressive …a much needed book"
(E.K. Gann)

"Nearly all accidents are caused by something the pilot did or did not do. And if the experienced air carrier pilots can make mistakes, less experienced general aviation pilots can certainly make mistakes, too…. The book's purpose is to enable all pilots to learn about the errors…to avoid making those errors ourselves." (From *Flying Out of Danger,* Preface)

In a text written with gripping realism, the author re-creates major accidents to show just where things went wrong and how they might have been avoided—the DC-8 out of fuel at Portland, the San Diego mid-air, the two jumbo jets at Tenerife, the 727 at Cincinnati, and many others.

AvvA, Inc.
735 Dolores St., Dept. B
Stanford, CA 94305

SHIP TO:

_____

Name

_____

Street Address   Apt.

_____

City   State   Zip

Book Title	Qty	Amount	TOTAL
VFR Flight Review		$8.95	
The Right Seat		8.95	
IFR Principles and Practice		8.95	
Flying Out of Danger		8.95	
ALL FOUR BOOKS (15% Discount)		30.00	
		Item Total	
CFI Certificate No. * _____		Less 25%*	
California Residents add Sales Tax:		6.5%	
Shipping: Add 75¢ per book			
		TOTAL	

*Active CFI's: Give CFI Certificate No. for 25% Discount

Method of Payment (Sorry, no COD's):

Amount enclosed: ☐ Check   ☐ Money Order $ _____

Please charge to my account:

☐ MasterCard   ☐ Visa
Account#

Expiration Date: _____

Signature _____

FULL REFUND IF NOT SATISFIED

AvvA, Inc.

735 Dolores St., Dept. B
Stanford, CA 94305

SHIP TO:

_____

Name

_____

Street Address   Apt.

_____

City   State   Zip

Book Title	Qty	Amount	TOTAL
VFR Flight Review		$8.95	
The Right Seat		8.95	
IFR Principles and Practice		8.95	
Flying Out of Danger		8.95	
ALL FOUR BOOKS (15% Discount)		30.00	
		Item Total	
CFI Certificate No. * _____		Less 25%*	
California Residents add Sales Tax:		6.5%	
Shipping: Add 75¢ per book			
		^ **TOTAL**	

*Active CFI's: Give CFI Certificate No. for 25% Discount

Method of Payment (Sorry, no COD's):

Amount enclosed: ☐ Check   ☐ Money Order $ _____

Please charge to my account:

☐ MasterCard   ☐ Visa
Account#

Expiration Date: _____

Signature _____

FULL REFUND IF NOT SATISFIED